THE LAST YEARS OF
A FRONTIER

THE LAST YEARS OF A FRONTIER

A history of the Borders during the reign of Elizabeth I

BY
D.L.W. TOUGH, B. Litt., M.A.

SANDHILL
PRESS

The Publishers wish to express their thanks to the
following: Mr. Geoffrey Suggitt for permission to
reprint the book. The many individuals, including
several ex-pupils of Mr. Tough, Leeds Grammar School,
The Old Leodiensian Association, Merton College, the
Yorkshire Post, all of whom helped to provide
biographical details about the author.

First published in Great Britain by
Oxford University Press.
© D.L.W. Tough 1928.

This reprint © 1987 Sandhill Press Ltd.,
Castleside, 40 Narrowgate, Alnwick, Northumberland,
NE66 1JQ.

ISBN 0 946098 06 9

Printed in Great Britain by Martin's of Berwick.

PREFACE

THIS book attempts a picture of the Borders as they were in their last years, an explanation of their state, and a narrative of the events of 1558–1603.

Queen Elizabeth and her counsellors, as well as the Scots government, treated Border affairs as matters of great importance. Modern English historians by their comparative silence, especially about the Laws of the Marches, show that they think that Her Highness was wrong. Readers of this book will be able to decide the question for themselves.

The author wishes to record his thanks to those named below for their generous assistance in various ways: The Warden and Fellows of Merton, the President of Corpus, Sir Charles Firth, Professor A. J. Grant, Dr. H. H. E. Craster, Mr. F. H. Lawson, and *the late* Reverend A. H. Johnson. None of these gentlemen is responsible for any errors which may have crept into the book, or for its Elizabethan inconsistency in the spelling of proper names.

The author's thanks are also due to Mr. J. H. A. Hart, B.D., former Fellow of St. John's College, Cambridge, and to the Reverend A. M. Hollis, M.A., Fellow of Hertford, for their sympathetic industry in reading the proofs.

D. L. W. T.

25 March 1928.

CONTENTS

LIST OF PLATES

(from photographs by the author)

LIST OF MAPS AND PLANS

BIBLIOGRAPHICAL INTRODUCTION

FOR the forty-five years preceding the Union of the Crowns the Border historian has mainly to rely on State Papers. These, unfortunately, are scattered, partly because the secretaries of that time regarded state papers as their own property, and partly because Mr. M. J. Thorpe, who edited the Calendar of State Papers relating to Scotland, abstracted some Border Papers and included them in it, while the editors of the first eleven volumes of the Calendar of the Foreign State Papers for the reign of Elizabeth included most of the other Border Papers for the period 1558–77. Most of the rest of those which are now public property are calendared in the two volumes of Border Papers edited by Mr. Joseph Bain. These are in the Public Record Office. The first twelve volumes of the MSS. of the Marquis of Salisbury at Hatfield contain many scattered papers, some of which were printed in full by Haynes or by Murdin; and other still more scattered Border Papers are in the Calendars of the Laing MSS., the Mar and Kellie MSS., the Home of Wedderburn MSS., the Athol and Home MSS., the Rutland MSS. (all in the Reports and Appendices of the Historical MSS. Commission), in the Hamilton Papers, in Rymer's *Foedera*, in the Addenda to the Domestic State Papers, and in the Calendar of Scots Papers edited by Messrs. Bain and Boyd. Their contents are necessarily miscellaneous, but consist for the most part of the correspondence of the Wardens, Bishops, and Deputy Wardens, and even of private persons; of the reports of Commissioners, Muster Rolls, lists of losses by Scots raids, accounts of the state of the fortifications at Berwick and elsewhere, letters from Elizabeth's ambassadors at Edinburgh, &c. To these State Papers must be added the Sadler Papers and the Correspondence of Robert Bowes. The Sadler Papers contain the letters written by Sir Rafe Sadler during the War of the Scots Reformation and the Rising

of 1569, and his accounts as Treasurer of the Army
during the latter period, together with a memorial concerning the Border service, dated 1559–60. Sir Rafe
(1507–87) was an experienced diplomatist and organizer
who had served Henry VIII and Edward VI in Scots
matters. Robert Bowes (1535?–97), son of a captain of
Norham and brother of Sir George Bowes, was a diplomatist who filled, to his financial ruin, the combined posts
of ambassador at Edinburgh and Treasurer of Berwick.
The correspondence covers but six years, 1577–83, and is
mainly about Scots affairs, but many other letters from
him are to be found in the Border Papers. It must be
noted that there is almost an entire lack of letters from
Scots Border officials to the Scots government, and vice
versa, but the latter is to some extent filled by the Registers of the Scots Privy Council, which contain numerous
entries relating to the Border policy of the Scots government, and are almost, excepting the Accounts of the Lords
High Treasurers, the only source for the very incomplete
list of Scots Border officers that can be compiled. Except
in the Hatfield MSS., where there are drafts of letters from
the English government to the Wardens, very few of such
letters remain, the correspondence which Hunsdon, the
Scroopes, Forster, and others received having apparently
perished. The loss is partly compensated by the Acts of
the Privy Council, which, though much less full than the
Scots Register, contain memoranda of instructions sent to
the Wardens.

In writing this book the author has relied on the Calendars of MSS. above named, except for the Bell MS.,
mentioned at the end of this introduction, which is un-
calendared, and for the Border Papers in the Public
Record Office. There are forty-two volumes of the latter,
and the last is an undated and anonymous folio of twenty-
one pages addressed to the Queen and explaining by
words and 'plattes' how to fortify the Borders by means of
'a certayne kinde of ENSKONCE'. The other forty-one are
letters and papers covering the period 1558–1603, and
are mostly in excellent preservation and quite legible.

The handwriting varies very much. Thomas, Lord Scroope's, is a large modern hand and rather untidy, while Eure's letters are in a small old-fashioned but beautifully neat handwriting. Sir R. Carey's style is mixed, mainly old; his brother John's is similar but less legible; Wyllughby's is quite modern and might almost be eighteenth or early nineteenth century; Sir W. Drury's is horridly untidy and hard to read, and Hunsdon's is old-fashioned but legible. The worst document of the lot, vilely written, is the undated general account of the Borders.[1] The documents, apart from those in Bain's two-volume *Calendar of Border Papers*, are almost entirely drawn from the Foreign Papers of 1558–77, but a few are from other sources, e.g. the Conway MSS. The calendaring is very good, the only common mistake is the misreading of 'Tinedale' for 'Tivedale' and vice versa, which occurs in the Foreign Calendar.

Contemporary English historians seem to have wrongly regarded the Borders as a backwater. Camden, whose history of Elizabeth is by far the best contemporary history of her reign, jumbled panegyric though it be, pays almost as little attention to the Borders, though he had visited them, as to the literature of his time. Holinshed and Stow are full on the Rising of 1569 and nothing else. Of Scots historians Leslie, whose work was written 1572–6, is the best of the Papists, but for Border history its only valuable part is the description of the Scots Borderers, their country, manners, and customs, valuable because he must often have passed through the Borders, sent agents thither and possibly accompanied the Queen when she journeyed in those parts. But, 'if we believe a MS. memoir by the son of Lethington', Ninian Winzet, a Papist schoolmaster of Linlithgow, wrote most of the book.[2] George Buchanan, the chief authority among men of the new religion, ended early and wrote little about the Borders. Lindesay of Pittscottie did the same. But, if Scots historians were scanty, Scots diarists, autobiographers, and memorialists were more numerous. Robert

---

[1] S.P. Borders, xx, 198–202.   [2] Lang, ii, 89, 91–2.

Birrel, burgess of Edinburgh, kept a diary, 1532–65, which shows no leaning to any Scots party; some unknown hand compiled a *Diurnal of Remarkable Occurrents*, 1513–75; another wrote a *History of James the Sext*, 1566–96; Sir James Melville of Halhill wrote Memoirs, 1549–93; Richard Bannatyne wrote Memorials about the years 1569–75. They say little about the Borders, except about well-known people like Mary's Bothwell; and David Moysie, if he wrote the Memoirs which go by his name, 1577–1603, says little more. On the other hand, James Melville, minister of Kilrenny, wrote a charming autobiography, called a Diary, which gives valuable pictures of religion in Berwick, the religion of Forster, and English feeling towards Scots. The so-called Herries Memoirs seem to have no independent value. Scots Border officers produced nothing to compare with the Memoirs of Sir Robert Carey, youngest son of Hunsdon and brother-in-law of Thomas, Lord Scroope, who visited Scotland, and was deputy in the West and Warden in the East and Middle Marches. The book gives a delightful account of the doings of an energetic Border officer and of his attempts to keep good rule. It is hazy about dates, because it was written about twenty-five years after his Border work was done, but it really shows us the man. No Scots Borderer produced a biography like that of Bernard Gilpin, 1517–83, by his pupil George Carleton, son of a Keeper of Norham and afterwards Fellow of Merton and Bishop of Llandaff and Chichester, which gives a clear view of the conditions under which a Border parson worked. The life of Lord Grey de Wilton, written by his son, 1562–77, contains nothing about his Border work and only a short account of his doings at Leith. Among other contemporary works must be noted the *Fyrste Boke of the Introduction of Knowledge*, 1547, by Andrew Boorde, clerk, physician, and traveller, who had lived in Scotland and knew the Borderers well enough to write a valuable though partisan account of them well worth comparing with that given by Leslie. In addition to Gilpin's Life we have, for the religious history of the time, the *History of the Kirk of Scotland*, by David Calderwood (1575?–1650), written at the end of his life and founded on Knox, Bannatyne, and Pastor Melville. With it may be compared the *History of the Church of Scotland* by Archbishop John Spotswood (1565–1639). Both books are political rather than religious and give little information about the religion of the Scots Borderers. Though there is no similar ecclesiastical history of England, the Surtees Society has published the *Ecclesiastical Proceedings of Bishop Barnes* of Carlisle and Durham (1532–87), which gives accounts of his visitations, and a volume of Depositions and Ecclesiastical Proceedings, being extracts from the records of the Courts of Durham and containing valuable evidence about the religious state of the diocese. Unfortunately no details are given to enable a comparison to be made between the number of offences and the estimated population, clerical and lay. The Camden Society has published in its ninth Miscellany certain letters from the bishops on the state of their dioceses in 1563–4.

For legal matters, besides the Bell MS. referred to in an appendix to this introduction, we have Nicolson's *Leges Marchiarum* and Rymer's *Foedera*, which three contain all the known Border treaties, and other information on March administration. The earlier texts in Latin are somewhat corrupt, but the Elizabethan laws are in English. Similar facts on administration are in M. A. Richardson's *Reprints of Rare Tracts*. The Acts of Parliament relating to the Borders are in Statutes of the Realm and the Acts of the Parliament of Scotland. The latter also contains some of the Border Laws.

For topography Camden's *Britannia* is the chief guide, though Camden was but 'little conversant' with Scotland. His journey was made about 1582, and his intention was to seek for Roman remains, accounts of which occupy most of his space. The 1610 edition contains maps of the three Border counties by W. Saxton, whose skill was primitive. Leland visited Morpeth, Alnwick, Berwick, and Carlisle, but his jottings are of small value. Speed's *Theatre of the Empire of Great Britain* (1611) adds little or nothing to

Camden except plans of Berwick, Newcastle, Carlisle, and Kendal, and large-scale maps of Holy Island and of the Farne Islands. A valuable survey of the Debatable and Border Lands in 1604 has been edited by R. P. Sanderson. The general lack of evidence for Scotland is well shown by Professor Hume Brown's extracts from the writings of *Early Travellers in Scotland* (1295–1689). Those who reached Scotland from England, except Aeneas Sylvius, seem to have hurried through the Borders for obvious reasons, or to have been interested only in hermits and in trees said to produce birds. Useful books on social life are the Household Books of Lord William Howard of Naworth, which were, however, slightly post-Elizabethan, and the Wills and Inventories of the Diocese of Durham, which throw much light on the backward state of the Borders. Harrison's *Description of England* is useless except for purposes of comparison. The writer was no traveller.

Among more modern authorities an excellent introduction to the whole subject is *The Wardens of the Northern Marches*, a Creighton Lecture by Dr. T. Hodgkin of Beal, which makes any one regret that so excellent a historian should, like Bishop Creighton, have devoted so much of his leisure to Italy, or to the history of England before 1066, rather than to the district of which he, like Creighton, was a native and a resident. The book, except the map by another hand, is beyond criticism. The only general history of the Borders of any length is by Ridpath: it is a good work for a pioneer, but neglects social and economic history almost entirely, being concerned almost exclusively with Anglo-Scots relations. Mr. Howard Pease of Otterburn has borrowed, with permission, the title of Dr. Hodgkin's lecture and produced a book which is worthy of mention because it contains the first attempt at a list of Wardens of the Marches. It does not aim at being a scientific history. There are several district histories. Raine's *North Durham* starts with a fine preface containing documents from the Cottonian MSS., and then becomes a parish history. The index is poor; two pages to a book of over five hundred pages. The *Northumberland County History* in course of publication is also parochial. Most of Hall and Humberston's Survey is printed under the several townships, and there are excellent descriptions of castles, for instance that of Tynemouth by Dr. H. H. E. Craster. The late Mr. C. J. Bates wrote a scholarly though popular *History of Northumberland*. The best-known work on Cumberland and Westmorland is that of Nicolson and Burn, which mangles and muddles the Bell MS. with Nicolson's *Leges Marchiarum* till the source of the quotations is lost. It contains invaluable lists of the Provosts of Queen's College, Oxford, and of the prebendaries of Carlisle, but a list of Wardens of the West March evidently seemed, to the authors, out of place in a history of two Border counties. R. S. Ferguson's short *History of Cumberland* calls forth the wish that he had written a work on the scale of Nicolson and Burn. The *Victoria History of Cumberland* devotes about six pages to the political history and nearly thirty to the ecclesiastical affairs of this period. There is a *History of the Border Counties* (of Scotland) by Sir George Douglas which is prejudiced, romantic, and uncritical, but other books on smaller districts are much better. The only volume published of R. B. Armstrong's *History of Liddesdale*, &c., is based on original research, but unfortunately ends at 1550. Sir Herbert Maxwell's *History of Dumfries and Galloway* contains an interesting chapter on the Maxwell-Johnstone feud of 1572–1620. G. F. S. Elliot's *History of the Border Elliots* is much more than a family history.

For architecture the best Scots authority is Macgibbon and Ross's five-volume work on Scots castles and fortified houses. It contains good plans and is most comprehensive. On a larger scale is the unfinished work of the late Mr. C. J. Bates, *The Border Holds of Northumberland*, a work of real critical ability with an introduction containing large extracts from contemporary surveys. The West March holds are well described in Mr. J. F. Curwen's

Castles and Towers of Cumberland and Westmorland. The proceedings of the local antiquarian societies published under the titles *Archaeologia Aeliana*, Proceedings of the Newcastle Society of Antiquaries, and Transactions of the Cumberland and Westmorland Archaeological and Antiquarian Society, contain useful papers too numerous to mention, and Miss R. R. Reid has published an extremely valuable account of the Rising of 1569, written from the point of view of the Northern Earls.[1] The most valuable town history is Creighton's *Carlisle*. There are two histories of Berwick: J. Scott's is good, but not precise enough in its references, and John Fuller's is mainly a statistical account of Berwick about 1799. R. Welford's *Newcastle and Gateshead in the Sixteenth Century* gives a picture of the most progressive part of the Borders.

In conclusion the writer, who has walked many hundreds of miles on the Borders and read good, bad, and indifferent guide-books, cannot help commending the late Mr. W. W. Tomlinson's *Comprehensive Guide to Northumberland*, Commander Robinson's *Guide to Berwick*, and Chancellor Ferguson's *Guide to Carlisle*. Mr. Tomlinson wrote another excellent book, *Northumberland in the Sixteenth Century*, based for the most part on the Calendar of Border Papers.

The MS. of Richard Bell.

This book, for the loan of which the writer is much indebted to the Dean and Chapter of Carlisle, is a folio of nearly two hundred and fifty leaves, most of which are covered on both sides with writing in an old-fashioned Elizabethan hand. The MS. has been rebound and is in a very fair state of preservation, but the title-page, if any, and folio 2, which contained 'the purports of the contents of this book', are missing, and so is the top right-hand corner of folio 248. A much later hand has added a table of contents which has the curious misreading 'commerce' for 'gunnerie'. Bell's writing is generally clear and neat, but folio 3 is hard to read because it has faded. This folio,

[1] Trans. R.H.S., N.S. xx, 176–201.

the first extant, contains a letter offering the book, which Bell calls the 'Memoriall of the Laite dissolved treatisies of truice and Lawes of Marches', to George, third Earl of Cumberland, who had brought Bell to the notice of Robert Cecil, first Viscount Cranborne, and thus obtained a royal pension of £20 per annum for Bell. This grant, dated November 13, 1604, for the maintenance of Bell, his wife, and family, was made in recognition of his services as Warden Clerk of the West Marches. He was for an unknown period, dating at least from 1585, Secretary to Henry, Lord Scroope, who died in office as Lord Warden in 1592, and all the evidence points to the conclusion that Thomas, Lord Scroope, his successor, kept Bell in office till there were no more Borders.[1] The last dated document in the book is dated April 1605, and, as Cumberland died on October 30 in that year, the date of the book is evident.[2] Folio 4 contains a dedication to James I, wherein Bell 'as one of the unworthiest yet oldest [warden clerk] whose time . . . is spent, bodie decrepit, and service decayed', presents 'this book of Marches' to the king 'as a poor mans myte'.

It was the Warden Clerk's duty to keep a copy of the various Border Laws for his Warden's use, and this MS. is probably a fair copy, with additions, of the book of March Laws kept by Bell. Folio 6 contains the grounds on which March Laws were established, and the ways of convicting thieves, and the next hundred and twenty-five, or so, folios contain the Border treaties and laws from 1249 to 1597. The text is not perfect, the Latin and the English are sometimes nonsense, and the laws of 1249 and 1448 are muddled, but it is the most complete set of Border Laws extant, and shows us probably a first copy of the actual book taken to days of truce, where the laws were administered. As an example of completeness it may be said that Bell gives twenty-four clauses of the Treaty of 1533 against ten in *Leges Marchiarum*. By collating these two with Rymer's *Foedera* a pretty perfect text

[1] Dom. 1603–10, p. 167; Bell, fol. 3, 157; C.B.P. i, p. 174, ii, 82, 99, 457, 669, 1504; Dom. Add. iii, p. 350.　　[2] Fol. 237.

might be made. The importance of the MS. lies mainly
in these laws and in information as to their administration, both of which were shamefully mangled by Nicolson
and Burn; yet later historians have found it easier to go
to the printed hodge-podge than to the MS. itself, and
some of them are not honest enough to say so. The
advantages of going to the MS. are, it is hoped, shown in
the sections on Border Laws. The rest of the book is
really a miscellany containing copies of documents
relating to Russell's death, Scots prisoners, pledges,
musters, and principal offenders, as well as of letters from
Francis Dacre, L. Carlton, and King James, and the text
of a Warden's patent and of the Bond of Association, &c.
Perhaps the most valuable of these miscellanea is the
advice given by Bell to Thomas, Lord Scroope, when he
succeeded his father as Warden. A few of the folios at the
end concern the pacification of the Borders, 1603–5.

LIST OF PRIMARY AUTHORITIES
CONSULTED

Accounts of the Lord High Treasurer of Scotland. Edinburgh, 1877–1916.

Bannatyne, R. *Memorials of Transactions in Scotland.* Edinburgh, 1836.

Barnes, *The Memoirs of Ambrose.* Durham, 1867.

Barnes, The Ecclesiastical Proceedings of Bishop. Durham, 1850.

Bell, R. (ed.). *The Fairfax Correspondence,* vol. ii. *Iter Boreale.* London, 1849.

*Bell, The MS. of Richard. Carlisle Cathedral Library.

Birrel's Diary (in J. G. Dalyell's *Fragments of Scottish History*). Edinburgh, 1798.

Boorde, The Works of Andrew. E.E.T.S. Ex. Ser. x. London, 1870.

Bowes, The Correspondence of Robert. London, 1842.

Brereton, Sir William, Bt. *Travels.* Chetham Society, 1844.

Brown, P. H. *Early Travellers in Scotland.* Edinburgh, 1891.

Buchanan, G. *Rerum Scoticarum Historia.* Edinburgh, 1727.

Calderwood, D. *History of the Kirk of Scotland.* Edinburgh, 1842–9.

Calendar of Border Papers. Edinburgh, 1894, 1896.

Calendar of Domestic State Papers, Elizabeth. London, 1856–71.

Calendar of Foreign State Papers, Elizabeth (1558–77). London, 1863–1901.

Calendar of Hamilton Papers, vol. ii. Edinburgh, 1892.

Calendar of Patent Rolls, Henry III. London, 1901–.

*Calendar of Patent Rolls, Elizabeth. In MS. in P.R.O.

Calendar of Scottish Papers (ed. Bain). Edinburgh, 1898–1915.

Calendar of Scottish Papers (ed. Thorpe). London, 1858.

Calendar of Spanish Papers, Elizabeth. London, 1892–9.

Camden, W. *Britannia.* Trans. by P. Holland. London, 1610.

—— *Annals of Elizabeth.* London, 1688.

Carey, Memoirs of Robert, ed. by G. H. Powell. London, 1905.

Carleton, George. *Life of Bernard Gilpin.* London, 1636.

Dalyell, J. G. *Fragments of Scottish History.* Edinburgh, 1798.

Depositions and Ecclesiastical Proceedings. Surtees Soc. London, 1845.

D'Ewes, S. *Journals of the Parliaments of Elizabeth.* London, 1682.

Diurnal of Remarkable Occurrents. Bannatyne Club. Edinburgh,
    1833.
Fiennes, Celia. *Through England on a Side-saddle.* London, 1888.
Grey de Wilton, Life of Lord, ed. by P. de M. G. Egerton. London,
    1847.
Haynes, S. *The State Papers of Lord Burghley,* 1542–70. London,
    1740.
Historical MSS. Commission. Calendars of—
    The Hatfield MSS. London, 1883–1915.
    The Home of Wedderburn MSS. London, 1902.
    The Laing MSS. London, 1914.
    The Mar and Kellie MSS. London, 1904.
    The Rutland MSS. London, 1888.
Holinshed, R. *Chronicles.* London, 1577.
Howard, The Household Books of Lord W. Surtees Soc. Durham,
    1878.
James the Sext, The History of. Bannatyne Club. Edinburgh, 1825.
Leland, The Itinerary of John (ed. L. T. Smith). London, 1907.
Leslie, J. *History of Scotland.* Scots Text. Soc. (ed. E. G. Cody).
    Edinburgh, 1888–95.
Lindesay of Pitscottie, *History and Chronicles of Scotland.* S.T.S.
    London, 1899–1911.
Lodge, E. *Illustrations of British History.* London, 1838.
Lowther, C. *Journal into Scotland* (1629). Edinburgh, 1894.
Melville of Halhill, The Memoirs of Sir James. Edinburgh, 1827.
Melville, Autobiography and Diary of Mr. James. Edinburgh, 1842.
Moysie, D. *Memoirs,* 1577–1603. Edinburgh, 1830.
Murdin, W. *State Papers of Lord Burghley,* 1571–96. London,
    1759.
Nicolson, W. *Leges Marchiarum.* London, 1747.
Parker, The Correspondence of Matthew. Cambridge, 1853.
Parliament of Scotland, Acts of the. N.P. vol. i, 1844, vols. ii, iii, 1814.
Pitcairn, R. *Criminal Trials.* Edinburgh, 1833.
Pitcairn, R. (ed.). *The Herries Memoirs.* Edinburgh, 1836.
Privy Council, Acts of the. N.S. vii–xxxii. London, 1893–1907.
Privy Council, Register of the Scots. Edinburgh, 1877–84.
Richardson, M. A. *Reprints of Rare Tracts.* Newcastle, 1847.
Rymer, T. *Foedera.* Edit. 2. London, 1737.
Sadler, The Papers of Sir R. (ed. A. Clifford). Edinburgh, 1809.
Sanderson, R. P. (ed.). *Survey of Border Lands,* 1604. Alnwick,
    1891.
Sharp, C. *Memorials of the Rebellion of 1569.* London, 1840.

Smith, T. *De Republica Anglorum* (ed. L. Alston). Cambridge, 1906.

Speed, J. *Theatre of the Empire of Great Britain.* London, 1611.

Spotswood, J. *History of the Church of Scotland.* Edinburgh, 1847–51.

*State Papers. Borders, 42 vols. in MS. in P.R.O.

Statutes of the Realm, vol. iv. N.P. 1819.

Stow, J. *The Annals of England.* London, 1605.

Wedel, L. von. *Journey through England and Scotland,* 1584–5. Trans. R.H.S., N.S. ix, 223–70.

Wills and Inventories. Surtees Soc. Durham, 1835, 1860, 1906.

Wills, North Country. Surtees Soc. Durham, 1912.

* These are manuscripts.

LIST OF SECONDARY AUTHORITIES CONSULTED

Abstracts of the Population of Great Britain. London, 1801.

Archaeologia. London, 1780–.

Archaeologia Aeliana. Newcastle, 1816–.

Armstrong, R. B. *History of Liddesdale.* Edinburgh, 1883.

Bartholomew, J. G. *Survey Gazetteer of the British Isles.* London, 1904.

Bates, C. J. *The Border Holds of Northumberland.* Newcastle, 1891.

—— *History of Northumberland.* London, 1895.

Bertie, G. *Five Generations of a Loyal House.* London, 1845.

Berwickshire. Report of Royal Commission on Monuments. Edinburgh, 1915.

Brown, P. H. *Scotland in the Time of Queen Mary.* London, 1904.

Brown, P. H. *History of Scotland,* vol. ii. Cambridge, 1905.

Cambridge History of English Literature. Cambridge, 1907–15.

Cambridge Modern History. Cambridge, 1902–11.

Clarke, G. T. *Mediaeval Military Architecture.* London, 1884.

Cox, J. C. *Parish Registers of England.* London, 1910.

Creighton, M. *Carlisle.* London, 1889.

Curwen, J. F. *Castles and Towers of Cumberland and Westmorland.* Kendal, 1913.

Dixon, D. D. *Upper Coquetdale.* Newcastle, 1903.

—— *Whittingham Vale.* Newcastle, 1895.

Douglas, G. B. S. *History of the Border Counties.* Edinburgh, 1899.

Dumfriesshire, Report of Royal Commission on Ancient Monuments. Edinburgh, 1920.

Elliot, G. F. S. *The Border Elliots*. Edinburgh, 1897.

Ferguson, R. S. *Guide to Carlisle*. Carlisle, N.D.

—— *History of Cumberland*. London, 1890.

Firth, C. H. *Ballad History of the later Tudors*. Trans. R.H.S., 3rd Ser., iii.

Fortescue, J. W. *History of the British Army*. London, 1910.

Fuller, J. *History of Berwick*. Edinburgh, 1799.

Gee, H. *Elizabethan Clergy*. Oxford, 1898.

Groome, F. H. *Ordnance Gazetteer of Scotland*. New edit. London, N.D.

Hodgkin, T. *The Wardens of the Marches*. London, 1908.

Hodgson, J. *History of Northumberland*. Newcastle, 1820–58.

Lang, Andrew. *A History of Scotland*. Edinburgh and London, 1912.

Lapsley, G. T. *The County Palatine of Durham*. New York, 1900.

Macgibbon, D., and Ross, T. *Architecture of Scotland*. Edinburgh, 1887–92.

Marr, J. E. *Cumberland*. Cambridge, 1910.

Maxwell, H. *History of Dumfries and Galloway*. Edinburgh, 1896.

Nicolson, J., and Burn, R. *History of Westmorland and Cumberland*. London, 1777.

Norman, F. M. *Guide to Berwick Fortifications*. Berwick, 1907.

Northumberland County History. Newcastle, 1893–.

Palace of History. Glasgow, 1911.

Pease, H. *The Wardens of the Marches*. London, 1913.

Pollard, A. F. *The Political History of England*, vol. vi. London, 1910.

Proceedings of the Newcastle Society of Antiquaries. Newcastle, 1857–.

Raine, J. *North Durham*. London, 1852.

Rait, R. S. *Anglo-Scottish Relations*. London, 1901.

Reid, R. C. (ed.). *History of Dumfries*, by Robert Edgar. Dumfries, 1915.

Reid, R. R. *The Rebellion of the Earls*. Trans. R.H.S., N.S. xx.

—— *The King's Council in the North*. London, 1921.

Richardson, G. B. *Plague in the North of England*. Newcastle, 1852.

Ridpath, G. *Border History*. Berwick, 1848.

Scott, J. *History of Berwick*. London, 1888.

Shakespeare's England. Oxford, 1916.

Tomlinson, W. W. *Northumberland in the Sixteenth Century.*
  London, N.D.
Tomlinson, W. W. *Guide to Northumberland.* London, N.D.
Transactions of the Cumberland and Westmorland A. and A. Society.
  Kendal, 1874–.
Transactions of the A. and A. Society of Durham and Northumberland.
  London, 1862–1905.
Victoria History of the County of Cumberland. London, 1901–.
Watson, G. *Bygone Penrith.* Penrith, 1893.
Welford, R. *History of Newcastle and Gateshead.* London, 1884–7.

ABBREVIATIONS USED IN REFERENCES

A.A.	*Archaeologia Aeliana.*
A.L.H.T.S.	*Accounts of the Lord High Treasurer of Scotland.*
A.P.C.	*Acts of the Privy Council.*
A.P.S.	*Acts of the Parliament of Scotland.*
Armstrong.	R. B. Armstrong's *History of Liddesdale.*
Autobiog.	*Autobiography and Diary of Mr. James Melville.*
Bannatyne.	R. Bannatyne's *Memorials.*
Barnes.	*The Eccles. Proc. of Bishop Barnes.*
Bates.	C. J. Bates's *Border Holds.*
Bell.	The MS. of Richard Bell.
Birrel.	Robert Birrel's *Diary.*
Brereton.	*Travels.* (Chetham Society, vol. i.)
Brit.	Camden's *Britannia.*
Brit. S.	Camden's *Britannia; Scotland.*
Brown.	P. H. Brown's *History of Scotland.*
Calderwood.	Calderwood's *History of the Kirk of Scotland.*
Camden.	Camden's *Elizabeth.*
Carleton.	Carleton's *Life of Bernard Gilpin.*
C.B.P.	*Calendar of Border Papers.*
C.H.E.L.	*Cambridge History of English Literature.*
C.H.M.	*Calendar of the Hatfield MSS.*
C.M.	*The Memoirs of Robert Cary.*
C.P.R.	*Calendar of Patent Rolls.*
C.R.B.	*Correspondence of Robert Bowes.*
C.R.M.	*Calendar of Rutland MSS.*
C.S.P.	*Calendar of Scottish Papers* (Bain).
Cox.	J. C. Cox's *Parish Registers.*
Creighton.	M. Creighton's *Carlisle.*
Curwen.	J. C. Curwen, *Castles and Towers of Cumberland and Westmorland.*
C. & W.	*Trans. Cumb. and Westm. A. and A. Soc.*
Dalyell.	Dalyell's *Fragments of Scottish History.*
D'Ewes.	D'Ewes's *Journals.*
Diurnal.	*A Diurnal of Remarkable Occurrents.*
Dom.	*Calendar of State Papers; Domestic: Elizabeth.*
Dom. Add.	Addenda to ditto.
D.W.	*Wills and Inventories.* Surtees Soc. 1835, 1860, 1906.

Eresby.	G. Bertie's *Five Generations of a Loyal House.*
F.C.	*Fairfax Correspondence,* ed. R. Bell.
Fiennes.	C. Fiennes's *Through England on a Side-saddle.*
For.	*Calendar of State Papers; Foreign: Elizabeth.*
Fortescue.	J. Fortescue's *History of the British Army.*
G.B.R.	G. B. Richardson's *Plague in the North of England.*
Gee.	H. Gee's *Elizabethan Clergy.*
Grey.	Egerton's *Life of William Lord Grey de Wilton* (Camden Soc.).
Ham. P.	*Calendar of Hamilton Papers.*
Herries.	*Herries Memoirs,* ed. Pitcairn.
H.J.S.	*The History of James the Sext.*
H.M.C.	Historical MSS. Com.
Hodgson.	J. Hodgson's *History of Northumberland.*
Holinshed, E.	*Holinshed's Chronicles, England.*
Holinshed, S.	*Holinshed's Chronicles, Scotland.*
Home.	*Calendar of Home of Wedderburn MSS.*
Laing.	*Calendar of Laing MSS.*
Lang.	Lang's *History of Scotland.*
Leges.	Nicolson's *Leges Marchiarum.*
Leland.	*Leland's Itinerary,* ed. L. T. Smith.
Leslie.	Leslie's *History of Scotland.* Scot. Text. Soc.
Lodge.	Lodge's *Illustrations of British History.*
Lowther.	Lowther's *Journal into Scotland.*
Mar & Kellie.	*Calendar of Mar and Kellie MSS.*
Marr.	J. E. Marr's *Cumberland.*
Melville, M.	*Memoirs of Sir J. Melville of Halhill.*
Moysie.	Moysie's *Memoirs.*
Murdin.	Murdin's *State Papers of Lord Burghley.*
Naworth.	*Household Books of Lord William Howard.*
N. & B.	Nicolson and Burn's *History of Cumberland and Westmorland.*
N.C.H.	*Northumberland County History.*
N.D.	Raine's *North Durham.*
Parker.	*Correspondence of Archbishop Parker.*
Pitcairn.	Pitcairn's *Criminal Trials.*
Pitscottie.	Lindesay of Pitscottie. *Chron. and Hist. of Scotland.*
P.N.S.A.	*Proceeedings of the Newcastle Society of Antiquaries.*
Ridpath.	Ridpath's *Border History.*
R.P.C.S.	*Register of the Scots Privy Council.*
R.P.S.	*Survey of the Borders,* 1604, ed. R. P. Sanderson.

R.T.	*Rare Tracts,* ed. M. A. Richardson.
Rymer.	Rymer's *Foedera.*
Sadler.	*The Sadler Papers,* ed. Clifford.
Scott.	J. Scott's *History of Berwick.*
S.P. Borders.	State Papers, Borders P.R.O.
Sharp.	C. Sharp's *Memorials.*
Span. Cal.	*Calendar of State Papers; Spanish.*
Speed.	Speed's *Theatre of the Empire of Great Britain.*
Spotswood.	Spotswood's *History of the Church of Scotland.*
Stat. Realm.	*Statutes of the Realm.*
Stow.	Stow's *Annals.* 1605.
Thorpe.	*Calendar of Scottish Papers,* ed. Thorpe.
Trans. R.H.S.	*Transactions of the Royal Historical Society.*
Travellers.	P. H. Brown's *Early Travellers in Scotland.*
Wardens.	Hodgkin's *Wardens of the Marches.*
Watson.	G. Watson's *Bygone Penrith.*
Wedel.	*Journey through England and Scotland,* 1584–5.

PART I

THE GEOGRAPHY OF THE ELIZABETHAN BORDERS

EVIDENCE of the general geography of the English Marches is fairly plentiful. Besides the undated and unsigned description in the vile handwriting of Thomas Phillips, Walsyngham's secretary, which was probably written about 1580,[1] there are Leland's *Survey* of 1538, or soon after, which is, however, meagre and often inaccurate, Camden's *Britannia*, and the work of Speed. These refer to all the Marches, but the valuable survey of Sir Robert Bowes and Sir Rafe Ellerker, made in 1541, unfortunately omits the whole of the West and parts of the other two Marches,[2] omissions which are partly supplied by John Udall's account of the West, which he wrote for Essex in 1598.[3] Raine printed a Survey of Norham and Islandshire dated 1561 or 1562.[4] There are various maps by Saxton in the *Britannia*, maps and plans in Speed, and a few unpublished maps, but Elizabethan map-making lacked accurate definition. Of the Scots Marches there seem to be no extant contemporary Scots surveys, and Camden is scanty, while Leland did not cross the Tweed. There are, however, an English military report of the West March written between 1563 and 1566 with reference to a possible English occupation of that district,[5] and Aglionby's report of 1592.[6] Otherwise a Border historian has to rely on stray references in state papers, accounts by travellers, and various contemporary historians, the most valuable of whom is Leslie, and supplement them with what his own eyes can see to-day. Large-scale maps are few, and not very helpful.

The English Borders were the three shires of Northumberland, Cumberland, and Westmorland, which were divided into three marches, East, Middle, and West.[7]

[1] S.P. Borders, xx, 198–202.   [2] Bates, i, 25, 29 et sqq.   [3] C.H.M. viii, 562–4.   [4] N.D. 15–27.   [5] Armstrong, cvi et sqq.   [6] C.B.P. i, 743.   [7] C.B.P. i, 76.

From Berwick to the head of Solway Firth is some 70 miles in a straight line, and between 110 and 120 along the actual frontier. About half of this is land, mostly in the Cheviots, the highest point being nearly 2,500 feet above sea-level, and the rest is formed by such streams as the Tweed, Liddel Water, Esk, Sark, and various burns. Northumberland lay 'after a sort enclosed in fashion of a Triangle, but not with equal sides', the ground itself being 'for the most part rough and hard to be manured', but becoming 'towards the sea and Tine by diligence and good husbandry . . . very fruitfull'. It contained 'in many places those stones, Lithanthraces, which we call sea coles'.[1] Of Cumberland Camden wrote: 'The country although it be somewhat with the coldest as lying farre North, and seemeth as rough by reason of hilles, yet for the variety thereof it smileth upon the beholders and giveth contentment to as many as travaile it. For after the rockes bunching out, the mountains standing thicke together, rich of metall mines, and betweene them great meeres stored with all kindes of wildfoule, you come to prety hilles good for pasturage, and well replenished with flocks of sheepe, beneath which againe you meet with goodly plaines, spreading out a great way, yeelding corn sufficiently. Besides all this the Ocean driving and dashing upon the shore affourdeth plenty of excellent good fish, and upbraideth, as it were, the Inhabitants there abouts with their negligence that they practise fishing no more than they doe.' [2] East Cumberland 'being leane, hungry and a waste', showed 'nothing but the spring head of South Tine in a moorish place'.[3] Westmorland lay 'among moores and high hilles reaching one to another' and was 'for the most part unmanured', but a narrow part of it between the Lune and Windermere was reputed 'fruitfull enough in the valleis', but had 'many felles with rough and stony rockes lying ever bare without grasse'.[4] Udall found the last two shires lay high and low, full of swift rivers, apt for good tillage, and sufficiently well pastured.[5]

[1] Brit. 799.   [2] Brit. 765.   [3] Brit. 786.   [4] Brit. 759.   [5] C.H.M. viii, 562.

The East Marches of England.[1]

This small district was 'that part of Northumberland which is next unto Scotland on the East side of England',[2] that is Norhamshire, Islandshire, Glendale, and Bamburghshire,[3] the two former of which, with Bedlingtonshire, were till 1844 parts of the County Palatine of Durham. The Marches began 'at a place called the Hanging Stone', marked in Saxton's map in the 1610 edition of *Britannia*, but not clearly, 'at the West end of the Forest of Cheviot, and so coming down by a little rinnel or brook, called Caudgate, which falleth into the river Tell, stretcheth, as the old borderers of the Middle March affirm, from the North side of Bewick lordship, down the Water of Warne to the Warneford, as the Lordships of Alnwick and Bamburgh are divided'. The east borderers maintained that 'the River of Ale maketh the division'.[4] Bowes and Ellerker were uncertain, but Hunsdon stated that his wardenry was some twenty-four miles long by sixteen broad, and apparently took the Aln as the boundary. Indeed about 1580 the opinion of the east borderers seemed 'presently to take place, part of Alnwick lordship being mustered with the East March'.[5] An undated manuscript (1574–96) showing 'the towns that partes the Este and Mydle Marches of Englande' does not settle the question. Chillingham, which is placed in the Middle March, mustered with the East at least three times during Hunsdon's tenure of office, and East and West Lilburn also broke the rule. An accurate map is thus impossible.[6] Two previous writers have published maps marking a boundary, without comment. They differ from each other and from those given here, which are based on muster rolls and on the above-mentioned document.[7] The publication of maps unrevised by the authors of the books which they illustrate is not new; Camden, for instance, would hardly have

---

[1] See Map I. [2] C.B.P. i, 76. [3] Sadler, ii, 288–9. [4] C.B.P. i, 76.
[5] C.B.P. i, 76. [6] C.B.P. i, pp. 17–20, 153, 157, nos. 253, 259; ii, no. 169;
C.H.M. v, 458 ; S.P. Borders, xli, fol. 237. [7] Maps II and III.

passed 'Mare Germanicus' (*sic*) as a description of the North Sea.[1]

The boundary 'foranenst' Scotland was the bounds of Berwick and then the Tweed. There were seven or eight ordinary fords [2] between Berwick and Norham, and others higher up, such as that between Wark and Coldstream,[3] but it must not be thought that the Tweed was no defence whatever, as those fords were dangerous in time of sudden

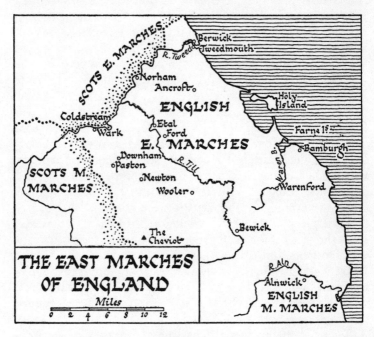

THE EAST MARCHES
OF ENGLAND
Miles
0 2 4 6 8 10 12

floods, which sometimes lasted for days.[4] When Sir W. Bowes crossed the Tweed in October 1597 it was 'so great' that the lives of some of his followers were in danger.[5] The thieves, however, took risks, and Wyllughby in 1598 wished to 'daume up' the fords as all the spoils were committed by way of them.[6] The country on both sides of the Tweed was very fertile [7] and the farmers do

[1] Map of Scotland in *Britannia*, 1610.   [2] See Plate IV.   [3] Bates, i, 64; Hodgson, III, ii, p. 200 note; A.A. xvi, N.S., p. 89 (1893).   [4] C.R.M. i, 42–3.   [5] C.B.P. ii, 776.   [6] C.B.P. ii, 980, 993.   [7] Brit. 779.

The Cowgate, or ' Carey porte ', from outside

The same, from inside

I. BERWICK WALLS

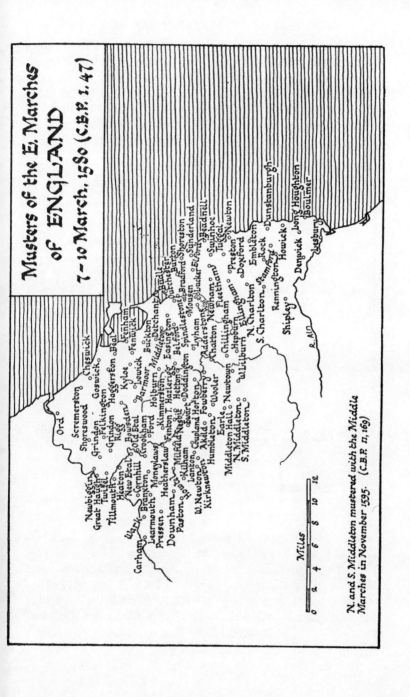

Musters of the E. Marches of ENGLAND 7–10 March, 1580 (C.B.P. I, 47)

N. and S. Middleton mustered with the Middle Marches in November 1595. (C.B.P. II, 169)

Miles
0 2 4 6 8 10 12

not seem to have raided each other's lands, but the thieves of Teviotdale raided both. None the less the March with its twenty-eight 'towns' was not undefended. The estimated number of castles in Northumberland varies from the twenty-six given by Speed (p. 87) to about a hundred. Many were mere towers intended for defence against sudden raids rather than for withstanding sieges, but three

Note. The document in S.P. Borders, xli, 237, contains no map. This map, based on the information therein, should be compared with Map II. ' Yerdell ' is now called ' Earle '.

of the most important Northumberland holds, Berwick, Norham, and Wark, were on the frontier of this March. Berwick,[1] 'the utmost towne in England, and the strongest hold in all Britaine', lay beyond the Tweed between a bend of the river and the sea-coast. Elizabeth, soon after her accession, 'enclosed it about in a narrower compasse within the old wall, with a high wall of stone most strangly

[1] See Plates I, II.

compacted together, which she hath so forwarded againe
with a counter scarfe, a bank round about it, with mounts
of earth cast up by mans hand, and open terraces above
head, that either the forme of these munitions, or strength
thereof may justly cut off all hope of winning it'. Its
Governor was always 'one of the wisest and most approved
of the nobility of England', and was also Warden of the
East March.[1] Opposite Berwick, at Tweedmouth, was a
tower which in 1542 was 'in reasonable good reparacions'.
It is not mentioned in the survey of 1560, and there is no
vestige of it now, though it was not pulled down till the
eighteenth century. It ought to have been strongly fortified to prevent its seizure by the French or Spaniards.[2]
Norham had a 'Castle [3] upon the top of a high steepe
rocke', fortified with a trench, 'in the utmore wall whereof,
which is of greater circuit, are placed sundry turrets in a
Canton toward the river: within there is another enclosure
or wall much stronger, in the mids of which riseth up the
Keepe of great heigth'.[4] It had been in a good state of repair and fortification in 1541,[5] and Sadler in 1560 thought
it 'the most convenient place of service for the Warden of
the E. March to lie at',[6] but the next year it was reported
as unserviceable except for spear and shield of the sudden,
though there was stone enough to repair it if the Queen
desired.[7] Ten years later Hunsdon feared that unless immediately repaired it would fall down that winter.[8] The
Privy Council talked of repairing it in 1578, but economy
won the day and in 1590 it was in ruins,[9] and, owing to
what Camden called 'the secure peace of our age', was
allowed to remain so,[10] though it should have been the
chiefest strength of the Borders if war had broken out
with the Scots. Full repairs would have cost nearly £1,800,
but only fifty-four shillings and ninepence was spent.[11]
Wark, a royal castle, 'of three wards whereof the utter-

---

[1] Brit. 816–17. See also C.B.P. *passim*, especially i, 554, which deals with
the walls; Fuller's *Berwick*, especially 355–7; S.P. Borders, xxxvii, 217; For.
iv, 580–2, 589; P. Hume Brown, *Early Travellers in Scotland*, 81; Brereton,
95.   [2] N.D. 245.   [3] See Plate III.   [4] Brit. 816.   [5] Bates, i, 38.
[6] Sadler, ii, 248.   [7] For. iv, 577.   [8] For. ix, 1153.   [9] A.P.C. x, 383;
R.T. iv, 225.   [10] Brit. 816.   [11] C.B.P. ii, 189, 295, 386.

most ward serveth for a barmekyn', was 'in greatt and
extreme decaye' in 1541, though Leland a few years before called it 'a meatly stronge fortress'. If repaired it
would have served to defend Glendale, the district to the
west of the Till, which was very fertile and well peopled,
but had not enough towers.[1] It had been thought that its
capture by the enemy would mean the destruction of the
whole frontier,[2] but when Rowland Johnson found it in
1561, 'ruinous being in most places fallen down', he thought
it useless as it was, or as it might be, as the very site was
subject to divers places within a quarter of a mile, and
there was no quarry near it anything worth.[3] In 1571 it
was reported as decaying very much daily, but in 1584 a
report of twenty-six pages was made on it, and as late as
1596 £300 was spent on repairs.[4]

The impregnable rock fortress of Bamburgh would
have been important if any of Mary Stuart's continental
supporters had dared to attack the coast, but they re-
frained, and so, like the decayed castle at Dunstanburgh,
it hardly enters into the history of this period.[5] Holy
Island, which had 'a pretty towne in it, with a Church and
a Castle', and under the town 'a good commodious haven,
defended with a Blockhouse situate upon a hill to the
South East', and the Farne Islands, some two miles from
Bamburgh, 'enclosed within the most deepe Ocean and
encircled about with craggy clifts' and containing a fort,
would also have sprung into prominence, but they were
neglected.[6] Ford and Etal castles were both in decay in
1541, and so was Wooler Tower which lay near 'a common entry and passage of the Scots for invading this realm
or making any spoil in time of war or troubles in time of
peace'.[7] Newton, Pawston, and Downham were also 'places
accustomed of defence for soldiers to lie in' and, with help
from Berwick and Wark, could 'keep in' the men of
Teviotdale, and drive them to forsake their own houses

---

[1] Bates, i, 30, 36, 331; Leland, ix, 67.   [2] For. i, 72.   [3] For. iv, 577.
[4] For. ix, 1604; S.P. Dom. Eliz., vol. xxviii, 95, 1. 2. 3. 4. 5; C.B.P. ii, 604.
For its importance compared with Berwick see S.P. Borders, i, 6.   [5] N.C.H.
i, 17, ii, 209; Brit. 815; Bates, 167, 223.   [6] Brit. S. 220-1; Speed 93;
C.B.P. ii, 176, 960; Brereton, 94.   [7] Bates, 33, 38-9.

and whole towns with little charges to the Queen.[1] In the East, as in other Marches, there were 'many small castles and piles', which, like Camden, 'I wittingly let passe: For an endlesse peece of worke it were to goe through them all one by one'.[2] The trouble was that their owners sought peace and quiet by leaving their houses to decay, and living farther from the frontier.[3] Besides towers there were fortified churches, at any rate at Ancroft,[4] where there was 'one pile builded to the end of the Church'.[5] It may thus be said that on the whole the East March was fairly well fortified, though its inhabitants did not think so, but sought government aid in 1596, pointing out that their March was but a third the size of either of the others, and adjoined two Scots Marches, both larger and more populous, having almost four hundred villages and steads to the hundred and twenty in the English East March, and that the Scots could invade it through a 'plaine champain countrey very nere adjoyninge, and sometimes by the river of Twede which is full of foordes'.[6]

The English Middle Marches.[7]

This was that part of Northumberland not included in the East Marches.[8] The frontier line was apparently the same as to-day, and the Cheviots,[9] which formed most of it, could not be crossed by an army with artillery, but there was plenty of room for large bodies of horse to enter the March near Harbottle,[10] and there were many passages convenient for the thieves of Liddesdale and Teviotdale.[11] Alnwick, a walled town with a 'goodly castle',[12] was the most important place in the northern part of the March, and close to it was Alnwick Abbey, the usual residence of the Warden.[13] The castle itself, which belonged to the Percys, comes but little into the history of this period, though seized by Forster in 1569, and afterwards, like Warkworth, much damaged by him. Harbottle Castle in

---

[1] C.B.P. i, 162.　　[2] Brit. 815.　　[3] Bates, i, 40.　　[4] See Plate IV.
[5] N.D. 19; Bates, i, 37, 53; P.N.S.A. 3rd ser., i, 185.　　[6] C.B.P. ii, 433.
[7] See Map IV.　　[8] C.B.P. i, 76.　　[9] See Plate III.　　[10] For. iv, 370.
[11] C.B.P. ii, 853.　　[12] Brit. 813.　　[13] C.M. 57; C.B.P. i, p. 215 (i); Dom. ii, p. 292.

upper Coquetdale was more important and might have been a real stronghold, lying as it did a hundred and fifty feet above the river at the top of a steep slope. However, it was kept in very poor repair, and by 1596 had become 'so ruyned' that its captain had to move for the winter and 'lye att Otterburne'.[1] Warkworth, another Percy castle, Morpeth Castle, and Newcastle itself also come but little into this story, though Newcastle and Warkworth were fortified by Forster against the earls in 1569.[2] Indeed Tobie Matthew asserted in 1599 that Newcastle was not in the Borders at all, but 'batable' between Northumberland and the Bishopric.[3] In Elizabeth's time Redesdale, which Camden found 'too voide of inhabitants by reason of depradations', and North Tynedale, both of which bred 'notable light horsemen' and had 'their hilles hard by, so boggy and standing with water in the top that no horsemen are able to ride through them', were the two chief cares of the Warden. Some allowance must be made for modern drainage, but many of these ways were dry and hard in the summers of 1911 and 1921 and impassable in the summer of 1927. To sum up, though there were numerous towers in the narrow valleys and along the east coast route, it is hard to conclude that the Middle March was as strong as its eastern neighbours said.[4] Taking Northumberland as a whole there were three geographical divisions, a coastal plain in the east, containing fourteen ports, creeks, and landing-places, uplands in the centre, and fells in the west. The men of the plain seem to have lived as settled a life as possible, but the hardness of the rest of the ground seemed to harden its inhabitants, who therefore 'addicted themselves, as it were, wholy to Mars and Armes'.[5]

The English West Marches.[6]

This was the counties of Cumberland and Westmorland,[7] of which the latter was too far from the frontier to

[1] C.B.P. ii, 466.   [2] Brit. 809–10, 812–13; Bates, 81; Leland, ix, 60, 63, 64; Brereton, 89–90.   [3] C.B.P. ii, 702, 1041.   [4] C.B.P. ii, 433; Brit. 802.   [5] Brit. 799.   [6] See Map V.   [7] C.B.P. i, 76.

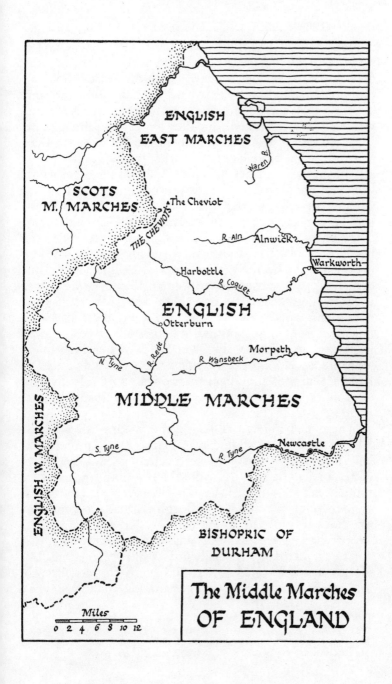

ENGLISH
EAST MARCHES

Waren B.

SCOTS
M. MARCHES   The Cheviot

THE CHEVIOTS   R. Aln   Alnwick

                                              Warkworth

            Harbottle
                        R. Coquet

            ENGLISH
Otterburn

                                    Morpeth
N. Tyne   R. Rede   R. Wansbeck

MIDDLE MARCHES

ENGLISH W. MARCHES

S. Tyne   R. Tyne   Newcastle

            BISHOPRIC OF
               DURHAM

                            The Middle Marches
Miles   OF ENGLAND
0 2 4 6 8 10 12

be important at this time. Its chief town, Kendal, was a place of great trade and resort, and its people had 'great trafficke and vent of their wollen clothes throughout all parts of England'.[1] Appleby had 'one broad street' and a 'castle aloft environed wholy almost by the river', but was 'slenderly inhabited', and, but for its antiquity making it the county town, it would have been 'little better than a village'. The shire had four market towns, seven castles, and twenty-six parishes.[2] Cumberland, on the other hand, with its 'goodly plaines' and 'prety hilles good for pasturage',[3] was all important. The sea frontier, Solway Firth, was hardly any protection according to Camden, for at every ebb the water was so low that for eight miles the borderers and beast stealers might easily wade it.[4] There is said to have been a ford as far west as Bowness. Camden, however, may not have known that the tide comes up Solway very fast, and in a south-west gale would have been dangerous even to those who knew the fords well. The land frontier of about twenty miles was largely formed by rivers, of which the Esk and Liddel water were easily fordable.[5] Happily before 1558 the Debatable Land, a fruitful source of disagreement, had been amicably divided, though its inhabitants were still very troublesome to both realms.[6]

There is ample evidence of the organization of the March for defence. The farthest strength adjoining Scotland and the sea was 'Rokele' Castle, the modern Rockcliffe, a small hold built by the Dacres on the Eden, three miles north-west of Carlisle. This was the most convenient residence for the steward of Burgh Barony, in whom 'lay all the safety of the West part of the Wardenry'. Its keeper had to see that the inhabitants were armed, and the fords guarded, especially at low tide.[7] The church at Burgh has a fortified tower, similar to that at Ancroft, and at Drumburgh was 'neither a castle nor tower, but a

---

[1] Brit. 759; Speed, 85.   [2] Brit. 761; Leland, ix, 47; Speed, 85.   [3] Brit. 765; Speed, 87.   [4] Brit. 775; Marr, 151.   [5] C.B.P. ii, 598, 1543; R.P.S. 12; Bell, 165.   [6] Bell, 164; C.B.P. i, 274, p. 102.   [7] Brit. 781; Leland, ix, 51; C.B.P. i, 76, 162, 274, 743; pp. 32, 392.

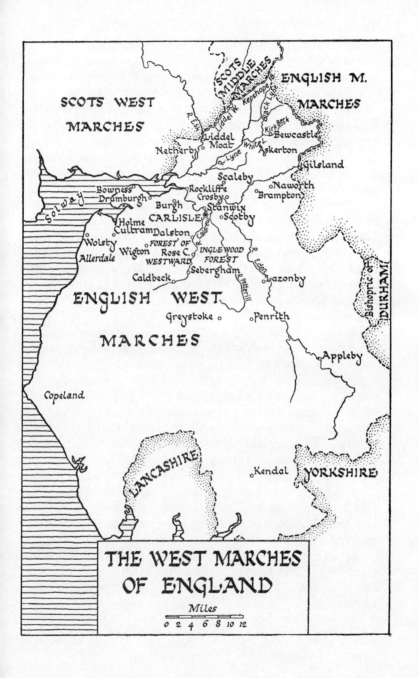

THE WEST MARCHES
OF ENGLAND

Miles
0 2 4 6 8 10 12

house of strength and very fit place of defence',[1] the remains of which now form part of a cottage wall. At Bowness was a house or tower belonging to the parsonage and adjoining a sea-creek. In 1593 it was a place of small receipt, yet very necessary for that part of the Border. Leland called it 'a lytle poore steeple as a fortlet for a brunt'.[2] Seven miles west by south of this was 'Woulstre' Castle, a quarter of a mile from a sea-creek, and about four hours by boat from Scotland. In 1580 it was said to need repairs estimated at £180.[3] The modern name is Wolsty. At Netherby and by Liddel Moat were 'howses' in which dwelt the Grames, 'very famous among the borderers for their martiall disposition'.[4] By their tenure they were bound to keep horse and gear and to watch the fords, but having intermarried with the Scots they were wont to bring them in.[5] The third place, next to the Moat, was the Queen's castle of Bewcastle,[6] 'standing in a wild and solitarie country'[7] between the White Lyne and Kirk beck, two tributaries of the Lyne, ten miles north-east of Brampton. The inhabitants of the district were 'rude for want of instruction and poor for want of stock, having more ground by a great quantity than they are able to store'. The castle had been 'the chief and only defence' of its district, but by 1583 it was almost a ruin, and in 1604 there was 'not any room thereof wherin a man may sit dry'. This neglect led to many Scots outrages.[8] Close to it was Askerton Tower, the men of which were supposed to keep watch and aid Bewcastle, services which they did not fulfil owing to local feuds. The steward of Gilsland was supposed to live there, and keep it without any help, but after 1569 it was 'sore spoiled . . . and worse governed'.[9]

At Carlisle lay the Warden, his deputy, and his constable.[10] The city was 'passing commodiously and pleasantly seated', 'betwixt the meeting of three rivers', the

[1] C. and W., N.S. xi, p. 242; Leland, ix, 51; Brit. 775.   [2] Brit. 775; Leland, ix, 50; Dom. Add. iii, 348–9.   [3] Dom. Add. iii, 349; Brit. 773. [4] Brit. 781.   [5] C.B.P. i, pp. 101–2.   [6] See Plate V.   [7] Brit. 778. [8] R.P.S. 35–6; C.B.P. i, pp. 69–70, 102, 393, nos. 174, 638, ii, 114, 131, 1081.   [9] Brit. 782; C.B.P. i, 162, 743, ii, 982.   [10] C.B.P. i, 743.

Eden, the Petterill, and the Caldew. It was 'fortified with
strong walls of stone', and had a castle, 'a place of great
respect', and a citadel. In the early part of the reign both
were in a parlous condition, but were repaired, and in
1598 Udall found them fit for defence against 'speer and
shelld'. The Deputy had charge of all service for the defence or offence, and in Udall's opinion the place was
weakly guarded and much neglected. Carlisle had a civic
life of its own, and much trade in cattle and stolen goods.[1]
At Stanwix, just north of Carlisle, the road crossed the
Eden by a wooden bridge, which was repaired by 43 Eliz.,
c. 16. There were really two bridges, as the Eden then
flowed in two channels.[2] This road led to Crosby, a barony
held by the Bishop, whose steward had to be ready to
guard the fords of Eden 'where of necessity the thieves
must pass' when any fray arose.[3] Next to this lay Scaleby
Castle. The tenants of the estate were able men, and in
their master's absence rode in both England and Scotland.
In 1583 the castle was said to be 'a strong house and a
fair, very well set for a captain to lie in,—yet it is not kept
by any soldiers, nor scanty any dwellers in it'.[4] Between
this and Scotland lay the Esk, inhabited on both sides
by the 'best Grames—under no government except the
Warden'. They were hard to restrain, but capable of doing
acceptable service.[5] West of Burgh lay 'the Holme lordship', or Holme Cultram, under a Steward 'who ought to
be resident within the Holme for the defence of the lordship'. It was a royal barony.[6] South of the Holme was
Allerdale ward which was safe if the Steward of Burgh
were careful; the inhabitants were liable for March days
or when sent for by the Warden. South of Burgh were
the barony of Wigton and the forest of Westward, under
the Earl of Northumberland's steward, who had to guide
and rule the inhabitants in case of service, and south-west
of it was Cauldbeck lordship, the tenants of which

[1] Brit. 778; C.B.P. i, 743; Dom. Add. ii, 431, 505, iii, 348–9; C. & W., O.S.
xv, 117 note; Creighton, 92, 124; C.H.M. viii, 562–4.   [2] Brit. 778; C. &
W., O.S. xv, p. 117 note.   [3] C.B.P. i, p. 393.   [4] C.B.P. i, pp. 22, 124,
393.   [5] C.B.P. i, p. 393.   [6] C.B.P. i, pp. 392, 430; Brit. 773.

appeared under a bailiff when the Warden sent for them.[1]
Between Cauldbeck and Penrith lay the barony of Grey-
stoke under a Steward whose services were used for March
days, and 'for watch and search'. There was a castle there.[2]
Between Westward and Inglewood forests lay Sebergham
under the Queen's bailiff, who led the tenants to the number required by the Warden when he sent for them. Next
came Dalston under a bailiff for the Bishop and others.
Its service was at Sebergham, 'but more to follow frays and
aid Burgh'.[3] The forest of Inglewood stretched from Penrith to Carlisle, and its tenants had to follow the Warden
for general or particular service.[4] At Penrith, 'a little
towne and of indifferent trade, fortified on the West side
with a castle', lay the Queen's steward, who was also in
charge of Lazonby, &c., and led the tenants to particular
and general service when required by the Warden.[5] Penrith itself is a good example of a border town with a
market-place in the centre and narrow lanes leading to it.
The cattle could be driven into the market-place and the
narrow lanes defended.

There remained all Westmorland and Coupland, which
were never called to service save by fire and beacon, or for
general service.[6] It is therefore unnecessary to lengthen
this dry catalogue by naming and describing Westmorland castles and holds. If it serves its purpose it will show
that this March was 'strong enough to defend themselves
against Scotland, and to offend them if need require', but
not strong enough for sudden service as most of the gentry
were non-residents, and those near by dared not put their
hands to it for fear of feud.[7] Naworth Castle [8] has not
been mentioned because, though important in the domestic
history of 1569–70, it seems to have had no place in the
subsequent defensive arrangements of the March. The
Bishop's 'proper fine castle', called Rose Castle, was in
1598 'a place of no strength',[9] and there were perhaps fifty
or sixty other holds, many of them in the south, and most

[1] C.B.P. i, p. 393.   [2] C.B.P. i, pp. 32, 392.   [3] C.B.P. i, p. 392.   [4] C.B.P.
i, p. 392.   [5] Brit. 776; C.B.P. i, p. 392.   [6] C.B.P. i, p. 393, ii, no. 1191.
[7] C.B.P. i, p. 393.   [8] Brit. 784.   [9] Brit. 778; C.B.P. ii, 1016.

of them unworthy of mention in this period. There were eight ports, creeks, and landing-places in Cumberland.[1]

The East Marches of Scotland.[2]

This was the county or sheriffdom of Berwick,[3] which adjoined England from Berwick Bounds to about a mile above Carham, and had but one opposite March. To the north it was separated from Haddingtonshire by the Lammermuir Hills and the Dunglass burn, and it fell roughly into two divisions, the Merse, a broad fertile lowland stretching from Kelso in the Middle March to Duns and Coldingham in the north and Berwick in the south, and the Lammermuirs and their foothills. The whole March was mostly in the hands of the Humes, but it is the Merse that concerns us most, and its chief strength was Hume, or Home Castle, one of the strongest holds in Scotland, standing on a rocky height seven hundred feet above sea-level, with an extensive view of the Merse and the Tweed valley. It lay most offensively for England, kept the greater part of the Merse in subjection, and if any foreign army entered Scotland it was well placed for annoying England, and ought to have been hard to capture.[4] Sussex, however, easily took it in 1570, and England held it for some time, till the Regent begged it back as one of the keys of the country, without which he could not 'contene' the disordered people in good obedience.[5] The modern castle is but an eighteenth-century sham, built of the debris of its real predecessor. The other key was Fast Castle,[6] so called, says Camden, because of its firmness and strength.[7] It was built on the top of an inaccessible cliff, on a promontory by the North Sea, about seven miles east of Cockburnspath. The adjoining cliffs are even higher than the platform on which the castle stood, and it must formerly have been reached by a drawbridge, but the cliff has slipped and partly filled in the abyss which separated the castle from the cliffs above. Very little remains of the

---

[1] Dom. Add. ii, 554.   [2] See Map VI.   [3] R.P.C.S. xiv, xcviii.
[4] C.S.P. iii, 209.   [5] C.S.P. iii, 197, iv, 726, 737; For. x, 1171.   [6] See Plate VI.   [7] Brit. S. 10–11.

castle, which, at its best, was rather a retreat than a place
whence England could be annoyed. Next in importance
came Eyemouth, the real key to Berwick, at which the
French fort was destroyed by treaty in 1561.[1] It lay on
the modern coast-guard station on the left bank of the
river, and, being but eight miles north of Berwick, was a
constant source of anxiety to England. Leslie says there

were many strong castles in these parts, but this is an
exaggeration. The people of the Merse were generally
quiet and gave little trouble to England, being rather
fellow sufferers with the English at the hands of the
Teviotdale thieves. The country was 'plentiful of corn',
not wheat but barley and oats, of which last very good
bread was made. There were few woods, and reeds or
straw were used for firing.[2]

1 For. iii, 281.   2 Leslie, 6, 10.

The Scots Middle Marches.[1]

This was the sheriffdoms of Roxburgh, Selkirk, and Peebles, and sometimes also 'the county of Liddisdaill',[2] though the last usually had a separate keeper.[3] From the Tweed above Carham to the Hanging Stone by the Cheviot this March adjoined the English East March, into which there were many easy routes, and from the Hanging Stone to a point some miles below Kershopefoot the frontier ran along the Cheviots opposite the English Middle March, and, for the last eight miles, opposite the English West March. The most notable route was probably that up Bowmont Water, over Cocklaw into Coquetdale, and the most notorious thieves came from Teviotdale and Liddesdale. Of Peebles, the most northerly county, we hear little that is bad, probably because it is near Edinburgh. There the Tweed ran through a dale 'replenished with sheepe that beare woolle of great request', and Peebles itself was 'a mercate town',[4] and a suitable place for levies to meet before going to the unruly parts of the Borders. Of Selkirk we hear even less, though levies met there also. Roxburghshire adjoined England, and its county town and castle were 'in a manner quite vanished and not to be seene',[5] but Jedburgh, 'a Burrough well inhabited and frequented',[6] Kelso and Hawick were towns of some importance; Kelso, in connexion with Francis, fifth Earl of Bothwell, Jedburgh for the Ferneherst family and for justice courts, and Hawick as the chief town of Teviotdale, of which Kelso was the second.[7] Teviotdale lay 'next unto England among the edges of high craggy hills . . . inhabited by a warlike nation which by reason of so many encounters in foregoing ages between Scottish and English' was 'alwaies most ready for service and sudden invasions'.[8] The Kers of Cesford and Fernieherst were the two most prominent families, and were sometimes at feud,[9] and loose men were abundant.

[1] See Map VII. [2] R.P.C.S. iii, 344–8. [3] C.B.P. i, 72. [4] Brit. S. 10. [5] Brit. S. 10. [6] Brit. S. 9. [7] C.B.P. i, 111, 186, 642, 940; Brit. S. 9; Leslie, 11. [8] Brit. S. 9; Leslie, 11. [9] C.B.P. i, 111, 197.

Cesford had 'twoe houses, Sesford fronting on England, and Hallidon in East Tivydale'.[1] The former lay on rising ground above Kale Water, six miles south of Kelso, on one of the main routes into England. It is now in ruins, but its plan was extraordinarily solid, the lower walls being over four yards thick, and there was also an outer curtain-wall and probably a moat. Of Holydean only a vault is

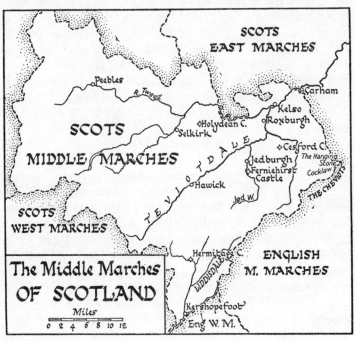

The Middle Marches OF SCOTLAND

Miles
0 2 4 6 8 10 12

left. Fernieherst Castle, in the valley of the Jed, two miles above Jedburgh, was partially destroyed by Sussex in 1570, but rebuilt just before the Union of 1603. Of the whole March, however, Liddesdale, especially the sur-names of Scott, Armstrong, and Elwood, was 'most offen-sive to England',[2] and its keeper, who was often in league with the raiders, had a secure retreat in the Hermitage, 'a very strong Castle',[3] on the left bank of Hermitage Water, between two tributary streams. The ground is not high,

[1] C.B.P. ii, 853.   [2] C.B.P. i, 743.   [3] Brit. S. 16; Leslie, 11.

Interior of a flanker

The same flanker, from the opposite direction

II. BERWICK FORTIFICATIONS

Norham Castle

The Cheviots, near the frontier-line

III. THE MARCHES OF ENGLAND

but very marshy, and several moats are still traceable, and are probably part of an extensive system of moats and mounds for the outer defence of the hold, there being no signs of a curtain-wall. The castle had very thick walls and could stand a siege unless heavy artillery could be brought against it, a difficult task in such a district. This Wardenry and its western neighbour troubled England most, and redress was very hard to get.[1]

The Scots West Marches.[2]

In 1578 this consisted of 'Galloway beneath and above Cree, Niddsdale, Annandale, Eskdale, Ewesdale and Wachopdale', or in other words, the Stewartries of Kirkcudbright and Annandale, with the sheriffdom of Dumfries.[3] For practical purposes, however, the Wardenry did not extend beyond Dumfriesshire, as is shown by a contemporary map of the country opposite the English West March,[4] which is dated 1590 and marks the towers and stone houses. The whole of the frontier was bounded by the English West March, and the Warden, like his eastern colleague, had only one opposite. Quite half his wardenry was upland covered with grass, heather, or peat, and the whole was divided into four dales. The Nith is a tidal river deep enough to allow fair-sized vessels to reach Glencaple, and its dale was 'sufficiently furnished with cornefields and pastures'. Dumfries lay near the mouth of the river, between two hills, and was 'the most flourishing town of this tract, which hath to show also an old castle in it'. It was 'famous for making of wollen clothes'.[5] The castle, which does not appear in this history, has left no traces, and the town was unwalled.[6] Carlaverock Castle, which lay amid the marshes near the river mouth, was described by Camden as 'a weake dwelling house of the Barons of Maxwell',[7] but Henry, Lord Scroope, was more correct in considering it 'a place of the greatest strength of any in these quarters',[8] though its importance was

[1] C.B.P. i, 595, 668.   [2] See Map VIII.   [3] R.P.C.S. ii, 678–9.
[4] *Archaeologia*, xx. 161.   [5] Brit. S. 17; Leslie, 12.   [6] C.B.P. ii, 527.
[7] Brit. S. 17.   [8] C.P.B. i, 349.

greater in Scots feuds than in offence against England.[1] Annandale was a district 'into which access by land is very difficult', and 'the places of greater note' in it were 'a castle by Lough-maben, three partes whereof are environed with water, and strongly walled, and the town of Annandale (*sic*) at the very mouth almost of the river Annan, which lost all the glory and beauty it had, by the English warre in the reigne of Edward VI. In this terri-

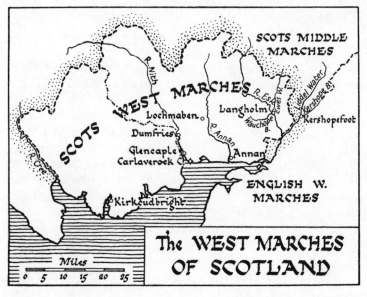

The WEST MARCHES OF SCOTLAND

torie the Johnstons are the men of greatest name; a kinred even bred to war'. So wrote Camden.[2] Lochmaben Castle was in Forster's opinion 'the King's chiefest strength' in that part.[3] Some of the lochs round it have been drained, but five remain, the one containing the promontory on which the castle stands being nearly half a mile long and a third of a mile wide. Like the Hermitage it was defended by an elaborate system of moats. Annan had had a royal castle before this time,[4] and its river was deep and tidal, and could take ships of a considerable size. The

---

[1] C.B.P. i, 845, 853.   [2] Brit. S. 16.   [3] C.B.P. i, 750.   [4] R.P.C.S. iii, 77.

Esk was 'a fair river', on which lay Langholm Castle,[1] probably a plain square tower, which is now an utter ruin. Ewesdale's inhabitants were reputed 'a civil people, and never ride in England', but they sometimes belied their character.[2]

The Wardenry was organized as follows. At Dumfries lay the Warden, the deputy, and the sheriff, to the second of whom the offence or withstanding of England was entrusted. A Captain, called the Keeper of Annandale, lay at Langholm, his service being 'opposite against Bewcastle, Esk and Leven, or Burgh at sometimes'. The rest of Annandale was defended by its surnames. In fact the whole wardenry generally had to defend itself owing to feuds.[3] It was said to have fewer inhabitants than the English West March, especially near the frontier, and nowhere within twenty miles of England was there strength in which an honest Scot could remain in safety, whereas a hundred men could lie at Rockcliffe, three-quarters of a mile from Scotland.[4] This did not prevent the Scots doing plenty of irregular damage to England.[5]

Between these three Marches on either side of the frontier the bounds were 'in debate in divers places where the two realms touch'.[6] The most important area, that between the two West Marches, some 7,403 acres in area, had been amicably divided in 1552.[7] Various attempts were made to divide the other pieces in a similar way,[8] but about 1580 it was stated that no 'composition' had been made since 1552 in spite of 'divers conferences and offers', so that there still remained in dispute 'three parcels between the Bushment hole and the Cauldron burn' in the East Marches, and doubtless others, but the manuscript ends abruptly at the foot of a page. These parcels were some 440 acres, of which forty were 'moorish and evil ground, and of little value, pastured indifferently'. The rest seems to have been pastured in common by the

[1] C.B.P. i, 197.   [2] C.B.P. i, 743, ii, 116.   [3] C.B.P. i, 743, ii, 527.
[4] R.P.C.S. iii, 77 et sqq.   [5] C.B.P. i, 681, pp. 558–9.   [6] C.B.P. i, 76.
[7] Bell. 164; C.B.P. ii, 598, 1453; R.P.S. 12, 16.   [8] C.B.P. i, 6; C.H.M. i, 1171, 1297; C.S.P. ii, 823.

two realms,[1] and there is no record of any further partition.

For the climate of the Borders in the sixteenth century we have little evidence beyond the generalizations of such people as Camden and Speed, who, not being Borderers, and possessing no meteorological records, must have written from hearsay or imagination.[2] It would be easy to write an account from nineteenth-century records and label it 'sixteenth century', but the harder course of collecting references from contemporary letters is more satisfactory, and is followed here. After making all due allowance for the weather as the grumbler's pet topic, it remains a strange fact that among the scores of references to the weather in Border letters there is but one appreciative remark, that made by Sussex, who wrote, on June 18, 1570, that while he was viewing the frontiers the openness of the air improved his health.[3] There are very few references to the spring, which must have begun late, but at least twice during this period the weather and waters were so outrageous and tempestuous that the movements of troops and of men proceeding to musters were seriously hindered.[4] Little also is to be found about the summer, but in August 1570 Sussex was forced to delay his raid owing to the rain and the greatness of the waters,[5] and there are a few other references to 'marvaillous stormes and rayne',[6] vehemency of rain whereby a river became too great to cross,[7] and 'extreamitie of wether' which prevented Buccleugh's dependants from raiding in England.[8] On the whole, therefore, the summers seem to have been good. For September, when autumn begins in the north, a southerner needed apparel such as he would not wear at home at that time,[9] and Sussex, another southerner, complained of the October cold in 1570 in Alnwick and Warkworth, especially as his chimneys would suffer no fire.[10] But on the whole the short northern autumns do

---

[1] C.B.P. i, 76.   [2] e.g. Speed, 85, 87; Brit. 776.   [3] For. ix, 1014.
[4] 1573, For. x, 870, 886; 1596, C.B.P. ii, 233.   [5] For. ix, 1196.   [6] July 1577, C.B.P. i, 16.   [7] August 1575, C.S.P. v, 183.   [8] August 1597 C.B.P. ii, 733.   [9] C.S.P. ii, 767.   [10] C.S.P. iii, 516.

not seem to have been bad except in 1573, when there was a tempest of rain such as there had not been for forty years. It continued for eight days and nights without a stop, besides much like weather for thirty days before. There was a marvellous spoil of the corn on the ground, and the tempest broke away a hundred yards of the old Berwick town wall towards the river.[1] Lord Eure mentioned that at the end of September 1597 the 'waters grew extreame raging and the weather intemperate'.[2] The northern winter—from October to March—was the cause of scores of remarks as to its ferocity, not all of them by southerners. At the end of October 1568 Norfolk wrote that he never saw worse weather for snow and frost in the south at Christmas than he saw during a journey from York to Alnwick.[3] Early in March 1565 there was so great a storm of snow that no one dared ride from Edinburgh to Berwick,[4] and when the snow fell it sometimes lay so long that no one could ride but on the beaten highways, which were slippery and dangerous, so that a man on foot made as much speed as a horseman.[5] When it melted quickly, or when heavy rain fell, the waters rose in the fords, and those who crossed risked drowning.[6] Sometimes travellers were held up for ten days,[7] and raids were sometimes postponed, but not always.[8] The worst winter was that of 1570–1. A storm began about the third week in November, and lasted well into February. On January 23 and 24 much snow fell, and that and the high tides endangered Berwick bridge, which was very badly damaged on February 6, and took over a fortnight to repair. For some time Berwick was cut off from communication with England, as 'the multitude of ice' made crossing by boat impossible.[9] In November 1584 Scroope mentioned a curious local mist in Liddesdale,[10] but, if silence is any guide, the winters were less severe on the west. Perhaps the whole subject of Border climate and

---

[1] October 1573, For. x, 1188.   [2] C.B.P. ii, 772.   [3] For. viii, 2608. [4] For. vii, 1017.   [5] C.S.P. ii, 922.   [6] For. viii, 2619.   [7] For. x, 126.   [8] C.B.P. i, 192, 499; For. ix, 1541.   [9] For. ix, 1514, 1543, 1570.   [10] C.B.P. i, 268.

weather from a southerner's point of view is best summed up by Wyllughby when he says: 'If I were further from the tempestuousnes of Cheviot hills, and were once retired from this accursed country whence the sun is so removed, I would not change my homlyest hermitage for the highest pallace ther.'[1]

It is said that statistics may be used to prove anything, and it may well be that an estimate of population based on statistics of doubtful reliability proves nothing. None the less some estimate of Border population must be made, and it seems best to base the English part of it on the Musters of 1584, the rolls of which have been preserved.[2] These, if properly taken, would include the names of all horsemen and footmen between the ages of sixteen and sixty. From the censuses of 1841 and 1881 it appears that the number of males between the ages is about 250 per thousand.[3] But allowance must be made for two sixteenth-century Border probabilities, first that in such an unsettled state of society the fencible men would have a higher proportional death-rate than in the nineteenth, and secondly that some of the able-bodied men were thieves and outlaws and did not attend the musters. It may therefore be safe to multiply the musters by five in order to get the total population of the districts mustered. This gives the following result:

March.	Muster return.	Estimated population in 1584.
East	2,986	14,930
Middle	7,603	38,015
West	8,350	41,750

To these totals additions must be made. In the East March was Berwick, the only place of which we possess a regular census, that of June 1565, when it contained 3,511 people, of which over 2,000 were soldiers, workmen, artificers, and labourers.[4] Part of the 2,000 were temporary inhabitants, but as the baptisms between 1584 and

[1] December 12, 1600; C.B.P. ii, 1299.   [2] C.B.P. i, 255; Bell, 174–6.
[3] W. Farr, *Vital Statistics*, 181; A. Newsholme, *Vital Statistics*, 3rd edit. 94.
[4] For. vii, 1232.

1603 averaged about 100 per annum, it is safe to say that the population of Berwick was 3,000.[1] Hunsdon's estimate of 7,000 in 1570[2] was either a bad guess or included temporary refugees. In the Middle March, Newcastle probably contained 10,000 people,[3] and Morpeth and Alnwick may have had 2,500 between them. In the West, Carlisle has been estimated at 5,000,[4] and Penrith, where the baptisms averaged 60,[5] and Kendal may have each had 2,000. The revised totals are—East March 17,930, Middle 50,515, West 50,750, or together 119,195. To estimate the population at 120,000 has not been difficult, to check the estimate is equally simple. The Census Report of 1801 contains an estimate of the population of 1700 based on the parish registers, which were very imperfect on the Borders before 1603, and other data. Its figures for that date are about 60 per cent. of those of 1801, and, if the figures of 1600 were about 60 per cent. of those of 1700, we get the following results:

	Estimate, 1700.	Author's estimate, 1600.
Northumberland	118,000	70,800
North Durham	5,700	3,420
Cumberland	62,000	37,380
Westmorland	28,000	16,800
Totals	213,700[6]	128,400

North Durham, that is the Shires of Norham, Island, and Bedlington, was part of the East and Middle Marches. It is impossible to separate the totals of the East and Middle Marches owing to the disputed boundary. It is clear that the two estimates, reached by entirely different methods, agree closely. There may be some accuracy in the coincidence, but if there is it must be remembered that the population was liable to sudden decreases from plague, the death-rate for some years being ten times the average. If Penrith is any criterion, the Border population decreased between 1584 and 1600.[7] For Scots population

[1] Berwick Registers.   [2] For. ix, 1153.   [3] A.A., N.S. iii (1859), 64.
[4] Creighton, 145.   [5] Registers, ed. G. Watson, 127.   [6] Appendix to
Report of 1801, 11.   [7] Watson, 127; Cox, 169.

estimates there is no reliable numerical evidence, but the Middle and West Marches of England far exceeded the opposite Marches in population, and the Scots East and Middle Marches far surmounted the English East March in the same way.[1] When the population of Scotland was 1,600,000, as it was in 1801, the Scots Border counties, excluding Kirkcudbright, had 132,705 inhabitants. In 1600 Scotland had possibly 600,000 inhabitants, and the East, Middle, and West Marches, 10,800, 14,000, and 20,000 respectively, a total of 44,800, which is possibly too low an estimate.

There remains the question of the influence of geography on the history of the Borders. It is the fashion nowadays to adopt a materialistic view of history and to try to give a geographical explanation of historical facts that would otherwise lack one. This is not new, for Camden traced certain attributes of the Borderers to their geographical environment. The present writer, as a pupil of the late Professor Herbertson, is not prone to underestimate the influence of geography upon history, but feels none the less that, for instance, the lack of a strong and settled government at Edinburgh was a more potent factor than geography in Elizabethan Border history and cannot be explained in geographical terms. The distribution of land-forms is bound to control the routes of armies, but, with one exception, the English armies in this period entered Scotland from Berwick or across Tweed or Solway, and no Scots army entered England, so there is no historical material in this period for a discussion of the Cheviot passes as routes for armies. But there is evidence of the routes taken by thieves, though, when it is remembered that the country was for the most part unenclosed, and that some of the rivers have been dredged and are therefore less easily fordable than in the past, it will not be difficult to believe that the thieves could make a raid and drive a prey in a great number of directions in spite of mountains and rivers. The opposite East Marches were separated by the Tweed, and Wyllughby stated that all

[1] C.B.P. ii, 433.

the Scots spoils on his charge were committed by way of the Tweed fords,[1] of which there were many. He may have exaggerated slightly, but his evidence is of more value than that supplied by the direction of the modern roads and Dr. Hodgkin's conjecture.[2] We should think that the fairly open country between Carham and the Cheviot would provide an easy route for the thieves, and historical evidence supports geographical theory, Downham, Paston, and Wooler being noted in 1541 as near common passages of the Scots.[3] In the Cheviots geographical theory points to a few well-defined passages and highways for thieves, such as that over Cocklaw, but historical evidence shows that between the Cheviot and Kershopehead there were no less than thirteen passages, while 'the passages of the Scottes all along Rydsdale' numbered twenty-three, and there were seven 'Tyndale passages westward'.[4] The Cheviots were not much of a barrier to raiders who knew them. On the west the frontier was mainly composed by the Solway Firth and various rivers easily fordable. To sum up, the raiders could come, and came from all quarters, and had a large choice of return routes. Any one who has watched a skilled shepherd in the Cheviots knows how easily an expert can control sheep amid the mountains. On one other point geographical theory might lead a careless historian astray. The Scots Cheviots give way to fertile valleys, the English continue as moorlands, hence the Scots were more open to English attacks than vice versa. The balance of historical evidence suggests, however, it might almost be said proves, that England suffered as much if not more than Scotland from enemy raiders. Geographers are curious folk. An author called G. H. Thompson christens C. Dacre's proposed line for a dyke between Carham and Chollerton 'The Raiders' Line', and states on the same page, 'This line . . . was seldom crossed by a mere raid'. That adverb would be hard to prove, but people who write of 'Jacobites in 1648, 1651' should be read with caution.[5]

---

[1] C.B.P. ii, 980, 993.   [2] Wardens, 5.   [3] Bates, 33.   [4] C.B.P. ii, 853.
[5] Hist. Assocn. Leaflet, No. 28, pp. 7, 11.

PART II

THE SOCIAL AND ECONOMIC CONDITION OF THE ELIZABETHAN BORDERS

CAMDEN travelled on the Borders, and, to use a vulgar phrase, 'saw life' there. One day, for instance, near 'Busy Gapp', 'a place infamous for theiving and robbing', he heard of some castles and set out to see them, 'but', he wrote, 'I could not with safety take the full survey of it, for the rank robbers thereabout'.[1] He found the Borderers, like their opposites, 'a notable light horsemen', particularly in North Tynedale,[2] and the roughness of the country seemed to him 'to have hardened the inhabitants', while the Scots by keeping them exercised in wars, and by intermingling their manners among them in peace time, had made the Borderers of both realms much alike.[3] Thus, like the Scots mentioned by Leslie, the English Borderers knew well the passages through mosses and marshes through which strangers could not safely pass, and had made their hold on them secure by felling trees and laying them across the ways and passages.[4] Like the Scots they were said to be loyal to the families of the old nobility, and Scroope wrote in 1570 that his wardenry was 'so addicted to a Dacre as, although I find no fault with them in any other service, they are not to be credited in this'.[5] This included the gentry as well as the commons, and even after Dacre's failure the commons still, in the Bishop of Carlisle's words, bore the image of a Dacre as a god in their hearts.[6] Forster, who was one of them, wrote 'we that inhabite Northumberland are not acquaynted with any learned and rare frazes',[7] and with rough speech went rough manners, the Borderers, according to Sir R. Carey, being given to liberty and 'lisentiusnes'.[8] Lord Eure found that they 'envyed the stranger, and could not lovinglie

[1] Brit. 800.   [2] Brit. 802.   [3] Brit. 799.   [4] Bates, 49.   [5] Dom. Add. ii, 202.   [6] For. x, 249.   [7] C.B.P. i. 180.   [8] C.B.P. ii, 593.

efforde pennyworthes' for his diet or his horses, except at
excessive rates. They were better at handling spears, &c.,
on horseback than Yorkshiremen, better riders in a chase
as knowing the mosses, and more nimble on foot.[1] A
certain Mr. Crackenthorp refused the living of 'Symond-
borne', thinking his body unable to live in 'so troublesome a place, and his nature not well brooking the per-
verse nature of so crooked a people'.[2] They did not all
value their word as highly as some say, and the Grames,
even when one of them 'offered to take upon hym Hectors
cloke', could not be trusted. All the Borderers in the
opinion of Thomas, Lord Scroope, were accustomed to
false swearing.[3] Valentine Browne found them both wise,
able, and stout men, so long as they were governed by
others not allied to their pretensions, but prone to make
long and boastful speeches about their great services to
the realm.[4] After hearing the evidence of residents, it is
well to turn to a visitor, John Udall, who in 1598 spent
some two months on the Borders, mainly in the west.[5] He
found the people strangely compounded, barbarous more
of will than of manners, active of person and speech, stout
and subtle, inclined to theft and strife, factious and seditious, full of malice and revenge, being nursed up in these
vices from their ancestors, apt to quarrel rather with blood
than speech, though scant of neither. Their situation in
close proximity to another nation gave them advantage to
traffic merchandise of the above kind. Considering the
idle disposition of the people, the weakness of their governors, and their geographical situation, he did not marvel
at the many outrages, factions, thefts, and murders committed, but rather wondered that there were not many
more, tending not only to civil broils, but also to matters
of state, so he concluded that their ambition was limited
to base subjects, just like carrion crows. They undertook
an enterprise with strong resolution easily turned into outrage, but if they once fell under justice there were not so
fearful nor miserable wretches living. They lived worse

[1] C.B.P. ii, 337.   [2] C.B.P. ii, p. 421.   [3] C.B.P. ii, pp. 142, 346, 369.
[4] Dom. Add. iii, 94–5.   [5] C.H.M. viii, 562–4.

than infidels, and the clown made the gentleman knave. Notwithstanding their gallantry some of them would sell their blood and death of their father for money, or, as they termed it, 'kynboote'; contrariwise the killer would submit himself naked upon his knees, holding his own sword by the point held to his breast, yielding the handle to his enemy's hand, and so with abject humility ask forgiveness. It is obvious that Udall looked upon the Borderers as savages, and so it is strange, in the light of the history of Elizabethan Ireland, that he should recommend mercy before strict justice except in capital cases. They were mostly brave, and under strict military discipline and a worthy governor, which in his opinion they lacked, he thought the frontier might be much strengthened. Probably his picture was overdrawn, because he wrote with his mind on the Grames and such-like surnames.

All the above remarks refer to the country folk, but the little evidence that exists about the townspeople is much more creditable. Melvill, who fled to Berwick in 1584, writes 'trewlie I fand sic fectfull professioun of trew Christianitie in Berwick as I haid never sein the lyk in Scotland'. He trusted the English so completely that he left his infant son for over a year in the care of Lady Widdrington at Berwick.[1] According to Fynes Moryson the men of Berwick were less grasping than the country Borderers, for if a man lent a good citizen sixty pounds he would give him 'a fair chamber and a good diet as long as he would lend them the money'.[2] Melvill was as favourably impressed with Newcastle as he had been with Berwick. He stayed in the house of a widow whose son-in-law 'was lyand seik of manie deadlie wounds, giffen him be the Scottes theives on the Border', and he and his party 'war verie well treated, and reasonablie'. 'At our departing', he concludes, he and his party 'gat bathe from the auld woman and her douchtar manie blessings'.[3] The cleavage of classes is thus obvious. There were civilized English Borderers who could sympathize with Scots, and regarded the loose Borderers of either realm with equal aversion.

---

[1] Autobiog. 171, 251.   [2] Travellers, 81.   [3] Autobiog. 17.

There is no evidence of the characteristics of the Scots Border townsfolk, chiefly because there were no Border towns in Scotland as big as Newcastle or Carlisle. But much has been written about the other Borderers. Andrew Boorde, an English physician who had studied and practised medicine in Scotland, published in 1547 *The First Book of the Introduction to Knowledge*.[1] In it he shows that no love was lost between him and the Scots, but, as he lived among them and claims to have gained their favour by his 'sciences and other policies', so that he knew their secrets, his report is worth consideration. He writes, 'The people of the country be hardy men, and strong men, and well favoured, and good musicians; in these four qualities they be most like, above all other nations, to an Englishman; but of all nations they will face, crack, and boast themselves, their friends and their country, for many will make strong lies'. The country, when he saw it, lay 'in much poverty and penury', and there were 'many outlaws and strong thieves, for much of their living standeth by stealing and robbing. Also it is naturally given, or else it is of a devilish disposition of a Scottish man, not to favour or love an Englishman.'[2] Camden, though he knew little of Scotland, had travelled enough on the English Borders to hear the current opinion about the Scots. It is possible that he entered Nithsdale and Annandale, but beyond saying that those dales nourish 'a warlike kind of men who have been infamous for robberies and depradations', he is content to quote Leslie. Of the Debatable Lands he says, 'the inhabitants on both sides, as borderers in all other parts, are a military kind of men, nimble, wilie, always in readiness for any service, yea and by reason of their skirmishes passing well experienced'.[3] The Northumbrian, Dr. William Bullein, who died in 1576, and knew what he was writing about, probably drew the character of Mendicus in his *Dialogue* from life. The remarks of Mendicus represent Northumbrian feeling at that time. He says, when taken for a Scot, 'I had better be hangad

[1] E.E.T.S., Ex. Ser. x, 1870.   [2] Op. cit. 59, 136–7.   [3] Brit. S. 17; Brit. 782; cf. Boece, ed. Bellenden, 1821, i, 27.

in a withie or in a cowtaile, then be a rowfooted Scot, for thei are ever fare and fase; I have been a fellow sharpe manne on my handes in my yonge daies, and brought many of the Scottes to ground in the Northe Marches, and gave them many griesly woundes; ne manne for manne durst abide my luke, I was so fell. Then the limmer Scottes hared me, burnt my guddes, and made deadlie feede on me and my barnes, that I have nethynge but this sarie bagge and this staffe, and the charitie of sic gud people as you are, gud maistresse.'[1] Probably the best, and certainly the fullest Scots authority is John Leslie, Bishop of Ross, whose evidence has been modernized as literally as possible.[2] He says the Borderers are 'in the greatest liberty and licence' and escape all punishment; and agrees with Boorde as to their extreme poverty, adding that they disdained agriculture, and sought their meat by stealing, not thinking it much odds whether they stole from Englishmen or from Scots. They had, however, a great abhorrence for shedding blood. The nobles among them were careful not to be too severe in peace time lest it should cost them dear in time of war, which was to them a second nature. The 'reivers' cared little for any force sent against them by the King; they knew the country, and, if driven out of the woods and mountains, fled to river banks and marshes whence they could lead their pursuers 'through certain difficult mires, which, albeit they be like green meadows above, and like fast earth appear underneath, yet when a man enters they shall gape wide and swallow him up in a manner to the depths'. Meanwhile the 'reivers' and their horses, both being wonderfully swift and agile, could pass where the King's footmen 'scarce dare follow'. For this reason the reivers' horses were not shod with iron shoes. Sussex's experience in 1570 confirmed these statements.[3] All border thieves were horsemen, and despised those who went on foot, and, if they had a speedy horse and clothes for themselves and their wives, they were not 'mickle careful for the rest of the household gear'.

[1] E.E.T.S., Ex. Ser. lii, 6. [2] Leslie, 10, 12, 97–102. [3] For. ix, 784.

Cannibalism and the slaying by women of men returned from a defeat Leslie thought rare, as the thieves were careful not to shed even their enemies' blood. But they thought that in time of necessity all the goods of all men were by the law of nature common to them and others, and they never said their prayers so carefully and fervently as when they had forty or fifty miles to drive a prey. The more perfect a man was in leading his prey home through difficult places, the more he was esteemed. Voluntary slaughter was seldom done save in revenge of some injury, and chiefly for the slaughter of some cousin or friend. From such cases arose feuds of tribe against tribe, which, though common to all Scotland, were found chiefly on the Borders. Infamy fell on any Borderer who broke his word, even to an enemy. Sir R. Carey gave three examples of this. He once found Sir R. Kerr as good as his word, and later the Armstrongs made him a promise 'which they did truly perform'.[1] Lastly in 1600 two sons of Scots lairds went to prison in Edinburgh Castle rather than go back on their words given to two Englishmen, or break the custom of the Border.[2] Elsewhere he described the Scots in general as 'a subtle desaytfull and beggerley people', while his brother, Sir John, thought them 'the most perverst and prowde nacion in the world'.[3] Sir W. Bowes wrote to Burghley in October 1597 saying the Scots 'both can or will say more for a falsehood than for my owne parte I can doe for the truth',[4] and Lord Eure found breach of assurance so common that he wrote that he must mend it 'as I may'.[5] The evidence is thus conflicting. Finally Leslie states that the Scots Borderers were musical, singing songs about the acts of their forefathers, which they had learned or composed themselves, and so eloquent were they that they could move the judges and even their most severe adversaries 'if not to pity, at least to wonder vehemently'. The men of the Merse were somewhat different, as they studied 'politic affairs' and were more expert in ordering a battle than the rest. It is curious that

[1] C.M. 50–1, 69.   [2] C.B.P. ii, 1195.   [3] C.B.P. ii, pp. 115, 315–16.
[4] C.B.P. ii, p. 347.   [5] C.B.P. ii, 454.

Ancroft. Church with fortified tower

Ford across the river Tweed, above Coldstream
(from the English bank)

IV. THE EAST MARCHES OF ENGLAND

Bewcastle. The castle, from the north

The same, from the south-east

V. THE WEST MARCHES OF ENGLAND

Leslie should omit one of the chief characteristics of the
Borderers, namely, that they thought it 'a liberty incident
to all nations to succour banished men',[1] and put this
theory into such thorough practice that their homes became
a regular refuge for alien fugitives.[2] In return Scots fugitives were received in England.[3] Betrayal was rare, and
the name of Hector of the Harlaw became a synonym for
Judas.[4] Cruelty to refugees such as the Countess of Northumberland was also rare,[5] but murders and tortures, if we
may believe the English witnesses who gave evidence at
the end of 1595 as to Forster's conduct as Warden, were
common. They said that in an hour they had counted up
among themselves a hundred and five true and able subjects who had been murdered in defence of their goods.
Huge numbers had been taken prisoners, 'which prisoners
hath been also extremely tortured and pinched, by thrust-
ing hot irons into their legs and other parts of their body,
and fettering them naked in the wilderness and deserts by
chains of iron to trees, whereby they might be eaten up
with midges and flies in summer and in winter perished
with extreme cold; other some used to set them upon a
crooked tree hanging over some deep water, sitting upon
a sharp harrow, whereby the prisoner is enforced, either
by moving to fall in the water and so to be drowned, or
else sit still upon the harrow pinched with extreme and
continual pricking of his flesh, which punishment is commonly termed amongst themselves "Paytes Jockes meare",
with sundry other unchristian devices to compel them to
promise greater ransoms'.[6] This may be false, but so bad
was the reputation of the Scots Borderers that even Francis,
Earl of Bothwell, when forced for safety to admit some of
them into his company, felt he must excuse himself to the
Synodal Assembly of Ministers then at Dunbar, and
promise to make them behave. 'It may', he concludes,
'be somewhat slanderous to us, and fearful to the common
people where we travel.'[7] It is not remarkable, therefore,

---

[1] Dom. Add. ii, 196.   [2] Dom. Add. iii, 45.   [3] For. ix, 565–6.
[4] Herries, 118–19.   [5] For. ix, 627.   [6] C.H.M. v, 477.   [7] H.J.S.
314.

that others traded on the Borderers' reputation to accuse them of robberies which they had never committed.[1]

After these general remarks it is time to discuss more particular objects such as the dwellings, clothes, food, and furniture of the Borderers. Nobles who lived within the Marches in no official position generally dwelt in their own castles, which they might use not only against the Scots, but also against their own sovereign. Such castles were Naworth, Alnwick, and Warkworth, the last of which has not been spoilt by later additions, and still has a fine keep. They were not typically Border or typically Elizabethan. In Scotland Home and Carlaverock castles may be put in a similar category. Other castles, such as Carlisle and Bewcastle, were the residences of Border officers, but there was not always an official dwelling, even for a warden. The gentry lived in towers, often nowadays loosely called 'peels'. 'There is not', wrote Camden, 'a man amongst them of the better sort that hath not his little tower or pile.'[2] Towers varied in size from that of Dacre,[3] which measures 66×45 feet, and is really a cross between a castle and a tower, to small buildings covering less than a quarter of that area. They have usually three stories above a vaulted basement, and good examples remain at Smailholm and near Canonbie (Hollows Tower). Neither has been spoilt by later additions, both are uninhabited, and the former has still its original roof. A description of them seems preferable to a mere generalization about their type. Hollows Tower[4] stands in a not very strong position on the edge of the steep bank of the River Esk. The slope from the front is more gradual, and on the other two sides the ground is almost level, but may have been marshy, and therefore difficult. The outside dimensions are $25\frac{1}{2} \times 33\frac{1}{2}$ feet, the full height to the top of the beacon nearly 60 feet, and to the bottom of where the roof was, about 40 feet. The walls are about $4\frac{1}{2}$ feet thick. The entrance is by a door at the ground level, but the original 'yett', which was probably of iron, is missing.

[1] C.R.B. clxix; C.S.P. vi, 321.　　　[2] Brit. 799.　　　[3] See Plate VII.
[4] See Plates VIII, IX.

On entering, there is a well-staircase to the right, and in front is another door leading into a vaulted chamber. The vault is about 11 feet high in the centre, and three shot-holes (the wall to the back of the house being unpierced) are the only openings in the walls. In this room stores were kept, and in an emergency a man might put his horse there, but cattle would have to be kept in a 'barmekyn' or outer ward enclosed by a high and thick wall. No foundations of such a wall are to be traced, but the absence of a shot-hole in the back wall of the vault may point to the existence of some kind of enclosure in that direction. The well-staircase, which is narrow enough to be easily blocked, leads to the first floor. This was the chief living-room and had two windows, a small one about a foot wide opposite the fire-place, and another about 2 feet wide by 4 feet high, with seats on either side, at the front. The room measures about $25 \times 16 \times 9$ feet. Above it is another room with a fire-place, then another room, and then the attic, a door from which opened on to the parapet. Above the attic is the stone part of a beacon, to which the fire must have been attached in an iron basket. The whole place is unhealthy and uncomfortable, but strong, except against artillery.

Smailholm Tower,[1] built on a basaltic outcrop, is more strongly situated, measures about 40×32 feet in area, is about 57 feet high, and has four stories. It lacks a beacon, but has an iron 'yett', and there is a hole in the first floor communicating with the vault, which could be made into two rooms by the insertion of an extra floor. The top of the basaltic outcrop was surrounded by a stone wall, part of which remains. There are also evidences of outbuildings, in front of the tower, at the foot of the basaltic cliff. There seem to have been outbuildings at Cockburnspath Tower, but perhaps they were merely cattle sheds, though they were probably something stronger, as the gentry are said to have kept their cattle in their houses in times of danger,[2] and the vaulted chambers would hardly have contained half a dozen. Some towers were entered by a ladder, the door being on the first floor. There were scores of

---

[1] See Plates X, XI, and plans on p. 40.   [2] Dom. Add. iii, 346.

towers, quite fifty, probably, in the small English East March.[1] Some of the towers, like Elsdon[2] Tower, are still inhabited and have only had their interiors and windows altered. Others, like Bonshaw and Embleton,[2] have been enlarged.

Bowes and Ellerker in their Survey of 1541 described the houses of the headsmen of Tynedale. These were the

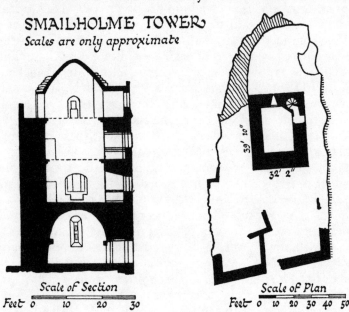

SMAILHOLME TOWER
Scales are only approximate

39' 10"

32' 2"

Scale of Section
Feet 0   10   20   30

Scale of Plan
Feet 0 10 20 30 40 50

chiefs of each surname, who led and answered for all the rest, yet their houses were built of wood, great strong oak trees cut square, strongly bound together and covered with great roofs of turves and earth. Thus they were very difficult to break into or set on fire. In Redesdale the chief men dwelt in richer but weaker houses.[3] Leslie says the more powerful Scots Borderers made towers 'of earth only, which can not be burnt, nor without great force of men of war down can be cast'. He calls them 'pailes'. The Cumberland farmer lived in houses of wood or clay, or, later,

[1] Sadler, ii, 288-9.   [2] See Plate XII.   [3] Bates, 49; C. J. Bates, *Hist. of Northumberland*, 217; A.A., 2nd ser., v, 118.

of rough unhewn stone, if near a quarry, or of second-hand stone if near a monastery or the Roman Wall. Where no stone could be easily got, a rough casing of board was set up, and into it was poured the clay in a semi-fluid state, layers of straw cut to the required size being laid on the wall every few inches. The house had two rooms on the ground floor, a living-room with a wide hearth intended to burn peat or logs, and a sleeping-chamber for the man and his wife. Over these rooms was a garret, reached by a ladder and open to the thatch, and in it the servants and younger members of the family slept. The door was invariably in the north-east, opening into a passage running north and south, dividing the dwelling-house from the byre, which opened from this passage on the left side. The only mason work needed was for the doors and windows; all the rest could be built by the owner with the help of his neighbours, 'boon-days' being customary when a house or building was to be made. The floor was usually of clay trodden hard as stone, and flags were used for the threshold and hearth. Huts of clay or brushwood covered with thatch, reeds, or turves sheltered the farmer's livestock.[1] The poor lived in houses 'such as a man may build within three or four hours'.[2] Leslie says 'their castles and pallaces are sheephouses and lodges which they commonly call "pailes", of whose burning they are not sore solaced'. They were probably clay huts, thatched with straw, containing nothing worth plundering, and scarcely worth setting on fire, though the thatch would burn and the walls fall to pieces. Of Scotland in 1584 Wedel wrote— 'the villages look very poor, the houses having stone walls not so high as a man, upon which the roofs are erected and covered with sod'. Celia Fiennes in 1695 found Scots houses worse than booths at a fair and so smelly that she preferred to lunch with her horses in the stable; the English houses she saw at Haltwhistle, though cleaner inside, were but little better built.[3] Brian Fairfax in 1659 found cows and hogs sharing the room with the family.[4] C. Lowther,

[1] C. & W., N.S. ix, 121–46.   [2] Boorde, *ut supra*.   [3] Fiennes, 169, 171–2, 174; Wedel, 248.   [4] F.C. ii; *Iter Boreale*, 157.

who visited Scotland in or about 1629, wrote: 'The houses of the Grames that were are but one little stone tower garretted and slated or thatched, some of the form of a little tower not garretted, such be all the leards houses in Scotland.' Of Langholm he wrote, 'we laid in a poor thatched house the wall of it being one course of stones, another of sods of earth, it had a door of wicker rods, and the spider webs hung over our heads as thick as might be in our bed'.[1]

The surveyor who mapped Dumfriesshire in 1590, after marking all the towers and stone houses, added, 'for the reste not put downe they ar but onsettes, or straglinge houses, th'inhabitants followers of some of these above described'.[2] In the towns such as Carlisle, Berwick, and Newcastle there are very few Elizabethan houses left. Wedel, who visited Berwick in 1584, says, 'The houses in the town are mean and thatched with straw.' In Scotland he found that the towns had no ramparts and the houses were built of wood, 'their outside covered with boards'.[3] Celia Fiennes states that the streets in Carlisle in 1695 were very broad and handsome and well pitched, but there were very few stone houses.[4] The absence of stone houses was probably general and accounts for the small number of survivals. For travellers and others there were plenty of inns, 74 in Berwick, one for every forty inhabitants, 137 in the East, and 123 in the Middle Marches in 1577.[5]

The dress of the different classes differed as much as their dwellings. In 1592 Sir Henry Woddryngton, a rich knight, possessed among other things, a 'dublitt and hose of tawnye sattan waved with gowld lace, £6 13s. 4d.', 'gowld buttons, £7 14s. 0d.', and a 'Sattan cloke, garded with velvett and gowld lace, £4'.[6] Sir George Heron in 1576 left a much simpler set of clothes, such as 'a damaske gowne xxxs., a velvett girkyn xxs., a peir of velvett breeches xxs., a satten dublitt xiijs. iiijd.'[7] Thomas Swinburne of Edlingham, Esquire, was better off, his clothes being

---

[1] Lowther, 10, 12.   [2] *Archaeologia*, xxii, 161.   [3] Wedel, 240, 248.
[4] Fiennes, 169.   [5] C.B.P. i, 21.   [6] D.W. ii, 227.   [7] D.W. i, 412.

valued at £9 in 1572, and comprising 'wone satten gown,
a velvett cote layde wyth sylver las, a satten doublet lade
wyth sylver lace, a payr of velvett slyvers wythe sylver las,
and a velvett hatt'.¹ William Anesley of East Shaftoe,
gentleman, had in 1573 'twoo jacketts xs., twoo dubletts
xs., twoo paire of hosse xs., foore shirtes xiijs. iiijd., one
hatt, one blake Spanish cappe vs.'² A Newcastle miller
had in 1585 'Two gownes and two brod-clothe jackettes
17s. 4d., one brode-clothe jerkyn, j lether jerkyn, and j
paire of longe hoes 8s. 4d., another lether jerkyn 12d.
Two lynnen shirtes 5s. 4d. A dagger a sword and a girdle
22d. A white russett cloke 2s. A payre of lether briches
and a jerkyn 4s. A cape 6d. Two paire of shorte hoes
8d.',³ and his eldest son had 'one blewe jackett, j blewe
jerkyn, j worsett jerkyn and j russett jerkyn 7s. A paire
of russett briches, a paire of white briches, a paire of knyte
hoes and a paire of carsey hoes 2s. 8d. A cape, a hate
and iij straken shirtes 4s. 4d., a prayer booke 3s. 8d.'⁴ In
1581 an old Berwick pensioner left a 'blacke clocke lynned
with bayes', a 'shorte gowne, ford with frycholle, and
lyned with lambe', 'a payre of grograyne briches and a
grograyne doblet, and a black dobleat of Doche fostyone',
'a payre of rosset breches of brod-clothe, a black fryse
jerkyn, lyned with blacke cotton, and a canevas doblet, a
payre of knyte hose', and some 'showes', a 'beste clocke
fassed with taffataye' and sundry gloves and weapons.⁵
Another, who was poorer, had in 1582 'Thre shertes
6s. 8d. Two dublets, 10s. Two payre of britches 12s.
Two paire of stockinges 3s. Two paire of shoes 16d. One
hatt 2s.,' some armour, a saddle, and a 'payre of bootes
12d.'⁶ Thomas Dawson of Elwicke, 'clarke', left in 1572
'thre long gowns xls., a cloke, ij jacketts and thre payre
of hosen, ij shertes xs.'⁷ A poor man with a large ward-
robe had in 1564 'his best Jacket iis. viijd.—his best hose
xijd.—his best dublatt xijd.—a nother Jackett xvjd.—a
secondari dublatt viijd.—a nother payre of hose viijd.—
a nother Jackett iiijd.—one old dublatt iiijd.', though his

¹ D.W. i, 372.   ² D.W. i, 392–3.   ³ D.W. ii, 113.   ⁴ D.W. ii, 114.
⁵ D.W. ii, 60–1.   ⁶ D.W. ii, 72–3.   ⁷ D.W. i, 379.

whole estate was £3 13s. 2d. net,[1] less than that of a
labourer whose dagger, sword, lamb, old buckskin doublet, and other goods were valued at £8 19s. in 1568.[2]
The 'rayment' of David Taylor, vicar of Bolham, was in
1583 valued at £1 6s. 8d. only.[3]

There is less evidence about female garments, but the
wife of the above-mentioned Newcastle miller in 1585
possessed 'a gowne 10s. One kyrtle, a petycote, one payre
of newe sleves, ij kerchyfes, and iiij railes 15s. 8d.', various
jewels, 'a violette froke 5s.', and 'a read hatt and a cape
2s.' Her eldest daughter had 'One stammell petticote,
and j brod-clothe savegard 20s. One petticote of house-
wyfe clothe and a savegard 11s. An upper bodye of
durance, a paire of newe blake hoes, and a new apron of
durance laid with laice 7s. 2d. A felte hatt, iij kerchiefs
and vij patletts 15s. 8d. Fyve paire of sleves, ij lynnen
aprens, a crose clothe, a kyfe and a silke belte 11s.',[4]
some of which are Greek to a modern man. Scots evidence is scarce for both sexes, but Robert Kerr of Ancrum Woodhead lost in 1573 three doublets valued at
£10, £7, and £3 Scots, and his wife's three best gowns
valued at £40, £20, and £20 Scots, and marvellous 'crea-
tions', as well as her three hats worth £3, £2 10s., and £2
Scots were stolen at the same time. They were rich people
for they possessed nearly 100 ounces of silver plate, eight
dozen Flanders pewter plate, and 'truncheouris', and forty
'furneist fedder beddis with scheittis coveringis coddis,
bousteris, blankattis,' &c.[5] Wedel noted that the Scots
horsemen he met in Berwickshire were not well dressed,
'as it is not their way'. 'The riders or gentlemen and their
servants wore long capes, as is the fashion there.'[6]

English evidence as to furniture is more plentiful and
ranges from the possessions of John Selby of Berwick,
who in 1565 possessed six feather-beds, three tablecloths,
twelve pewter plates, six towels, but only two chairs,[7] to
those of Thomas Dawson, clerk, whose whole furniture
was 'a coverled and a mattresse', 'a paire of bedstocks

[1] D.W. i, 224–5.   [2] D.W. i, 290.   [3] D.W. i, 393–4   [4] D.W. ii,
113–14.   [5] R.P.C.S. ii, 269–70.   [6] Wedel, 241.   [7] D.W. i, 236.

wth the hangings, a fether bed wth the bolster', 'three chists, a chaire, a forme and two kaykes of waxe'.[1] In the above lists of clothes and furniture it is the absence of certain articles rather than the presence of others that is noticeable. Shirts and nightshirts are rarely mentioned, and it seems possible that adult Borderers had their undergarments sewn on and removed them as seldom as the children of the slums of modern London. There is certainly little to suggest that personal cleanliness was thought a necessity, or was even a rare virtue. Among household stuffs carpets, except in the sense of table-cloths, were unknown. It is doubtful whether matting was used in the north before 1624.[2] In many rooms the furniture must have been made in situ. The study of the inventories as a whole gives a man a very low idea of the civilization of the north even when compared with the contemporary south. Books were very rare, though the great-nephew of a Bishop did possess the *Booke of Marters* in addition to a Bible.[3] Pictures seem unknown, and there are but few mentions of tapestry or hangings. The case is made worse by the fact that we have not the wills and inventories of the lowest class.

The English Borders, unlike most of the country districts of England, did not produce enough food for the consumption of the inhabitants. The Merse supplied Berwick with beef, mutton, veal, pork, and all kinds of 'pullyn' without which the garrison could not live.[4] Sometimes, for example in 1565 and 1595, the Scots were forbidden by their own officers to bring any victual into Berwick and the town was threatened with starvation, which in 1595 was prevented by promises to sell grain to the Scots when it was plentiful.[5] This grain was not Border grown but came by sea from Yorkshire, Cambridgeshire, Norfolk, and Lincolnshire.[6] Northumberland occasionally provided a little grain, and Suffolk supplied Berwick with butter and cheese.[7] On one occasion grain

---

[1] D.W. i, 378–9.   [2] Naworth, 216–17.   [3] Bates, 386.   [4] C.B.P. ii, 77.   [5] C.B.P. ii, 77, 178; For. vii, 1462.   [6] C.B.P. ii, 571; A.P.C. xiii, 351; xxx, 409–10.   [7] A.P.C. xxv, 39–40.

was brought from Hamburg to Berwick.[1] In April 1578 barley and oats and beans were sent from Somerset and Dorset to relieve a famine in the West March, but arrived too late.[2] In September 1596 there was a similar great dearth at Berwick, followed by disease and deaths.[3] The Scots Borderers, apparently, grew most of their own food, and lived mainly, according to Leslie, on flesh, milk, cheese, and parched barley known as 'sogne beir or org-mount', having 'little use of bread . . . good beer . . . or wine', and not taking much delight in either of the latter. In the houses of such men as William Kerr of Ancrum might be found 'clarett', 'quhyte wyne', and 'oy d'oleif', which the Borderers thought it worth their while to steal.[4] When C. Lowther lodged at Langholm in 1629 he found the following good victuals, 'mutton, midden fowle, oat bread cakes on the kirtle baked the fifth part of an inch thick; wheat bread, ale, aqua vitae'. He notes that the fire was 'in the midst of the house'.[5] Evidence of the amount of food eaten by civilians is lacking, and there seem to be no extant ration lists for the garrisons of such castles as Home or Lochmaben, but Berwick evidence is abundant. Theoretically a soldier's allowance of food was most generous. Each day he had a twenty-four-ounce loaf of wheaten bread at a penny, a pottle of beer, apparently about two-thirds of a gallon, at a penny, two pounds of beef or mutton at $1\frac{3}{4}d.$ a pound from Midsummer to January and $1\frac{1}{2}d.$ from January to Shrovetide, half a pound of butter and a pound of cheese. This extract from the victualler's contract for 1575 applied only to meat-days.[6] Eleven years later each man got bread, meat, and beer as above, but nothing else on meat-days, whereas on fish-days the rations were bread and beer as above, with half a pound of butter or a pound of cheese, or a quarter of a 'codd' or of 'linge a reasonable pece', or seven or eight 'white hearinges or red'.[7] In 1597 he got twelve ounces of bread, three pints of beer, $\frac{3}{4}$ lb. of cheese, and $\frac{1}{4}$ lb. of butter, or

[1] A.P.C. xxix, 469.   [2] A.P.C. x, 181–2, 203; C.H.M. ii, 528.   [3] C.B.P. ii, 377.   [4] R.P.C.S. ii, 269.   [5] Lowther, 11.   [6] For. xi, 336. [7] C.B.P. ii, 459.

a pound and a half of beef instead of the last two, at a cost of $5\frac{1}{4}d$.[1] In 1595 there were three fish days a week.[2] The decrease in the ration was probably due to the increased prices. There was a big rise between 1591 and 1595, wheat going up from £1 to £2 a quarter, oxen from £4 to £5. 10s. each, butter from £3 to £4 a barrel, &c., &c.[3] It must not be supposed, however, that the men got their full rations, as the victualler was often either inefficient or dishonest. In 1574, for instance, the garrison complained that their bread and beer were deficient in quantity and of an inferior quality. The victualler excused himself by supplying elaborate calculations showing that he was a heavy loser on each item of his contract. He seems, however, to have recouped himself by advancing money to soldiers at 33 per cent. interest for three months.[4] In February 1595 John Carey complained that the administration of the victualler's office grew daily worse. Beer had gone up 33 per cent., and as for the horse corn and other provision, 'we are fedd only with hope', he wrote.[5] In March 1597 the horse garrison had neither oats, beans, nor peas, and none in prospect. The men had long eaten nothing but rye bread, though the Queen paid for the best of all things. She was said to be so 'cossened' by the officials of the palace that the food was such as neither man nor horse could eat 'but for pewer neede'.[6]

In the Elizabethan Borders there were many industries which had not become specialized. Thieving, for instance, was a recognized occupation, but the professional thief could and did occupy his spare time, which was often long, in farming of one kind or another. Examples could be multiplied, and the following words must be read on the understanding that the various occupations must not be regarded as water-tight compartments. The three most important methods of getting a living illegally were stealing, piracy, with which wrecking may be incorporated, and coining. Stealing, the most important, was to a great extent a seasonal occupation. The thieves, wrote Sir R.

[1] C.B.P. ii, 713. [2] C.B.P. ii, 53. [3] C.B.P. ii, 130. [4] For. x, 1643. [5] C.B.P. ii, 24. [6] C.B.P. ii, 545.

Carey in 1597, 'will never lightly steale hard before Lammas
(August 1) for fear of the assizes, but being once past,
they returne to their former trade, and, unles in such
years as they cannot ride upon the wastes by reasons of
stormes and snowes, the last moneths in the yeare are
theyr cheiffe time of stealling; for then are the nightes
longest, theyr horse hard at meat and will ride best, cattell
strong and will drive furthest. After Candlemas (February 2) the nightes grow shorte, and cattell grow weaker,
and oates growing dearer, they feed their horses worse,
and quickly turn them to grasse'.[1] After further experience
he found that the chief time for stealing was from Michaelmas to Martinmas (November 11), for, he says, 'then are
the fells good and drie and the cattle strong to dryve'.[2]
Christofer Dacre gave October 1 and April 1 as the limits
of the chief time for thieving.[3] Thomas, Lord Scroope,
writing in November 1595, says, 'the depe of wynter and
most unquiet season is now come on us', and adds that
raids were nightly increasing,[4] when, according to Sir R.
Carey, they should have been decreasing. In bad winters
the cattle became so weak and the ways so deep that they
could scarce draw an empty cask and were not worth stealing,[5] but there are instances of cattle being stolen and
driven off after Martinmas and even soon after Candlemas.[6] The long nights were the best time, and the longest
in Berwick was over seventeen hours,[7] and though 'stormye
and contageous wedder' sometimes stayed thieves of both
the realms,[8] some thieves were dauntless, and the Taits of
Teviotdale burnt two houses at Downham during the
record storm of February 1571.[9] It is impossible accu-
rately to work out the incidence of raids as the dates and
times of day are often not mentioned in the bills. Nor is it
possible to say whether moonlight was a factor of importance. Day raids were not uncommon. To sum up, the
Border thieves were no ordinary thieves. Many young
men adopted the trade because their district was over-

---

[1] C.B.P. ii, 745; cf. For. v, 229, vii, 753.   [2] C.B.P. ii, 1121.   [3] C.B.P.
i, 746.   [4] C.B.P. ii, 172.   [5] For. i, 311.   [6] C.B.P. i, 668.
[7] Brit. 816.   [8] C.B.P. i, 192, 499.   [9] For. ix, 1541.

populated and the tenements consequently small. They had a queer ethical code and doubtless felt quite justified in what they did. In a similar way Drake was no ordinary pirate, and like him the Border thieves sometimes stole with the Queen's or King's permission, though there is no record of her sharing the plunder or knighting any of them. Raids were made by bodies of men numbering sometimes a hundred or more, and national enmity vied with poverty and lust for gain in causing them.

Some of the Border seaports were frequented by pirates, and at Berwick they were so openly maintained in 1574 by some belonging to that town that it caused evil blood among the Scots. Some of the maintainers belonged to the garrison. Scots pirates were at work on the west coast in 1575, and, in March 1577, Lord Maxwell, the Scots Warden, and John, Lord Herries, were said to be in league with them.[1] In the winter of 1577-8 a commission inquired into piracy in Northumberland, but its fines for goods landed there and for food supplied to pirates amounted to the small sum of £20.[2] A list made in the following March, however, includes the names of 155 people in Northumberland, mostly poor fishermen, who dealt with pirates, and fines varying from 3s. 4d. to £2 13s. 4d., and adding up to £147 1s. 10d., were imposed.[3] Piracy was combined, if not with wrecking, at least with the plunder of wrecked ships,[4] and, as in 1580 there were still pirates in Tynemouth,[5] more vigorous action was taken, and two pirate barks were captured by a ship fitted out by the Corporation of Newcastle.[6] This coincided with Scots complaints against Berwick soldiers for committing piracy. Bowes's inquiries satisfied him that two of the accused soldiers were innocent, but the Scots remained suspicious, and the innocence of the third man was not clear to Bowes.[7] In 1583 piracy reappeared in the west, and Richard Musgrave of Carlisle was accused of receiving goods. He sent a certificate, signed by the

[1] For. x, 1497, 1507; C.S.P. v, 31; C.H.M. ii, 76; R.P.C.S. ii, 603-4.
[2] Dom. Add. ii, 529-30.   [3] Dom. Add. ii, 541.   [4] A.P.C. xi, 447.
[5] C.H.M. ii, 823.   [6] A.P.C. xii, 129.   [7] C.R.B. xl, xli.

J.P.s of the coastal districts, certifying that none had been illegally landed for seven years.[1] In 1586–7 the Scots made numerous complaints, none of which could be proved against Borderers.[2] By the end of the period the pirates of the district were described as Dunkirkers, though the ships were victualled in Scotland, and most of the crews were said to be Scots.[3]

Coining was not uncommon; some of the best soldiers in Berwick garrison, men with wives and children, made a practice of counterfeiting Scots money, and were leniently treated by Hunsdon in 1569.[4] This leniency may have been the cause of a fresh outbreak about 1575 when Scots money was again coined.[5] Coiners were at work in the English Middle Marches in 1590,[6] and in 1596 one of the Grames of the English West March kept a 'coyner' at work in the top of his own house and 'in Geordy marks sheyld in the myllers howse end'.[7]

The majority of the peaceable borderers, and of the thieves during the close season, were farmers. The feeding and breeding of beasts was their most important work, and their wills and inventories show that cattle, horses, and sheep were their most numerous animals, though hogs, goats, and geese are also mentioned. Wedel notes that the Scots horses 'were small and bad looking, saddles and bridles as well, the latter having no bits'. Cows, as nowadays, were given such names as 'Throssell' and 'Cherrie'. Bee-keeping was not uncommon.[8] Harrison says that the English oxen were particularly big, some of them bigger than a man of mean or indifferent stature.[9] Some of the more enlightened Border farmers of to-day hold, if they have any opinion at all, that the breed was small till the eighteenth century. In the absence of any evidence, such as how many cattle were required for a day's meat ration for Berwick garrison, the question seems insoluble. The Border papers are silent about the slaughter

---

[1] C.R.B. ccxvi; Dom. Add. iii, 96–7.   [2] C.H.M. iii, 391–2, 398, 412, 422, 427, 446, 555, 572, 597, 611; C.S.P. ix, 215.   [3] C.B.P. ii, 1457, 1466. [4] For. ix, 383.   [5] C.S.P. v, 209, 226.   [6] C.B.P. i, 673.   [7] C.B.P. ii, 285.   [8] D.W. i, 335, 365–6, 378–9, ii, 112, iii, 99; Wedel, 241. [9] Holinshed, 109.

and preservation of cattle for winter food, but frequently allude to the custom known as 'summering' in time of peace. 'Here every year', wrote Camden, 'round about in the wastes as they term them, as also in Gillsland, you may see, as it were, the ancient Nomads, a martial kind of men, who from the month of April, lie out scattering and summering (as they term it) with their cattle in little cottages here and there, which they call sheals or shealings.'[1] Summering lasted till August[2] and was 'theire chefest profitt', but sometimes had to be abandoned for fear of raids in force.[3] In the Harbottle district 2,200 acres were given up to this use in 1604.[4] That Survey also records that farmers 'till, reap and mow each their own ground particularly, and after the first crop they eat all in common without stint or number, except in some places where the tenement lieth in several'.[5] The year's work began with ploughing as soon as the frosts were over, some of the winter having been spent in threshing. Haymaking was sometimes half over before the end of July,[6] and then the cattle were put in the fields till food became deficient. Meanwhile the crops of grain were reaped. It is not always possible to tell the proportion of grains sown on the fields of those whose wills and inventories have been preserved, because 'hard corn' may mean 'wheat' or 'rye'. Oats were the commonest crop, followed by barley, of which 'bigg', the four-rowed variety of the six-rowed or winter barley, was found most suitable for the northern climate. 'Beare', the six-rowed kind, was also grown, and the terms were sometimes used loosely. Rye was probably the third crop in order of size, and wheat was sown, though not much of it. 'Peasse' were grown as cattle food, though in time of dearth men ate them.[7] In summer the farmers collected turves and peat for fuel.[8] Wood was too scarce, and was doled out to tenants for the necessary repairs of the houses. No land seems to have been set apart for afforestation.[9]

[1] Brit. 816; cf. C.B.P. i, 217, 305.   [2] Speed, 89.   [3] C.B.P. ii, 611–12, 618.   [4] R.P.S. 104.   [5] R.P.S. 52.   [6] C.B.P. ii, p. 159.   [7] D.W. i, 335, 365, 367–8, iii, 165, &c.   [8] R.P.S. 75, 77, 108, 112.   [9] R.P.S. 74–5; see also C. & W., N.S. ix, 121–46.

According to Leslie, the Scots Borderers did 'utterly contemn' to till their ground in peace time, fearing war, though the ground itself was fertile. This was untrue of the Merse, and there is evidence that Scots illegally sowed corn on the English side of the frontier. They also depastured their cattle in England, and the English were equally guilty of this breach of the Border Laws. In Scotland the corn 'was not kept in barns, but stood in heaps'.[1]

Berwick and Carlisle were the only places through which goods might be sent into Scotland, and were therefore considerable market towns. Newcastle had some trade with the Continent, and a trade in coal; and the men of Kendal had 'great traffic and vent of their woollen cloths throughout all parts of England'.[2] The rest of the Border towns were chiefly market towns where agricultural produce, cattle, and horses were sold. Copper mines were worked at Keswick and Newlands, 'where likewise black lead is gotten',[3] and 'sea-coles' were 'dragged up' in great plenty to the great gain of the mining districts of Northumberland.[4] There were salmon fisheries in the Tweed, Solway, and elsewhere, but the men of Cumberland neglected them.[5] A large number of Scots were employed in the English Marches as shepherds, salmon-fishers, and colliers.[6] These Scots, and the Scots pedlars, who were licensed to sell bridles, saddles, daggers, spears, stirrups, skins for covering coats of plate armour, and steel bonnets and bonnet-coverings, were reputed to be spies. The merchants of Berwick and Carlisle complained of them for trade reasons, but Henry, Lord Scroope, said they had caused the price of linen and other goods to be lower, and thus benefited the poor. In the end the English Government tried to stop the traffic.[7] As a last resort an honest Borderer might be driven to beg, and, if he could get the support of an influential man like Lord Eure, and show that his house had been burned and wasted by the

---

[1] Wedel, 247–8.   [2] Brit. 759.   [3] Speed, 87.   [4] Brit. 779.   [5] Brit. 765.   [6] C.H.M. i, 1269; C.B.P. i, 571, 806, 810; C.S.P. v, 664.   [7] Dom. Add. ii, 411, 418; C.B.P. i, pp. 142, 145.

Fast Castle, from the cliffs to the south

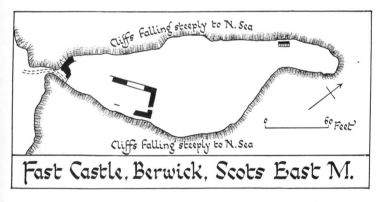

Cliffs falling steeply to N. Sea

Cliffs falling steeply to N. Sea

0   60 Feet

Fast Castle, Berwick, Scots East M.

Fast Castle. Ground-plan

VI. THE EAST MARCHES OF SCOTLAND

Dacre Castle, from the NNE.

Dacre Castle, from the south

VII. DWELLINGS

Scots to his utter undoing, the council might grant him a licence to beg elsewhere.[1]

The legends about 'Merrie England' are not applied to the Marches even by the most romantic pseudo-historians, but the Borderers had many forms of outdoor recreation. The rich indulged in hunting and hawking. James VI occasionally visited his East March to hunt with Lord Hume, and the English Wardens found that three or four couples of hounds 'for the hayer' formed a useful introductory to present to him.[2] Thomas, Lord Scroope, also delighted in hunting, and Wyllughby found it not only an excellent pastime, but also a means of spying out his wardenry.[3] Hunting in the opposite realm was illegal. Scotland was famous for certain kinds of hawks, such as goshawks, 'tarselles gentle and marlyons', and the English wardens were generally glad to receive them as presents.[4] Hunsdon, however, was reported to take 'als gret plesure to caus hang thevis as uyer men in halking and hunting'.[5]

There is no evidence that English nobles played football, but the Scots lords did, and the game caused feuds. On May 29, 1583, R. Bowes wrote, 'some quarrel happened the other day betwixt Bothwell and the Master of Marishal upon a stroke given at football on Bothwell's leg by the Master, after that the Master had received a sore fall by Bothwell'. It took James VI some time to reconcile them.[6] Bothwell kept up the game and was 'oppinly on Esk' with other traitors 'playand at the futt ball' in October 1592.[7] The game was sometimes played six a side, and followed by hard drinking. A Scots team might come to play Bewcastle, but would hardly venture farther into England.[8] The chief riders used to attend matches, and there was no close season, games being played on Sundays in June. The meeting of undesirable spectators gave opportunities for the plotting of murders, such as that of Sir John Carmichael.[9] In England attempts were made to

---

[1] C.H.M. vii, 529–30.   [2] C.B.P. ii, 232, 236, 239.   [3] C.B.P. ii, 360, 1085.   [4] C.H.M. iii, 632; C.B.P. i, 245, ii, 1220.   [5] C.S.P. v, 208.   [6] C.R.B. ccviii; C.S.P. vi, 489.   [7] C.B.P. i, 783.   [8] C.B.P. ii, 1066.   [9] C.M. 46; Pitcairn, ii, 363–4.

stop Sunday games during service time, by keeping players in jail for a week and then making them do penance in the parish church.[1] The game was very rough and had no regular rules.[2]

Horse-racing, which was almost if not quite unknown in the south, was very popular in the Marches, and especially appealed to the undesirable classes. Bothwell, for instance, in 1593, in spite of Scroope's proclamation against recetting him, 'openlie shewed himselfe uppon Gaterlie moor at a horserace there'.[3] Sometimes there were quarrels and horses were slain.[4] Buccleugh and the Grames took a keen interest in the sport, the former in 1597 especially, when he was organizing forays to welcome the English Commissioners.[5] This did not prevent respectable people, like Thomas, Lord Scroope, from attending races on well-known courses.[6] In north-west Cumberland the two chief courses were at Langwathby Moor for the country folk, and at Kingsmoor for the citizens of Carlisle. Two racing bells are preserved at Carlisle, one dated 1599, and the other probably forty years older. They must have taken the place of challenge cups.[7] In the Middle and East Marches of England there must have been less racing, but Wyllughby, when Governor of Berwick, entered horses. Horse races were also held at Strokstruther in Teviotdale, and in 1602 brawls took place in which pistols and hackbuts were used.[8]

Salmon fishing at Berwick was a trade, and perhaps the fish were netted as they are nowadays,[9] but by the Solway, says Camden, 'the inhabitants thereabout on both sides with pleasant pass time and delightful sight on horseback with spears, hunt salmons whereof there is abundance'.[10] Dancing and bowling were common enough to be forbidden to unmarried parsons, probably because the meeting-place was usually a tavern. Popish abrogated holidays were also forbidden, and no fairs or markets were to be

---

[1] Barnes, 119.   [2] C.H.E.L. iii, 22.   [3] C.B.P. i, 853.   [4] C.B.P. ii, 600.   [5] C.B.P. ii, 307, 577, 600.   [6] C.B.P. i, 831.   [7] C. & W., O.S. xii, 188; C.B.P. i, 309.   [8] C.B.P. ii, 1162; R.P.C.S. vi, 259. [9] C.B.P. i, 806, 810.   [10] Brit. S. 17.

held on Sundays.[1] Archery is scarcely mentioned in Border documents.[2] In towns bull-baiting was probably carried on. There were bull-rings in Alnwick and Brampton, but no literary evidence is forthcoming. In Newcastle there were occasionally stage plays,[3] and perhaps the English players who entered Scotland in 1599 and caused 'sume littyll stear betwen the Kynge of Scotland and his minesters', who had forbidden them to play and preached against them,[4] played at Border towns on their route. There is no record of betting at horse races, but cards were played for stakes of ale or money, especially among the outlaws. Dice were popular among the men of Berwick garrison.[5]

With so many outdoor occupations and recreations the Borderers should have lived to a ripe old age, but for two things, deaths by violence and deaths by plague. 'Plague' is a vague term which seems to have included all epidemic diseases which ran an acute course and caused a heavy death-rate. Its first appearance in the Elizabethan Borders seems to have been in November 1568, when it was brought from Edinburgh.[6] In the following February there was at Newcastle an epidemic of burning ague, cousin-german to the plague and fatal in twenty-four hours. At the same time Berwick was suffering from a new disease called 'hyves', akin to small-pox and a younger son to the plague. Hunsdon's and the Marshal's were the only houses free from it, and there was no physician in the district.[7] In August 1570 there was a new sickness of 'hotte fever', which ran sore in the English Middle March. It was said not to be plague, but was fatal in two days and left marks on most of the corpses.[8] At the same time plague visited Newcastle, but not Berwick, which was again troubled by burning ague. Many fell sick, but few died, such as had good keeping recovering in eight or ten days.[9] In 1576 plague was again in Newcastle, and in 1577 thirty-eight inhabitants of Hawkshead, a Cumberland village, died of

---

[1] R.T. vi, no. 4.   [2] C.S.P. iv, 501.   [3] A.A. iv, 233–4.   [4] C.B.P. ii, 1126.   [5] Sadler, ii, 388; C.B.P. i, p. 415 (1); Brit. 818.   [6] C.H.M. i, 1211. [7] For. ix, 116; C.H.M. i, 1277.   [8] C.S.P. iii, 411.   [9] For. ix, 1183.

a pestilent disease brought by a stranger.[1] In October 1579 the plague was in Berwick and in sundry parts of the East and Middle Marches whither Scots resorted. The Scots council, therefore, stopped intercourse with England, and the disease did not spread beyond the frontier. It was not a serious variety, for, though it spread into sixteen or seventeen houses in Berwick, only forty-two people died of it, and not one soldier in pay.[2] In July 1580 there was in Edinburgh and Berwick a disease which began with pains in the head or eyes, and sores in the throat and breast, in the nature of a cold. Almost every one in Berwick caught it, but few, or none, died, and very few died in Edinburgh, where there were three or four thousand cases at once.[3] In October 1583 plague broke out in Tynemouth, spread to Newcastle, and was 'sprynkled here and there in many places of Northumberland'. The gentry were terrified and the musters hindered.[4] In 1588–90 there was a great visitation at Newcastle, during which business was at a standstill and 1727 people died. By March 1590 it began to cease there, but was greatly dispersed throughout the district, especially at Alnwick, and put men in marvellous fear. In 1593 plague was again at Newcastle.[5] About May 1596 'a marvelous and straunge sickness' broke out in Newcastle, and many were infected and died.[6] In the following January it suddenly increased, and by July was dispersed throughout the district, so that the judges held no Assizes there.[7] By August Berwick was 'allredey belegard about with the plague' to its very gates, and likely to suffer from famine.[8] It spread to most of the neighbourhood, and by September was all over the Borders, reaching Edinburgh in October, but Berwick apparently remained free from it.[9] In November it was still increasing in Carlisle, 'notwithstanding Mr. Maiore his dewtifull care to prevent the same', and it was not till January that it began to cease there.[10] But it did not really

[1] C. & W., O.S. xi, 158; G.B.R. 15.   [2] C.R.B. xi; C.S.P. v, 439. [3] C.R.B. xxxix.   [4] C.P.B. i, 114.   [5] C. & W., O.S. xi, 158; G.B.R. 15; C.B.P. i, 663.   [6] C.B.P. ii, 266.   [7] C.B.P. ii, 466, 480, 492, 675.   [8] C.B.P. ii, 718.   [9] C.B.P. ii, 743, 755, 788.   [10] C.B.P. ii, 819, 844, 890.

end then, for in July it had 'toutched' the deputy warden's servants about him, and in September Scroope wrote that it was 'greatly disperced and hot, wherby most of our people is dead, and divers of my men'.[1] It was over by the end of the year.

Ignoring the inscription in St. Andrew's Church, Penrith, which gives impossible figures, and confining our attention to the parish registers, we find that between October 14, 1597, and December 15, 1598, there were 608 deaths from plague in Penrith, where the average number of deaths was fifty. In Kirkoswald the death-rate increased from ten to fifty-one.[2] This was the greatest visitation in the period. The last was in 1602, and was severe enough to prevent the Assizes being held in Northumberland.[3] It is marvellous that any one survived, such was the neglect of sanitary precautions and the insufficiency and inefficiency of physicians in the north. When a family had died the house was sometimes purified,[4] but the heaps of clay, filth, dung, and ash which lay in the streets of such towns as Berwick[5] gave the plague every chance. It was thought that plague might be caught from patients, or from articles used by them, for a letter from Leigh, when his house was infected, was not shown to the Queen, but there seems to have been no idea that the disease could be rooted out by sanitary improvements, or was caused by dirt. It was regarded as the 'visitacion of God'.[6]

Border Tenures really form a special and very perplexing subject, any detailed treatment of which is outside the province of a general history. All tenants, whatever their tenures, were liable to fight for their lands, and there was no lease in Northumberland but with provision to find horse and armour for each tenement, to be held by an able man.[7] A few examples may make things clearer. In Wark and Harbottle the principal freeholders held of the Queen, by knight's service, and 'were at the command of the keeper to serve in field on horse or foot for defence of the

---

[1] C.B.P. ii, 969–70, 991. [2] C. & W., O.S. xi, 158–86; Cox, 169; Watson, 127–9. [3] G.B.R. 21–2. [4] D.W. i, 113–14. [5] Scott, 303. [6] C.B.P. ii, 819, 970. [7] C.B.P. i, 78.

Border lands in as strict a manner as any of the customary tenants'. If unfurnished they were apparently liable to forfeit their holdings.[1] Some tenants, for example those in Tynedale, claimed to hold their lands 'by title of tenant right'. They were bound to serve like the above free-holders, but might sell all or part of their holdings, and could not be evicted if unfurnished.[2] Tynedale tenements were divided equally among the male children when their father died, thus causing loss of service, and forcing youths to become thieves for lack of sustenance.[3] Lease-holders often held their lands at small rents, their military service being taken into account. For example, the men of Bewcastle were said to pay just over one per cent. of the yearly value of their lands.[4] Sometimes leases of lands were given to heirs as rewards for Border services done by their fathers.[5] Some tenants held by copyhold, but the courts were not always orderly kept.[6] The muster rolls show that, with and without excuse, many tenants evaded their obligations. Evidence about Scots Border tenures is scanty. In 1565 it is noted that a certain John Carruthers held lands within six miles of the frontier 'subject to continual service, and to sustain horse and gear for defence of the realm, whereunto the inhabitants of the incountry are not so daily astrictit'.[7] Lands at Canonbie were said in 1576 to be held 'be sic men as were providit and reddy at all tymes for the service and accumpanyeing of the Wardanis of the West Marche at dayis of Trew and outherwayis for defence of the realme'.[8]

There remains the perplexing question of dialects, for which contemporary evidence is scanty. Boorde, who had lived on the Borders, wrote, 'But the South part of Scotland, and the usual speech of the peers of the realm is like the Northern speech of England. Wherefore if any man will learn to speak some Scots—English and Scots doth follow together'. Elsewhere he wrote, 'In England there be sundry speeches besides English. . . . There is also the

---

[1] R.P.S. 57–8; C.B.P. ii, 268.   [2] R.P.S. 51; C.B.P. ii, 613 (4).
[3] R.P.S. 85; C.B.P. i, p. 23, ii, 268.   [4] C.B.P. i, 162; R.P.S. 21.   [5] C.H.M. iii, 158.   [6] R.P.S. 124.   [7] R.P.C.S. ii, 432.   [8] R.P.C.S. ii, 542.

Northern tongue, the which is trew Scottish, and the Scots tongue is the Northern tongue'.[1] In W. Bullein's Dialogue the Redesdale beggar is taken for a Scot by 'Uxor'. This evidence leads to the conclusion that it was hard to distinguish, by his speech, a Scots Borderer from an English Borderer. Personal observation nowadays is of doubtful value, as people move so easily, and three centuries of inter-marriage separate us from 1603. But a Londoner can distinguish between the speeches of Dumfries and Carlisle, though both, like that of Bewcastle, are Scots to him. The difference between speech at Harbottle and Jedburgh is clear, but in the East Marches the difficulty increases. The Berwick dialect, to a Londoner, is Scots, and is hard to distinguish from that of the other bank of the Tweed. Farther south comes the easily recognizable Northumberland 'burr', and then the 'Newcăssle' twang, which to some ears is horrible. The halting conclusion is that, in spite of what Boorde says, a Scot would easily betray himself to the local ear of the sixteenth century in the West and Middle Marches. If he came from the Merse he might escape detection more easily in the East March.

[1] Op. cit. 137-8, 121.

PART III

THE RELIGION OF THE BORDERERS

[The author believes that the facts hereinafter stated are true. The ethical and doctrinal opinions expressed are those of contemporaries, most of them in official positions.]

THE East and Middle Marches of England were part of the see of Durham, and the West March, except an area attached to Chester, formed the see of Carlisle. In Northumberland there were about forty-six parishes, in Cumberland fifty-eight, and in Westmorland twenty-six.[1] The incumbents had an uphill task. The Borders in the sixteenth century had produced a few learned men like Nicholas Ridley and Bernard Gilpin, who was born at Kentmere in Westmorland, and was afterwards vicar, first of Easington, and then of Houghton-le-Spring, where his heart was troubled by the desolation of the Church and the ignorance of the common sort. This desolation appeared most of all in Northumberland, especially in Redesdale and Tynedale, where, about 1556, the Word of God was never heard to be preached but by Master Gilpin, who journeyed thither once a year. To remedy the lack of learned men able to preach God's Word, he 'builded a school, allowing maintenance for master and usher', and privately instructed some of the best pupils himself. He also maintained scholars at the University. Though his work was so conspicuous that the Queen, on Bedford's recommendation, offered him the see of Carlisle, which he refused, and that Sir William Cecil visited him at Houghton on his way back from Scotland, and though he did settle many feuds and went about doing good, his work was but a tiny drop of oil poured on an ocean of ignorance.

The Elizabethan settlement was not well received by

[1] Brit. 161–2, 763, 788, 822.

the Borderers, who knew little about the 'truth in Religion' lately rediscovered. Almost all the influences to which they were subject were opposed to it. Gilpin himself only conformed lest he should be a means of making others refuse.[1] It is difficult to discover the sentiments of the people; they may or may not have been in sympathy with their old clergy. Those clergy had been, in a sense, a papal garrison, yet when the Oath was administered in 1559–64 most of them took it. The Board of Visitors began its work at Durham on September 1, 1559, and sat at Newcastle on September 27 and Alnwick on September 30. Some of its members, like the Earl of Northumberland and Sir Henry Percy, were of doubtful orthodoxy, and it may be that their secret influence rather than the example of Gilpin, so influenced the clergy that of the 145 who appeared (there were thirty-five absentees) only two were deprived, one of whom held the Border living of Bothal. Perhaps, like the Earl, they thought they were merely conforming temporarily. At Carlisle on October 3 and 4, and at Penrith on October 6, there was also little opposition. Only two of the sixty-five clergy who appeared were deprived, though thirty-five were absent. Again it is likely that many, relying on the Dacres, did not regard their oaths as permanent.[2] Knox would hardly have regarded them as true and faithful preachers such as were necessary to unite the hearts of the Borderers in God's fear.[3] Both the bishops, Tunstall and Oglethorpe, were deprived, and died in 1559, and the sees were vacant till March 1561. A further commission was given to the Earl of Rutland to inquire into illegal congregations and conventicles in the north, and to administer the Oath of Supremacy, apparently only to those who had refused it or been absent before. The bishops also visited their dioceses, and Best found the Oath generally taken, though some recusants sheltered themselves under the nobles; but Pilkington met with more opposition. None the less in 1559–64 there were only five changes among the clergy of

---

[1] Carleton, 1, 63–4, 69–73, 79–80, 87, 89, 133.   [2] For the facts, but not for the opinions, see Gee, 71–89.   [3] C.S.P. i, 488.

Carlisle diocese, and nineteen in Durham, two of which, Bothal and Wooler, were in the Marches.[1]

Sadler had wished for a greater change. The see of Durham was rich, and he thought that much of its revenues might be put to secular uses, but proposed that 'two or three godly and learned men should have convenient entertainment either by yearly stipend, or by some spiritual promotions of the said bishopric, to preach and teach the Word of God for the better instruction of the ignorant people, which is a thing needful and necessary in the North parts, and specially in Berwick'.[2] Knox spoke of the need for a preacher in Berwick, where the curate could not live on his pay,[3] but actually there was one new minister per March and nothing is known of his credentials. It is not surprising then that, though Pilkington found more gentleness from the Earl of Westmorland and Lord Eure than he looked for or felt he deserved, and had only two refusals of the Oath from J.P.s in the summer of 1561, the Bishop of Carlisle was at the beginning of 1562 lamenting the prevalence of Papistry in his diocese and the confidence among Papists of a coming change which alienated quite away the people's hearts which were quieted before.[4] In 1563 many Scots priests crept into England minding, it was said, to do no less mischief than they had done in Scotland, and among them was a notable friar whom Sadler thought the greatest liar that ever was, with one exception. These men worked for less pay than Englishmen, and were aided by the importation of books and scholars from Louvain and other places.[5] Bedford thought that some restraint was necessary, or the Popery rooted in the north would bring forth evil.[6]

In 1564 the bishops held a general inquiry into the religion of J.P.s, and, in England as a whole, half of the 852 received favourable reports, and only about one in six was a hinderer of the established faith. The town J.P.s,

[1] Gee, 38, 158, 166–71, 273, 276.   [2] Sadler, ii, 282–4.   [3] C.S.P. i, 488; For. iv, 774.   [4] For. iv, 771 and note.   [5] For. vi, 768, 839; C.S.P. ii, 9; C.H.M. i, 1024 (14); Camden Misc. ix, Letters from Bishops, 67. [6] For. vii, 266.

except in Newcastle, were more hostile than the rural ones. On the Borders the state of affairs was different. Of the East March the Bishop wrote: 'My lord of Bedford sais that in his charge there is never a justice of peace nor none he can commend as mete for that purpose.' Forster could recommend twelve for appointment, and complained of three only. The Bishop's report on Newcastle, where the Mayor and ten aldermen were J.P.s, was satisfactory. In Cumberland nine justices, including Lord Dacre, got bad reports; six, including the Bishop, were marked good; and eight, including the Warden and his brother, were recommended for appointment. In Westmorland nine were not good, four good, and seven were recommended for appointment, but the Bishop was loud in his complaints against the noblemen's tenants, who did not dare to be known to favour 'the religion' for fear of losing their farms.[1] The J.P.s were not dependent on their theological views for their living; the clergy were, yet they got very little pay and were overworked. In many parishes, especially in Northumberland, the vicars had to serve from two to five chapels, and some of the parish churches had no vicars at all, but were served by vagabond Scots exiles. The Queen drew large revenues from some parishes and paid a lewd priest £4 to £5 a year to serve them, or put in no vicar at all.[2] Pay was one of the chief causes of the decay of religion in the north, but the Government would not see it. Thus, when guarding against dangers that might arise from the Darnley marriage, it sought to destroy lewd books from beyond the seas, and to banish dishonest and unconformable curates, but utterly neglected to provide the only likely means of obtaining suitable clergy for the north, where, in Bedford's opinion, only Scroope, Forster, and Sir H. Percy favoured 'the religion'.[3]

To the danger of a people full of Papistry, yet 'mere ignorant of religion and altogether untaught',[4] was soon added the danger of Mary Stuart's presence. And to

[1] Camden Misc. ix, Letters from Bishops, 48–51, 65–7, 73–80; C.H.M. i, 1024 (11), (14).   [2] Dom. Add. i, 577–8.   [3] For. vii, 1224, 1509.
[4] C.S.P. ii, 668, 829.

these dangers were joined those of economic distress caused by absenteeism, the temporary suspension of the wool trade with Flanders, and the dissolution of the monasteries. Thus, when the Earls rose against the new men, the people, as Gilpin had foreseen 'by certain evident signs',[1] so liked their cause of religion that they flocked to them in all places, and such as were in person with the Queen's forces were so ignorant, superstitious, and altogether wholly blinded with the old popish doctrine that their hearts were with the rebels, and Sadler felt sure they would fight faintly. Gilpin and Pilkington fled, but there was hardly any fighting.[2] When the rising was over, Gargrave urged that religion must be put in better stay, and the Papists in more fear, or quiet would be shortlived. He recommended the encouragement of the Ecclesiastical Commissioners to proceed. The Queen seems to have thought that the instruction of the rebels by discreet preachers in open sermons before they appeared before the commission would do good. Ignorance, as Gilpin knew, was the cause of many being found in the rebel camp, but sermons in such circumstances would hardly enlighten it.[3] However, for a time things seemed to improve, and the Bishop of Carlisle could assure Burghley that God had mightily prospered his simple ministry among his savage people, so that, except in four parishes, where there was neither fear, faith, virtue, knowledge of God, nor regard of any religion, no one openly repined against religion, refused to communicate, shunned sermons, or openly spoke against the established faith.[4] It is not unlikely that hanging, rather than preaching, was the cause of this. Burghley was not impressed by it, and ordered the Bishop and Scroope to search for vestments concealed in their charges,[5] and another inquiry was held into the cases of all known and suspected Papists;[6] but the traffic in beads, Agnus Dei's, friars' girdles for women in travail, hypocritical and abominable idolatrous pictures, &c., went on

---

[1] Carleton, 99. [2] Dom. Add. ii, 111, 139; R.T. i, 210; Sadler, ii, 325. [3] R.T. i, 218, 251; Carleton, 102. [4] Dom. Add. ii, 367. [5] Dom. Add. ii, 414. [6] C.S.P. iv, 501.

as before, though the penalty for selling them might be death.[1] It must not be concluded that the Government wished to be cruel. Scroope, for instance, in 1574 had arrested two Papists, one a priest, for religion, and was ordered by the Privy Council to free them if they could be brought to conform, but otherwise to proceed according to law.[2]

Bishop Barnes was an optimist, and, on his translation from Carlisle to Durham in 1577, wrote to Burghley lauding his new flock for its civil obedience and excellent conformity, and himself for having driven the numerous mass-priests out of his diocese into Yorkshire and Lancashire. It is clear, however, that some of them were still 'reset' in the Middle March. He considered the men of Northumberland 'far more pliable to all good order than the stubborn churlish people' of Durham, and the clergy showed a 'good readiness to apply their travells to their calling'. Only two Northumberland men, as against six men of Durham, were reported for refusing to attend church.[3] Soon after his entry into his new see he set to work to hold a visitation, and in January and February 1578 his Chancellor was in Northumberland calling the clergy, schoolmasters, &c., before him, excommunicating such as were absent as contumacious, and giving the Bishop's charge. The clergy were to learn St. Matthew's Gospel in Latin, or, if they did not, in English. Some of the Bishop's score or so of injunctions were counsels of perfection, but others were practical. All popish ceremonies like masses for the dead, non-prayer-book baptismal rites, and holiday services were to cease. Popish articles were to be removed, and popish paintings 'perjetted' over with lime. The sacrament was to be administered at least once a month, all over fourteen being obliged to partake of it thrice a year, and a catechismal test was imposed on communicants, godparents, and would-be brides and bridegrooms. A yearly examination was to be held in Lent, and the clergy were to teach children weekly

[1] Dom. Add. ii, 416.   [2] A.P.C. viii, 314.   [3] Barnes, x, quoting Strype, ii, 482–3; Dom. Add. ii, 519–20; A.P.C. x. 78–9.

and report those parents who would not send them. No fairs were to be held on Sundays; no taverns to be open during Divine Service; no clergy to keep concubines or frequent taverns or dances; no archdeacon to commute penance for money-fines, &c.[1] The offences with which his ecclesiastical courts dealt in 1577–87 varied very much. A clerk accused of adultery was ordered 'ad purgandum se duodecima manu' and succeeded; a woman charged with fornication had fled and was excommunicated; absentees from the Easter communion had to do penance in their usual dress with a white sheet over the same; players of football during the Sunday services were fined and did penance in church. A Scots woman who was a scold, sellers of fish on Sundays and holy-days during church-time, talkers in church, non-resident vicars, church-wardens who let the church fabric decay, &c., were also dealt with.[2] In 1579 Barnes held a second visitation, and summoned the clergy to chapters at Newcastle and Alnwick, where they were examined in 'their progress in learning and studying the Scriptures', St. Matthew's Gospel being the set book. At Newcastle three of thirty-nine performed their task well and sixteen imperfectly; at Alnwick twelve of fifty-four did well and three imperfectly. The complete failures included William Hall, who had been Rector of Elsdon since 1543, and his curate. In Durham thirty-nine of ninety-six did perfectly, and yet, out of the three hundred and three extra sermons which the Bishop ordered to be preached, only eighty-eight were to be in Northumberland. St. Luke's Gospel was set for the Visitation of 1580.[3]

In 1580 the papal campaign began in earnest, and on the capture of Campion in 1581 Hunsdon wrote from Berwick advising severity, 'for trewly my lorde the papystes wax prowde and arrogante bothe men and women especyally in these north partes'.[4] Early in that year a dozen or more had been arrested for hearing mass at

---

[1] Barnes, 13–28, 29–46; R.T. iv, no. iv.   [2] Barnes, 113–42.   [3] Barnes, 62–72, 76–97; Elsdon Registers, Newc. Soc. of Antiquaries, 76.   [4] C.B.P. i, 102.

Warkworth Castle, and the Keeper of Tynemouth Castle had fled to France or Spain for some mischief.[1] A more vigorous search for Jesuits was started next year, and, though they were plentiful, yet, being backed and comforted from Scotland, they found it fairly easy to pass through the Borders with their miscellaneous luggage which included breviaries, 'certen instrumentes to drawe forth teethe', and looking-glasses which hid cipher letters.[2] Except for the capture of Boast, an important prisoner, neither Scroope nor Forster had much success.[3] An influence on the anti-papal side was Melvill, who, while spending the winter of 1584–5 at Berwick, got a licence from Hunsdon's cousin, 'the good Lady Widringtoun . . . to teatche in a certain hous of the town thryse in the ouick'. Lady Widdrington attended his sermons.[4] In the early summer of 1585 the Wardens were again ordered to inquire into the cases of recusants and to search their houses for armour and weapons. Scroope only found two, but in Forster's office some of the Papists were exceedingly arrogant and would 'by no means be perswaded to heare the Worde of God', even when urged by the Warden. His religion must have seemed curious to a Papist if he was in the habit of doing what he did when Melvill dined with him, for then he suddenly 'began bothe to glorifie God in recompting what he haid wrought already, and to prophesie concerning the stay of foull wather and of the pestilence', &c.[5] In 1586 the search for Jesuits was continued, and they were said to remain in Forster's Wardenry and find it easy to cross the frontier. They were much encouraged by Lord Maxwell, Earl of Morton.[6] Papistry in Northumberland was less open than it had been, but the Papists were there all the same, and in great expectation. They evidently had dispensations, for some of them that had of late 'reset' seminary priests made not dainty to come to the communion.[7] In 1587 Bishop Barnes died,

[1] C.S.P. v, 741.   [2] C.B.P. i, 126, 144.   [3] Dom. Add. iii, 104–5, 118; C.B.P. i, 126.   [4] Autobiog. 197.   [5] C.B.P. i, 313, 328; Autobiog. 227.   [6] C.B.P. i, 404–9, 412, 420, 458.   [7] Dom. Add. iii, 191–2, 231.

Hollows Tower. The beacon

Hollows Tower from the SW.

VIII. DWELLINGS

Hollows Tower. Window in first-floor room

Hollows Tower. Staircase and doors to first and second floors

IX. DWELLINGS

leaving Northumberland, in spite of his labours, 'most wretched and miserable enough to burst the heart of a well-meaning pastor, so small assistance for public religion, and the state, both ecclesiastical and civil, nowhere less . . . in this realm or the next; the place exceeding chargeable in peace, and in war doubly dangerous, yet, if God send it, it would be welcome'.[1]

Less than a year after his death open war came, and the defeat of the Armada did not shatter the hopes of the Papists. Jesuits and seminary priests were still 'reset' especially in the west, and the people fell daily from 'the religion', and inclined to Papistry, 'by the lewde perswacions of Jesuits and semynarie Priests repairing unto them secretlie',[2] and 'searchers' employed to discover them had hard usage from their friends 'especially in those North parts give(n) only to revenges'.[3] None the less recusants with popish books were taken, some of them on their way to Ireland, and the most dangerous were sent to York for proceedings.[4] This policy was shown on inquiry to be not altogether unsuccessful. Forster noted that five recusants in his office had conformed, but most of them left the country, lurked in secret places, or kept their houses shut. Only forty-eight warrants were taken out in the Middle March, but the accused were hard to catch unless starved till they came out of their secret conveyances and close corners made in walls.[5] The sheriff seems to have been very slack, and Tobie Matthew and his three fellow commissioners journeyed to Newcastle and found no one to meet them. This impunity led to further conversions to Popery, especially among the Earl of Westmorland's tenants.[6] It is possible that the Border officers did not do their utmost, as prisoners were 'chargabell', and their chances to escape a cause of anxiety.[7] Tobie Matthew felt that he lived in a place 'where a man would be loath to be that could be anie where els in anie safe and reasonable

[1] Barnes, xii; C.B.P. i, 515, 519; A.P.C. xv, 127.   [2] A.P.C. xvii, 264–5; Dom. Add. iii, 270, 321.   [3] A.P.C. xxi, 40.   [4] Dom. Add. iii, 324–6; A.P.C. xxii, 482.   [5] Dom. Add. iii, 285, 339, 342–4.   [6] Dom. Add. iii, 344–5, 377.   [7] C.B.P. i, 919.

condicion'.[1] But Burghley had no intention of letting the recusants alone, unless they would withdraw twelve miles from the frontier or sea-side, and reside with their friends under sureties.[2]

He did not see that the root of the trouble was that the Borderers were offered no alternative religion to Popery. 'True religion', wrote Sir W. Bowes from Newcastle in November 1595, 'hath verie little place, not by the unwillingness of the people to heare, but by want of meanes, scant three able preachers being to be found in the whole country. False and disloyall religion hath taken deipe root, and that in the best howses, increasing daily by the number and diligence of the semynaries, with more liberty resorting hither, being driven from other places of both the realms'.[3] In the next year Lord Eure complained of the local 'want of knowledge of God'. The churches, he said, were mostly ruined to the ground, and ministers and preachers were 'comfortles to com and remaine where such heathenish people are'. Melvill would have agreed with this view. 'Gif the Hiland and Bordour Kirks war planted, there wad be less thift', he said.[4] Tobie Matthew, on the other hand, grieved as he was at unlicensed minstrels drawing youths from evensong, so that every Sunday in some place or other was 'consecrated to Bacchus', did not know how to mend matters. He advised, and obtained, a renewal of the Ecclesiastical Commission for dealing with recusants, but when it reached him he found it so altered and abridged as to be useless.[5]

The other Commissioners, appointed to meet the Scots Commissioners to settle Border disputes, were authorized in 1597 to inquire into the religious state of the Borders.[6] They found that there were twenty-six recusants in Cumberland and twenty-one in Westmorland who had been presented to the Grand Juries at the Assizes for the last five years;[7] that certain churches, including that at Bewcastle, had been decayed for over sixty years, and the

1 C.B.P. i, 942.   2 Dom. Add. iii, 453-4.   3 C.B.P. ii, 171.
4 C.B.P. ii, 255; Autobiog. 400.   5 C.H.M. vi, 62, 72, 167, 176-9;
C.B.P. ii, 402, 442, 541.   6 C.B.P. ii, 610.   7 Dom. Add. iv, 354.

names of the patrons were unknown; that Lanercost church
had been decayed for three or four years, and Kirklinton
for twenty. This evidence must have influenced them in
favour of the first article of the Treaty of Carlisle,[1] by which
it was agreed that good ministers should be planted at
every Border church, and the churches repaired.[2] This
new idea was unfortunately expensive, and when the West
March gentry and many of their wives came dutifully to
the communion on Ascension Day—a proceeding which
did not prevent those of them who were J.P.s from dealing
with Jesuits in a careless or partial way—the Commissioners seem to have been so much impressed that they
forgot to urge that the first article should be put into practice, and, despairing of the conformity of the ill-affected,
advised more strict proceedings than had been used hitherto.[3] Tobie Matthew's further suggestions were useless,
and the only valuable thing he did was to agree with the
Bishop of Carlisle that non-resident clergy must be called
home.[4] Experience had shown him, he said, that lenity in
religious matters did little good and severity no harm, so
he wished the penalties on recusants to be duly levied,
that no respect for persons should be shown, and that the
Bishop, especially assisted and advised by the Ecclesiastical Commissioners, should be allowed to proceed uncon-
trolled according to law, within his own flock 'for whom
he, not others, must answeare to God'.[5] Some anonymous
suggestions were much more valuable. The Queen out of
her abbey lands, tithes, &c., in Northumberland might
maintain preachers and three grammar schools. She might
remove all non-resident ministers and others, 'whoe cannot preach', holding benefices worth £40 a year. Lastly,
no recusant, or recusant's husband, should hold office in
the county.[6] Another anonymous paper of the same date,
though directed against Lord Eure, agreed with him that
ignorance was at the root of religious decay, and stated
that there were not four preachers in Northumberland, no
grammar school, and not one man in five thousand who

---

[1] May 5, 1597.   [2] C.B.P. ii, 613, 622 (1).   [3] C.B.P. ii, 626.
[4] C.B.P. ii, 631.   [5] C.B.P. ii, 646, 659.   [6] C.B.P. ii, 746.

sent his son to a university.[1]   Tobie Matthew's attitude
seems to have been the cause of a Jesuit conspiracy against
his life which was discovered in the spring of 1599.[2] At
the end of that year Henry Robinson, the new Bishop of
Carlisle, sent Cecil a report on his diocese. He found more
recusants than he expected, but alleged that there were
even more in the small part of Cumberland in the see of
Chester. Eight or nine had just conformed and most of
the gentry were sound in religion, and the poorer sort
willing to hear, though pitifully ignorant. As causes he
suggested the weakness and carelessness of the clergy, the
decay of church buildings, and the lack of suitable clergy.
Most of his priests were utterly unlearned and unable to
read English truly and distinctly. He said his predecessor had instituted unfit men presented by others, but
it is hard to think that godly and capable men would work
for stipends the highest of which was twenty nobles.[3]
Nine months later he wrote to ask for a Commission for
repressing recusants, not noting that it might be useless
unless the other abuses were reformed. He thought that
if the 'principalest' felt the smart of civil justice they
might be humbled, or at least that the canker would not
spread farther.[4] At the end of the year the Privy Council,
hearing that the number of recusants had increased, and
that over 150 had been convicted at the last Assizes in
Northumberland, wrote to the Wardens and Sheriffs.[5]
Next year Sir R. Carey brought many before the Commissioners, of whom he was one, and some conformed and
others were not hopelessly obstinate. Only one refused to
say 'Amen' to a prayer for the Queen, and he was imprisoned and reported to the Privy Council.[6] The Council
on May 5 ordered the Archbishop of York and fifteen
other Commissioners to take the oaths of all manner of
spiritual persons in the northern province, punish those
who were absent from church, &c.[7]

Thus the first article of the Treaty of 1597 was for-

---

[1] C.B.P. ii, 881.   [2] C.B.P. ii, 1051.   [3] Dom. v, 362.   [4] Dom.
v, 468.   [5] A.P.C. xxxi, 26–30.   [6] Dom. v, 553; C.B.P. ii, 1331.
[7] Dom. Add. i, 510; Rymer, ix, 611.

gotten. It is not easy to say that the religious condition of the north had improved during the reign. Money was the chief cause of the failure. Repression paid its way with fines, and a credit balance could be shown in terms of hard cash. Church-building and adequate ecclesiastical stipends, to say nothing of the foundation of schools and scholarships, would have been very costly. In fifty years' time it might have shown a handsome profit, even in a pecuniary sense, but the Government wanted quick returns and would spend little or nothing, while the introduction of marriage among the clergy dried up one of the chief sources of money for learned foundations. Thus the educational experiment was postponed, as it has been postponed, at any rate in its entirety, ever since, and the proposal to build churches was likewise shelved. Taking Berwick as an example, it will be found that the Mayor and others had petitioned the Crown for money for a new church as early as June 1584, the old church being small and ruinous, so that people went to ale-houses instead. Nothing was done then or in 1597 when John Carey and others sent a new petition saying that preacher and people often ran out of the church during service for fear of its falling during a storm. Not even in 1600, when John Arden, or Harding, died intestate, and it was suggested that his estate should be used for replacing the church, which would only hold a quarter of the population, was a new church built. The ultimate destination of the money is unknown.[1]

In the history of the Scots Reformation the Borders were a backwater and a refuge, and played no prominent part. Leslie says 'neither have they notwithstanding, now vainly fallen from the faith of the Catholick Kirk as many others have done',[2] and in that condition the West March, at least, remained till the end. A Convention at Edinburgh in January 1559 decided to place superintendents over the various ecclesiastical districts. At Edinburgh there was to reside one whose province included the Merse and Tweeddale, at Jedburgh another, over Teviotdale, Tweeddale, and

---

[1] C.B.P. i, p. 143 (10); ii, p. 505, nos. 1176, 1178, 1202.   [2] Leslie, 101.

the Forest of Ettrick, and at Dumfries a third to look after
Galloway, Carrick, Nithsdale, Annandale, and the rest of
the western dales. They were not to be suffered to 'live
idle lives as the bishops had done heretofore', but were to
move after three or four months in one place, and visit
their whole bounds, preaching thrice a week at least, trying the diligence of behaviour of the minister, and looking
after the poor and the manners and instruction of the
young, &c.[1] In July of the same year Knox was quite confident that if Cecil would license a godly Berwick preacher
to preach in Scotland he (Knox) could 'obtain unto him
the favour of the most part of the gentlemen of the East
and Middle Borders'.[2] He was not given the chance, but
the parts he named were the most suitable Border soil for
the new seed. Lord Hume, who was very powerful in the
East, refused to attend mass with Mary on her return in
August 1561.[3] With the West it was far otherwise. Certain English Papists had a common passage through the
Borders, and Knox met one of them at Dumfries.[4] Scots
priests likewise passed into England when things were too
hot for them in their own country, and this interchange
continued throughout the period, and Popery remained
open in the west.[5] In 1574, as neither the Commissioner
for Nithsdale, nor the Reader, would hold a Christmas
service, the people set up a reader of their own to do so,
but it is not stated that he held a popish service.[6] In 1580,
however, it is recorded that the schoolmaster at Dumfries
'did read to his scholars the Roman catechism'.[7] The
climax came in 1584 when at 'Glencluden' Abbey, Maxwell, Earl of Morton, and Lord Herries with divers
gentry and others to the number of two or three hundred
heard mass. Mass was also celebrated in Morton's house
at Dumfries and the town preacher forbidden to preach.
Some of the mass-priests were Englishmen. For this
offence Morton was committed to Edinburgh Castle.[8] In

---

[1] Spotswood, i, 342–3.   [2] C.S.P. i, 488.   [3] For. iv, 455.   [4] C.S.P.
i, 1152.   [5] C.S.P. i, 9; For. vi, 768, 839: ix, 658; Dom. v, 362; C.B.P.
i, 458, 474, 515, 519: ii, 1349.   [6] Calderwood, iii, 351.   [7] Spotswood,
ii, 267.   [8] Calderwood, iv, 489; C.B.P. i, 404–9, 411–12, 420.

January 1587 the King sent one of his chaplains with
Lord Hamilton, the Lieutenant, to make Maxwell and
others subscribe the articles of religion professed in Scotland, but he 'flatlie denied' to do it, and remained the
centre of the Papist conspiracies, having frequent intelli-
gence from English Papists.[1] Next year Herries and fourteen others of the West Marches were mentioned as
'Papists, apostates, maintainers, entertainers, and professed
favourers of Jesuits'. At Dumfries there was 'no resorting
to hear the Word there, no discipline . . . all superstitious
ryotousness at Yuile and Pasche', &c. No kirk had been
planted there. Of the Merse and Teviotdale Calderwood
wrote, 'The principal men of the country corrupt in religion', and mentioned Lord Hume as one of them, '. . . the
whole people ready to revolt from the Evangel because
they see the prince careless thereof . . . Manie supersti-
tions, pilgrimages, and keeping of holy days' took place,
he said, and he named five Papists and stated that 'the
greatest part of the kirks want ministers, and the Word
altogether vilipended by the gentlemen of the country'.
The state was thus similar to that of the English Borders,
and the remedy, 'the planting of kirks with qualified
ministers', was applicable to both realms.[2] These accounts
were written in 1588, and might, with perhaps some little
reservation for the east, be taken as true in 1603. On the
west there was likewise no change. As late as November
1601 certain inhabitants of Dumfries were summoned
before the Council to answer for 'the saying and heiring of
Messe and prophaning of the Sacramentis; the reset and
suppleing of Jesuittis, seminarie preistis, excommunicat
and traffiquing Papistis'. Among those accused of 'reset'
was Herries, who had to give a bond of £5,000, Scots, not
to 'reset' Jesuits again, and to aid the minister at Dumfries
in the discipline of the kirk.[3]

[1] C.B.P. i, 474.   [2] Calderwood, iv, 657–8, 662, 671; Autobiog. 400.
[3] R.P.C.S. vi, 312, 326–7, 335, 717.

PART IV

THE WARDENS OF THE MARCHES

THE Commission of an English Warden is best studied by comparing two versions from different Marches, that of William, Lord Grey de Wilton, of the Middle March, dated December 22, 1559,[1] and that of Henry, Lord Scroope, of the West March, dated April 6, 1563.[2] They are almost the same. In the general preamble the Warden is given 'potestatem et speciale mandatum faciendi et exercendi omnia et singula quae ad officium guardiani sive custodis pertinent ibidem, prout antea . . . in hac parte rationabiliter fieri et exerceri consuevit', by the authority of sovereigns from Richard II onwards. The documents may be divided into some fourteen clauses which define the Warden's powers as follows:

1. To correct, reform, and amend everything done 'contra formam treugarum'.

2. To castigate and punish delinquents according to their demerits by imprisonment and distresses on their lands, goods, and chattels wheresoever found.

3. To take cognizance in all suits, pleas, and debates, in imprisonments, spoils, and rapines, and other hostile acts (and to hear and determine them). The bracketed words are in the Bell MS. only.

4. To hold Warden Courts and Sessions in his March, as well within liberties as without, and to inquire into persons offending 'contra formam treugarum', and also into offenders against orders made by the Warden or his deputy by authority of his office, and to punish them.

5. To levy fines 'et alias obligaciones' incurred for crimes as in the preceding section, and to punish those who disobeyed, by means which seemed to him expedient, and, if they persisted, to notify the Queen and Council that they might provide suitable remedy without delay.

[1] Grey, 53 et sqq.   [2] Bell, fol. 196 ff.

(Grey's copy adds 'prefatis libertatibus et omnibus aliis quam in hiis quae ad dictas treugas et ordinaciones marchiarum predictarum concernunt semper salvis'.)

6. To inquire into persons who practise with enemies of the realm, and to punish them.

7. To hear and settle by March law and custom 'querelas, placita et debata prevocata'.

8. To set watchmen and others 'ad explorandum' against hostile incursions, at the cost of the lieges and by their consent as aforetime.

9. For the safety of Berwick when likely to be attacked, to defend it and save it, and to muster all fencibles from sixteen to sixty in the March (in and outside liberties), and to see all men furnished and properly mustered. The punishments were to be imprisonment, and such others as seemed good. (The Bell MS. omits the words in the brackets and adds Carlisle.)

10. To conclude abstinences with his opposites, from week to week or month to month in the Queen's name. Deputies to do the same.

11. To nominate and make two deputies, and two 'warden serjeants', and other necessary officers under him according to custom.

12. To hold the office with its appurtenances, profits, &c., from the date named, during the Queen's pleasure.

13. To be paid his salary and the salaries of his deputies and 'warden serjeants' from the Treasury on March 25 and September 29 in equal parts.

14. To have the obedience of all lieges, and their help as was seemly.

The Warden of the East March was usually Governor of Berwick and had a separate commission. This, to judge from Lord Grey's, which is dated November 5, 1560,[1] was short and vague, and gave the same rights as had been held by former governors, with the result that there were disputes, especially in Wyllughby's time.

The Warden having 'charge as generall, in all affaires under her Majestie for the lawes of marches, according to

----

[1] Grey, 53.

the auncient Border lawe and severall newe treatisse',[1] had great powers, but they were limited, though it was sometimes mentioned in Acts of Parliament that they should not abridge his authority.[2] First, his powers were limited to his own March; for example, the Warden of the East could not arrest those under the government of the Middle March, though the Earl of Northumberland stated in 1596 that there were contrary precedents.[3] The transgression of this custom by Eure in that year involved him in a dispute with Scroope,[4] and Sir R. Carey upheld his own jurisdiction against Wyllughby's aggression in 1601, when the latter sent his officers into the Middle March.[5] But within his own office there were few exemptions from the Warden's authority, and contumacious subordinates were sometimes sent up to Court, reprimanded, and sent back to submit to the Warden.[6] Secondly, though the Warden's patent gave him the right to choose his own deputies, to whom he left all particular service either for defence of England or offence against Scotland, except on important occasions when he acted himself,[7] the Government sometimes interfered. In one case the Privy Council wrote to a man appointing him deputy Warden, but it was usually content 'to rest uppon' the judgement of an experienced Warden.[8] The powers of a Governor of Berwick were more vague. Apparently the Crown appointed the Gentleman Porter,[9] but Wyllughby during his short term of office brought the whole question into acute controversy. He claimed the right of making cannoneers, which was also claimed by the Master of Ordnance, and also of making lieutenants of the companies, and councillors, and the master-smith, besides displacing and appointing captains. He seemed bent on absolutism, but learnt just before he died that the appointment of councillors at Berwick belonged to the Queen.[10] John Carey, his successor, found his powers curtailed and was not made 'absolute

[1] C.B.P. i, 743.   [2] 43 Eliz., c. 13.   [3] C.B.P. ii, 231.   [4] C.B.P. ii, 452.   [5] C.B.P. ii, 1317.   [6] A.P.C. xxv, 251.   [7] C.B.P. i, 743. [8] C.B.P. ii, 775, 787, 798, 1334, 1347; A.P.C. xviii, 227, xxxi, 259.   [9] For. x, 952-3.   [10] C.B.P. ii, 958, 1252-3, 1258, 1273, 1338-9, 1384.

governor', but none the less as late as December 2, 1602,
he claimed the right to appoint captains.[1] The deputy's
authority ceased when the Warden died.[2] Thirdly, the
Warden's power was limited in international matters,
cases of slaughters having for a long time been referred to
the Princes.[3] Nor might he supply men to help his opposite pursue traitors, without a definite commission from
his own sovereign.[4] Lastly, his powers within his own
March were limited, not only in viewing castles and ordnance,[5] but also in judicial matters. The murderers of the
parson of Ford at Alnwick were kept for the Judges of
Assize, and the Warden could not withdraw a case from
their jurisdiction without writing to Court. In actions of
debt, too, unless both parties, or at least the defendant,
were inhabitants of the March, the case was to come
before the ordinary judges. Even then Berwick became a
refuge for debtors, and the Warden defended the practice.
Newcastle, on the other hand, claimed not to be 'subject
to admirall jurisdiccion'.[6] In 1584 Hunsdon successfully
opposed Walsyngham's attempt to order the Scots exiles
to be received in Holy Island, 'for that the Jurisdiction of
the place did of right belong to him, as Warden of the
East March'.[7]

The duties of an ideal warden are well summed up in
a paper on 'Remedies of divers decays on the Borders',
dated 1597.[8] They were as follows: To keep monthly
'trews' unless prevented by the weather; in default of the
Scots Warden, to give letters of reprisal and assist the
parties grieved; to prosecute English fugitives harboured
in Scotland, and deal with the Scots Warden to proclaim
Scotsmen harbouring them; to demand, at each day of
'trews', redress against murderers, burners of houses, per-
jurors, and those 'thrise fyled'; to do his best to file on his
honour, if his opposite did the like, and otherwise to give
the equivalent only; to make no delivery except at 'trews'

---

[1] C.B.P. ii, 1470, 1527.   [2] C.B.P. ii, 314, 329, 1390–1.   [3] C.S.P. v,
197.   [4] C.B.P. i, 314, 321.   [5] C.B.P. ii, 439, 445; C.H.M. iii, 654.
[6] A.P.C. ix, 291, xvii, 79, xxx, 718–19; C.B.P. i, 429, ii, 1267–9; Leges, 110.
[7] Camden, 293.   [8] C.B.P. ii, 746.

on receiving the like; to seize the goods and flocks of Scots depasturing in England; to punish those who 're-setted' Scots, or had Scots servants; to keep a Warden Court half-yearly or oftener; to give yearly account to the auditor and receiver, of escheats for March Treasons; not to deny challenge to any man convicted of March Treason; to enlarge none convicted of March Treason, without the Queen's warrant or pardon; to cause his gaoler and 'warden serjeant' to answer all escapes; to take oath yearly at open Assize to perform the above. But besides these, and the supervision of watches and seeing that castles were kept in good repair, the Warden had an equal number of other duties, as follows: to view the Marches and determine grounds about which there was variance with Scotland;[1] to examine complaints about land, and settle them if he could;[2] to see statutes like Philip and Mary's Enclosure Act carried out;[3] to sit on various commissions like that about the Dacre lands in 1589;[4] to assist against recusants;[5] to see special messengers were furnished with post-horses, &c., for speed;[6] to examine cases of coining;[7] to interfere in Scots politics by keeping the Scots Borderers at home;[8] to employ spies and a system of secret service on various occasions and matters like James's matrimonial plans,[9] Maxwell's practices,[10] and others;[11] to spy, even on Englishmen, when necessary;[12] to stop men getting into Scotland;[13] to act for the Sheriff when the office was vacant;[14] to meet only with the Wardens of Scotland;[15] to hold consultations with English ambassadors proceeding to Scotland;[16] to keep good rule, even by practising with the gentry of the Scots Borders if it could not be otherwise kept;[17] to continue in office till his successor came and published his commission, on which occasion an

---

[1] For. v, 469.   [2] A.P.C. xiv, 41, 145, xv, 163, xix, 55, 281, xx, 347, xxi, 248.   [3] For. iv, 370.   [4] Dom. Add. iii, 266.   [5] C.B.P. ii, 1331. [6] A.P.C. xxx, 23.   [7] A.P.C. xxii, 388.   [8] C.B.P. i, 206, 212, 216. [9] C.S.P. vi, 51.   [10] C.B.P. i, 458, 461.   [11] C.B.P. i, 220, ii, 4; A.P.C. vii, 313, ix, 246, x, 377–8; For. viii, 237, 761, ix, 1514, 1895; Dom. Add. ii, 164; C.S.P. v, 98; C.H.M. iii, 541, vi, 220.   [12] A.P.C. vii, 16.   [13] C.B.P. i, 442.   [14] Dom. Add. iii, 166.   [15] Camden, 217.   [16] For. vii, 723; C.S.P. i, 530.   [17] For. viii, 2184.

inquiry was usually held into the state of the wardenry.[1] In pursuit of this ideal the Warden met with various hindrances, apart from Scots raids and those mentioned above. At Berwick and Carlisle the municipal authorities were troublesome,[2] and liberties were a nuisance. Lord Grey complained that, as soon as he banished whores or thieves from Berwick, they were received into the liberties of Norham and Islandshire where he could not touch them. He also found it impossible to get any service out of those shires.[3] Sometimes, even when acting on a special commission sent by the Privy Council, a warden was open to complaint if he 'cessed' townships in another wardenry for spoiling a ship.[4] Lastly he stood in fear of the Queen and Council, and was often obliged to inquire the Queen's pleasure in international and domestic matters.[5] The office was burdensome, and it is easy to agree with Valentine Browne that a warden ought to have been a wise and severe man with no alliances in the country over which he ruled.[6] For the East March, he thought, a southerner was necessary, but a southerner laboured under certain disadvantages. Forster knew how to get letters into Scotland in the shortest possible way; but a southerner, with no Border lands, was more likely to do justice indifferently and to show no awe of the Scots.[7] Strength and ability to make an impression were necessary for dealing with Englishmen as well as with Scots, and deputies often had serious troubles during the absence of a warden.[8] When the West March was vacant in 1592 the character of an ideal warden was drawn up. He was to be a man of wisdom and good policy, zealous to suppress offenders and defend good subjects, loyal above suspicion in religion, able to choose good officers, and no favourer of malefactors either from familiarity or kinship. And even a man with all these qualities would need some force of his own besides the authority of his office, and, unless he were a noble, the offices of Warden and of Captain of Carlisle

---

[1] C.B.P. ii, 154; Dom. Add. iii, 350.   [2] For. iv, 212, viii, 1705.
[3] For. iv, 1070.   [4] For. v, 288.   [5] For. viii, 2234.   [6] For. vi, 410.
[7] For. ix, 547; C.S.P. ii, 821.   [8] For. iv, 212.

should be divided.[1] A 'nobleman of especially trust' was the best choice, as, in Elizabethan times, nobility of birth was usually a real recommendation. With the exceptions of the Careys, who were scarcely exceptions as they were the Queen's cousins, and of Forster, all the permanent Elizabethan Wardens were nobles; and the three outstanding failures, Dacre, Forster, and Eure, were all northern men.

The question of the Warden's salary is somewhat perplexing. In the East Lord Grey as Warden got £424 per annum in 1560[2] and Wyllughby £420 in 1600;[3] and to this must be added an equal amount as Governor of Berwick, and various perquisites and allowances which made the combined offices worth between £1,000 and £1,100 a year,[4] in Hunsdon's time. Out of this the Warden had to pay each of his two deputies £10, £2 to each land serjeant, and the wages of horsemen, sometimes as many as forty.[5] Lord Grey's patent for the Middle March gave him £333 6s. 8d. a year[6] and Forster got £300 for himself, £10 for each of two deputies, £2 for each of two warden serjeants, and £26 13s. 4d. for the Keepers of the castles of Tynedale and Redesdale.[7] Lord Eure stated in 1595 that his father, grandfather, and great-grandfather, and Lord Wharton, had had £500.[8] At Carlisle the fees were £400 net for the Wardenry, and £221 for the Captaincy, with allowances for deputies and serjeants, and occasionally pay for horsemen.[9] The value of money in 1558 is hard to estimate, but it was probably worth quite ten times as much as in July 1914, so the fees do not seem inadequate. Yet the office of Warden was not popular, especially with southerners, who regarded it as exile. Bedford made frequent requests for his discharge,[10] and Hunsdon, soon after taking office, learnt why: 'for pleasure and profit', he wrote, 'there is none in it, and less thrift'. He said he could live as cheaply in London, and his wife found house-

[1] Dom. Add. iii, 323.   [2] For. iv, 347.   [3] Eresby, i, 535.   [4] C.B.P. ii, 333; C.H.M. i, 1253; C.M. 80.   [5] C.B.P. ii, 1308; C.M. 80; Dom. iv, 539.   [6] Grey, 57.   [7] C.B.P. ii, 122.   [8] C.B.P. ii, 131. [9] C.B.P. i, 781, 785, ii, 1533; Dom. Add. iii, 335, 341; C.M. 25; C.H.M. iv, 240; cf. Bell, 171.   [10] For. viii, 528, 697, 1331.

keeping very expensive, namely £21 a week, without the wages of the stable servants and others. So great was the need for economy that, even when he entertained a distinguished foreigner at supper, no silver was used on the table, but 'only tin dishes and wooden plates'. The Warden's household numbered forty, and its cost was increased by the daily resort of captains, lieutenants, pensioners, and others who looked to be fed.[1] Hunsdon found a solution in non-residence, but, unless he and his wife exaggerated their expenses, as Elizabethan officers sometimes did, the other wardens, who were usually resident, must have found their office unprofitable, and been tempted to seek illegal profits such as Forster was accused of making. There is, however, no evidence that any Warden was in Spanish or French pay. The deputy's office was also unpopular.[2]

When Andrew, Lord Stewart of Ochiltree, was made Warden of the Scots West March on November 2, 1597, he was given power to hold Warden and Justice Courts anywhere in his March; to take and try all 'resets', witchcrafts, slaughters, thefts, &c., or any capital crime, except cases of redress against England; to be accompanied by lieges against thieves and to 'trews'; to make courts of redress for bills given in to the King; to receive fugitives, &c., to obedience; to charge the Keepers of four of the King's houses to make the same open to him; to stop the export of cattle and sheep to England. In doing this he was to have indemnity for any slaughters he might commit.[3] By Act of Parliament Scots Wardens had been given the power to make sufficient deputies,[4] but the whole subject of the powers of Scots Border Wardens and other officers has been already described by Mr. R. B. Armstrong.[5] The curious point about his description is that he says the office of Warden was much coveted and sought after by great barons and nobles on the Border, but gives us no evidence for the statement,[6] and on the other side

---

[1] C.H.M. i, 1210–11; Wedel, 240.   [2] For. viii, 1017.   [3] R.P.C.S. v, 424–5.   [4] A.P.S. ii, 214, 1489 c. 6.   [5] Armstrong, i, 2–13. [6] Armstrong, 2.

Smailholm Tower.   Iron 'yett'

Smailholm Tower, from E. by SE.

X. DWELLINGS

Smailholm Tower. First-floor room

Smailholm Tower, showing vaulted roof

XI. DWELLINGS

mentions two instances of Wardens who wished to resign.[1] The office had ceased to be hereditary before Elizabeth's time.

The question of fees at once shows the comparative poverty of Scotland. The ordinary fee for the Warden of the East March and of the Middle March was £100 Scots.[2] This was too little, and in May 1564 Lord Hume, on applying for an increased allowance, was granted a Warden fee 'extending to ane hundred pound', and a yearly pension 'extending to four hundred pounds'.[3] By 1579 the salary had decreased to 'ane hundreth pundis money of our realme', but in that year George Hume of Wedderburn, a commoner, was Warden.[4] In the Middle March in 1584 Sir Thomas Ker of Ferniehurst, who was Warden as well as Keeper of Liddesdale, was granted £1,000 a year as he had been ruined by his long troubles.[5] He was only in office eight months. Sir R. Kerr of Cesford told Sir R. Carey in 1598 'that he never had fee of the King for his mayntenance'.[6] Sir John Maxwell as Warden of the West March was paid £333 6s. 8d. in 1562,[7] and for each of the three years 1573–6, John, eighth Lord Maxwell, received £600.[8] In 1587 Lord Herries got £100 'as for the ordinarie fee appointit for the using of the said office' with £500 as a yearly pension 'for his supporte and better using of the said office'. He was also to be paid £216 13s. 4d. a month for raising twenty-four horse.[9] Payment was not made in cash, but wardships, reliefs, escheats, &c., falling to the king in the West March were 'disponed' to Herries for a reasonable composition to be allowed to him for his fee and the wages of certain horsemen.[10]

It is hard to estimate the value of Scots money in Elizabethan coin. In 1562 Lord Hume stated that by old custom £4 Scots was equal to £1 English, but Grey disagreed with him.[11] In September 1570 Randolph valued

[1] Armstrong, 2, note 3, 7, note 1.   [2] A.L.H.T.S. x, 212, 304; xi, 54, 88, 167, 220–1.   [3] R.P.C.S. i, 278.   [4] Home, 49.   [5] R.P.C.S. iii, 699.   [6] C.B.P. ii, 998.   [7] A.L.H.T.S. xi, 167, 221.   [8] R.P.C.S. ii, 543.   [9] R.P.C.S. iv, 188.   [10] R.P.C.S. iv, 222–3.   [11] C.S.P. i, 108.

the Scots pound at nearly eight shillings,[1] in April 1583 R. Bowes put it as low as 2s. 9d.,[2] and in June 1589 Burghley put it at 5s.[3] The average is about five shillings. This shows that the Scots Wardens were ill-paid. Like the English office the Scots Wardenship was unpopular and unprofitable. The fee for the West March, that 'great and cummersum office',[4] had to be raised in order to get any one to accept it.

[1] C.S.P. iii, 452.   [2] C.R.B. cxcii.   [3] C.H.M. iii, p. 421.   [4] R.P.C.S. iii, 82.

PART V

BORDER WARFARE

IN Elizabeth's time there was no open war with Scotland, and the two English risings of 1569–70, and such fighting in the Scots civil wars as took place in the Marches had no Border peculiarities on the purely military side. On the other hand the invasions of Sussex and Scroope in 1570 were unique in size for this period, but were merely punitive expeditions which met with no resistance, the Scots preferring to thresh their corn, carry off their cattle and valuables, and unthatch their houses.[1] They, perhaps, filled their stone towers with peat and set it smouldering to save them from being blown up, but Sussex certainly destroyed some of them. There seem, however, to have been no attacks on towers like that described by W. Patten, Londoner, who went into Scotland with Somerset.[2] Towers were attacked at other times by various methods. Buccleugh in 1596 'with fyer to the dore' smoked the tenants out of one, and, though they had guns, powder, and bullets, they made little resistance.[3] Later in the year Buccleugh took a tower by forcibly burning and bursting in the door and the 'irone yeat'.[4] Stone towers sometimes resisted successfully when the Scots had hewed up the gates of the 'barmekyn' with axes.[5] Sir R. Carey had a method of his own. He set his men to work to the top of a tower 'and then to uncover the roof, and some twenty of them to fall down together, and by that means win the tower'.[6] The most certain way of taking a castle was to use artillery, but it was not easy to transport. There is no good account of the method of defending a tower, but the obvious way was to put the cattle inside the 'barmekyn', put the best horses in the vaulted chamber with the stores, take a stock of provisions upstairs, unless there was a trap-

[1] For. ix, 801.   [2] Dalyell, 35–6.   [3] C.B.P. ii, 332.   [4] C.B.P. ii, 399.   [5] C.B.P. ii, 431.   [6] C.M. 27.

door from the first floor into the vault, shut and secure the
iron 'yett', and roll a stone part way down to close the well-
staircase. These staircases were so built that, as a man
ascended, his right hand was inside and his sword-play
impeded. Having secured the lower stories the inhabitants might fire at the attackers from the upper windows,
but the parapet at the top of the tower made a better
fighting platform. Some towers had shot-holes in the
vault, but the ground covered by the guns must have been
small.

There were hardly any attacks on towns, using the word
'town' in its modern sense, but Sussex burnt Hawick, and
Cesford, threatening Berwick, made 'ladders of roopes in
fashion as the tackle of a shipp, with iron hookes at the one
end, and plomettes of lead at the other'.[1] Berwick was,
after the first few years of this period, secure against anything but surprise, treachery, or siege, and the besiegers
would have had no chance unless they had held command
of the sea. The fortifications, made after the Italian model,
were unique in the island, and no assault could have hoped
to succeed against walls twenty yards thick and quite
twenty feet high, defended as they were by moats, and a
system of bastions and casemates from which the attacking
troops could be doubly enfiladed.

The most common form of Border warfare was raids,
which were usually made by night. The Scots were sometimes very daring, and in August 1596 got as far as Alnwick, the strongest town in the Middle March, took the
watches, broke open the stables, and carried horses and
oxen clean away.[2] The essence of such an attack was
surprise, as the town was walled. Day-forays were made
on places, like Gilsland, nearer the frontier;[3] others were
made in force, and had murder and destruction, as well as
booty, for their objects.[4] Apart from the keeping of an
efficient watch, and the lighting of beacons, if aid were
needed from elsewhere, the safety of the country against
raids lay in its readiness to follow its officers against the

[1] C.B.P. ii, 435.   [2] C.B.P. ii, 351.   [3] C.B.P. ii, 330.   [4] C.B.P.
ii, 602.

raiders.[1] A young and energetic Warden, like Sir R. Carey, could do, and did much to diminish raids by resisting them and making counter-raids.

The Elizabethan age was a period of transition in the history of 'furniture'. As early as May 1544 Hertford and others reported to Henry VIII that the Scots Borderers 'love no gonnes ne will abyde withyn the hearyng of the same'.[2] From this it might have been expected that the 'hackbut' would gradually and by no means slowly supersede the bow. None the less in January 1560 Huntley urged that the English army about to enter Scotland should bring one or two thousand bowmen.[3] Ten years later there were a great many archers in the musters against the northern earls,[4] and the 'shott' sent from the south for Sussex's punitive expedition were so ill furnished that he would have preferred good archers.[5] In 1572 Huntyngdon was ordered to maintain the laudable and allowable use of the longbow,[6] and in the raid of Reidswyre the Scots used arrows.[7] We still possess the muster rolls made in February 1581 in Scroope's March.[8] The jack, a sleeveless tunic usually of leather quilted and sometimes plated with iron, the steel cap and the spear predominate near the frontier, the bow and the bill, a kind of halberd, in districts farther south, and there are not a dozen guns, though there were nearly 400 'Harquebushes' in store at Newcastle at that time. In Eskdale and Cumberland Wards there were 83 bowmen to some 2,000 men with jacks and steel coats, steel caps, spears or lances;[9] and in Leith Ward over 1,000 bowmen and billmen to 171 men furnished with spears or lances.[10] In April 1583 the light horsemen of the West March, excluding gentlemen, freeholders and their servants, were mustered and 374 out of 601 were furnished.[11] These light horsemen wore defensive armour on the back and breast, had iron caps, carried lance and buckler, or sometimes a bow, and

---

[1] C.B.P. i, 743. [2] Ham. P. ii, p. 390. [3] Thorpe, 126. [4] Dom. Add. iii, 111. [5] Dom. Add. iii, 268. [6] C.S.P. iv, 501. [7] For. xi, 275. [8] C.B.P. i, 90–4. [9] C.B.P. i, 90. [10] C.B.P. i, 92. [11] C.B.P. i, 159.

were mounted on 'nags' probably nearer thirteen than
fourteen hands high.[1] Some of them had swords.[2] There
is unfortunately no mention of their method of fighting
in Elizabethan Border papers. We have notes of musters
held in September 1584, when, of 15,133 foot in the
English Marches, 2,500 were archers, 2,500 billmen,
827 had jacks or spears, and 1,347 spears only. The 7,959
returned as unfurnished included the 5,277 men of the
Middle March who were all certified without mention of
furniture. In the East March, which was all of it near
Scotland, there were no bowmen.[3] The musters of horsemen were carefully compared with those of 1580, and
there was found to be a decrease in the numbers furnished,
and (in the East March only) in the total. From 1,148
(323 of them furnished) the number had in four years gone
down to 813 (267 of them furnished). In the Middle
March the furnished horse had decreased from 1,145 to
819, and the unfurnished had increased from 525 to
1,507. The West March numbers were more constant
but smaller.[4] Guns were not mentioned, though horsemen's pieces, calivers, and pistols, and footmen's 'shott'
were said, about this time, to be desirable.[5] As time went
on the bow decreased in favour and 'shott' gained in
reputation. In September 1587 the Council recommended
that of 200 foot specially levied for Border defence, 40 per
cent. should have 'shott or harquebuse', 20 per cent. 'pykes
with corseletes', 20 per cent. 'bowes', and the rest 'hal-
bardes or good black billes'.[6] Yet among the munitions
sent north in 1588 were but 100 muskets with rests and
'bandilers', to 1,000 pikes and 100 bills, and only ten
were issued, compared with 460 pikes.[7] Again in 1592
among munitions sent to Berwick were 1,000 bows, 300
'musketts', and 300 'callivers',[8] and when R. Lowther
asked for munitions for Carlisle he named 'bowes, spears
and pykes, of every sorte 200'.[9] Even when harquebuses
were sent they seem to have been left to decay in large

[1] Fortescue, i, 114–15.   [2] C.B.P. i, 159.   [3] C.B.P. i, 255.   [4] C.B.P.
i, 255.   [5] C.B.P. i, 162.   [6] C.B.P. i, 539.   [7] C.B.P. ii, 444.
[8] C.B.P. i, 744.   [9] C.B.P. i, 777.

numbers;[1] and the lighter 'weapon of calyver' was said to be of little use in the west,[2] perhaps because it was expensive and troublesome to keep up. Calivers, however, grew in proportion to bows in Berwick armoury. The official proportion was 200 calivers to 300 bows, pikes, and halbards, but Eure had only 90 serviceable 'musquettes' in 1596.[3] Calivers cost 20s.; bows and pikes but 3s. 4d., but the price of arrows rose from 2s. to 2s. 6d. a sheaf in three years.[4]

Musters were held irregularly, and the first and last general musters of which figures have survived are apparently those of October 1565 and May 1593. It is well to compare them.[5]

	1565.		1593.	
	Furnished.	Unfurnished.	Furnished.	Unfurnished.
Horse . .	2,799	45	5,707	1,591
Foot . .	3,225	4,913	8,905	4,443
Scots . .	—	166	—	—
Totals . .	6,024	5,124	14,612	6,034
Gross totals	11,148		20,646	

In 1584 the gross total was 18,940,[6] so the increase was fairly regular. Yet in places near the frontier there had been a large decrease; by 1593 the Norham and Islandshire foot had decreased from 320 to 130.[7] Berwick garrison was mustered quarterly, at any rate after 1575.[8] In the early years of the reign it had numbered about 1,000,[9] and by 1600 the numbers had decreased to under 500.[10] There are apparently no extant Scots Border muster rolls.

Artillery was kept at Newcastle, Berwick, Carlisle, and a few other places like Tynemouth Castle, Holy Island, Wark, and Norham, but Berwick had most of it.[11] All the artillery in these places was Crown property, and very little was in private hands, though Leonard Dacre had

---

[1] C.B.P. i, 828.   [2] C.B.P. ii, 472.   [3] C.B.P. ii, 283, 467.   [4] C.B.P. i, 832, ii, 283, 289.   [5] N.D. xxxiii; Dom. Add. iii, 350–1.   [6] C.B.P. i, 255.   [7] Dom. Add. iii, 350.   [8] A.P.C. ix, 27.   [9] For. vii, 1232.   [10] C.B.P. ii, 1193.   [11] C.B.P. i, 958.

some at Naworth in 1570. In Scotland the evidence
points to the existence of more private artillery. English
artillery was sometimes lent to Scots for their civil wars
and for the quieting of their West March.[1]

It remains to mention watches and beacons. The
placing of watches on the frontier itself was the first step
in defence against raids. No scheme possible with the
scanty population of the sixteenth century could have
prevented small bodies of Scots stealing into England, but
it was easier to detect their return to Scotland, especially
when they were driving cattle, though it might then be too
late to take effective action. A system of watches was carefully drawn up by Lord Wharton, anno 6, Edward VI,
and a book of them was kept and followed by the Wardens
till 1592 or later.[2] This book was printed by Bishop
Nicolson.[3] The West March watches must have occupied
the time of over 300 persons, excluding searchers, and the
Middle March required more. For the East March,
excluding searchers, 218 watchmen were required by
night and 17 by day, apart from the watch in each town.
The watches began normally on October 1 and ended on
March 16, but the Warden could extend them at both
ends if he thought fit. The unpleasantness of the job,
and the fact that it was unpaid, sometimes caused strikes,[4]
but when the watches were well kept they were effective.[5] Sometimes certain fords were dammed, in order
to release some of the watchers.[6] A system like Lord
Wharton's may have existed in Scotland, but no details
seem to be extant.

In conjunction with this system of watches was a system
of beacons. The Scots, says Leslie, used to 'kindle bleises
in tour heidis or higher places . . . to let see when danger
is.'[7] There seems to be no list of Scots beacons in this
period except that of 1588, in which 'Windie Edge' and
Hume Castle are mentioned,[8] but this was not designed
against English raids. There is a list of Northumberland

---

[1] See Bell, 183–5.   [2] C.B.P. i, p. 413.   [3] Leges, 147–218.   [4] C.B.P.
ii, 831.   [5] C.B.P. ii, 458, 699.   [6] For. iv, 503; ix, 507; C.B.P. ii,
1010.   [7] Leslie, 10.   [8] R.P.C.S. iv, 306–8.

beacons dated 1549,[1] and a West March list of 1468,[2] which show that beacon sites were chosen as carefully as places for the watch, and alternative routes were usually provided in case of fog. Watchmen were placed beside the fires. There must have been about fifty recognized English Border beacons, and a large number of smaller ones could be lit on 'tour heidis'. There was, however, no general lighting of Border beacons in this period except in 1569, 1570, and 1588.[3]

[1] C.R.M. i, 37–8.   [2] Curwen, 333.   [3] C. & W., O.S. xiv, 139–43.

PART VI

INTERNATIONAL BORDER LAW AND CUSTOM IN 1558

THE term 'Laws of the Marches' is vague. To most people it has meant Nicolson's *Leges Marchiarum*, but it was really much more comprehensive.

Richard Bell, the last Warden Clerk of the West Marches of England, in *The Memoriall of the laite dissolved treatises of truice and Lawes of Marches* says: 'The lawes of the Marches were maid and established upon three speciall groundes. The first upon Jus Gentium which ruleth all amongst people and nations, and thereunto were adjoined certaine principles of the Civill Lawe. The second was procured by the evill and corrupt manners and untowardness of the subjects of the realms which brought out in tyme certaine treatice advised and agreed upon betwene the princes for to represse the insolences of theaves and truce breakers. The third were the customs contynuallie used on the borders in certaine cases, as well not comprehended in the foresaid lawes and treatises as also in the execution of things conteyned in the same.'[1] But besides these international treaties and customs, and besides certain agreements between opposite Wardens which applied to their own Marches only,[2] there was a domestic department of Border Law.[3]

The whole subject is thus very complicated and has therefore been shirked by many people. Nicolson and Burn, for instance, though they had Bell's MS., reduced the treaties to a code, giving as their sole reference 'Nicolson's Border Laws, passim'. They say they did this to avoid perplexities and frequent repetitions, and perhaps they succeeded in so doing, but they utterly failed to give an adequate idea of the Laws and Customs of the Marches.[4]

---

[1] Bell, 6.   [2] e.g. Bell, 89.   [3] See Parts ix and x.   [4] See N. & B. I, xiii–xxiii.

Repetition and errors are scarcely avoidable, but the giving of full references should lead to their ultimate detection.

When in 1592 William Fielding, servant to Henry, Lord Scroope, searched by Burghley's orders 'amongst this multitude of writings for such books of March Laws and Border Causes as remain', he found some eight sets of treaties and 'two confused tracts of treaties', one apparently of 1559, and the other of Edward VI.[1] A modern inquiry, though handicapped as regards custom, cannot fail to be more successful in collecting written laws.

In dealing with international Border Laws it seems best to make, first of all, an attempt at a code of the 'Laws and Customs of the Marches' as they stood at Elizabeth's accession. The difficulty is that some of them seem never to have been written down, but they are mentioned in the treaties as if well known, and, as it is said that the commissioners in some cases did not intend 'by these presents to make any abrogation or alteration in time coming of the old Laws and Customs',[2] and in other cases no mention is made of the matter, it seems safe to try to make a code from the former laws and such few customs as Bell mentions,[3] and to conclude that that code was in force in 1558. This will enable us to judge what changes were made after 1558, and perhaps also to understand the reason for those changes.

The materials for the international code are as follows:

1. 1249, Apr. 14. The 'Laws and Customs' as written down when twelve knights and one Warden from each realm met 'ad recognoscendas leges et consuetudines Marchiarum'.[4]

Nicolson and Burn[5] consider this a Scots forgery designed to show Edward I that the two realms were on an equal footing in his father's reign. It is true that there are only twenty-two commissioners named, and that one of them, Robert de Clifford, was unborn. They contend,

---

[1] C.B.P. i, 474, 778, 782.   [2] Leges, 74, 1553, § 4.   [3] Bell, 6–7.
[4] Leges, 1–7; Bell, 7 (clauses 9–13 lost); A.P.S. i, 83*–86*.   [5] I, ix–x

however, that there is no evidence for the existence of any
of the English signatories. But there is. On January 10,
1249, Robert Malenfant was old enough to have a son
pardoned for murder, and on September 16, 1255, at
Carham, Sampson de Coupland was exempted for life
from being put on assize, &c., against his will.[1] The
treaty, therefore, may be genuine, and the point is that,
though almost all its provisions were out of date in 1558,
Bell regarded it as genuine.

2. 1346, Oct. 30. A treaty, after the battle of Durham,
or Neville's Cross, for the settlement of the Scots Border.
This was interpolated in the Ayr MS. by a later hand and
contains nothing of apparent importance for the reign of
Elizabeth.[2]

3. 1384, Mar. 15. An indenture made 'at the Water
of Eske beside Salom' between Sir Henry Percy, Earl of
Northumberland and Archibald Douglas, Earl of Galloway.[3] This is perhaps a mere private agreement between
two Wardens for the furtherance of justice, and fixes dates
for Trews and provides against one side doing 'skaith' to
the other in the interim.

4. 1448, Dec. 28. 'The Statutes and use of Merchis
in time of werre', ordained in Black Archibald of Douglas's
days and his son's days, collected in 1480, December 18,
by Earl William of Douglas, when he assembled the lords,
freeholders, and eldest borderers and made them swear, at
'Lynclowden' to put in writing the statutes that had been
in use at the former date.[4] These have no English authority, and, as war statutes, hardly apply to Elizabeth's day.
Bell puts them before those of 1449, thus showing that he
believed their date.

5. 1449. A peace made by six English and four Scots
commissioners.[5] Many of the clauses are new and have
no special reference to the Borders.

6. 1464. A peace made by seven English and five
Scots commissioners at York. It was to last till sunset on

---

[1] C.P.R. Hen. iii.   [2] A.P.S. i, 180, note 1.   [3] A.P.S. i, 349–50.
[4] Bell, 11–13. The first part of the preface is missing. A.P.S. i, 350–2.
[5] Leges, 9–16; Bell, 14–24.

October 31, 1479.[1] This is mainly a re-enactment of that of 1449 with certain additions.

7. 1473, Sept. 28. An indenture made at Newcastle. This mainly concerns the method of holding certain days of Truce.[2]

8. 1486, July 3. An indenture made by six English and six Scots commissioners.[3] This was made at London and nine clauses of it are verbatim copies of number 6. Much of it concerns the whole realms.

9. 1528, Dec. 14. A peace made at Berwick.[4]

10. 1533, Oct. 1. An indenture made at Newcastle.[5] Peace was to last for a year, and the laws of 1528 were to be used in redressing 'attemptates'.

11. 1534. A peace made by five English and two Scots commissioners to last for the lives of the two princes and for a year after the death of the first of them.[6] Nicolson omitted the last fourteen of the twenty-four clauses and dated the treaty a year too early.

12. 1551, June 10. A peace made by four English and four Scots commissioners, which was not in any way to diminish or contradict that of March 24, 1549, between England and France.[7] Nicolson's text is in English and he dates it 1549. The other two are in Latin and contain an extra clause on Shipwreck, after the one which Nicolson numbers 13.

13. 1551. Bowes in his 'Form and Order of a Day of Truce'[8] gives a set of laws which he implies he got from the treaty of 1551. He must, however, have relied largely on his memory as commissioner.

14. 1553, Dec. 4. Two English and two Scots commissioners met 'for the good of peace, reformation of disorders, and better maintenance of quietness and good rule upon the Marches of both the said Realms'.[9] The result was the first real code of Border Laws for peace time since that of 1249.

[1] Leges, 16–45; Bell, 25–38.   [2] Rymer, xi, 788–91.   [3] Bell, 38–44; Rymer, xii, 285–91.   [4] Rymer, xiv, 278 ff.   [5] Rymer, xiv, 480. [6] Leges, 45–55; Bell, 45–60; Rymer, xiv, 529 ff.   [7] Leges, 56–71; Bell, 62 ff.; Rymer, xv, 265 ff.   [8] R.T. iv, 2; N.D. xxii, ff.   [9] Leges, 71–83; Bell, 75 ff.

15. 1556. Commissioners met and made ordinances at Berwick.[1] This last pre-Elizabethan meeting was really an attempt to clear up the great disorders and number of unredressed bills then extant. The agreement of October 20 referred only to the West Marches, and was temporary.

It is necessary to note that, though the Bell MS. came at some time into the possession of Joseph Nicolson, Bishop Nicolson, his uncle, did not use it in compiling *Leges Marchiarum*. He used, however, three transcripts which he believed to have been made soon after the last treaty (1597).[2] It is clear that he did not use the Bell MS. as he omits fourteen clauses of the treaty of 1534, does not copy the marginal notes to the treaty of 1563, and omits an important proviso at the end of clause 33 of the treaty of 1597. The Bell MS. has not been used, hitherto, in any but a slipshod manner, though its value, owing to its author's position and experience, is undoubted.

The laws contained in these treaties bound Englishmen and Scots, and out of them the following code of international Border Laws and Customs has been made, the text of Richard Bell being followed, except where otherwise noted.

Bell's 'briefe extract of the sumarie of the articles of trewes condiscended upon in divers princes times' only goes back as far as Henry VI.[3] With reference to the Russell case of 1585, Dr. Colmar quoted 'Treatie, H. 6, art. 2; H. 8, art. 2, 3', and Scroope and others 'Treaty H. 8, art. 4'.[4] The Wardens kept a book of all the treaties between the realms,[5] and it was probably from the West March copy that Bell compiled the part of his manuscript relating to them.

[1] Bell, 86 ff.   [2] Leges, vi–vii.   [3] Bell, 239–46.   [4] C.B.P. i, 359, 367.   [5] C.B.P. ii, 133.

A PRE-ELIZABETHAN CODE OF THE INTERNATIONAL 'LAWS AND CUSTOMS OF THE MARCHES'

1. *Slaughters.*

When a subject of one realm murders a subject of the opposite realm and complaint is made to the offender's Warden, 'like process answere and execution shall be thereunto with all expedicōn made done and administered as in the treatye of peace for such attemptat is provided and conteyned, and according to the auncient Lawes and Customes of the Borders', neglect of the said law having been the occasion of great disorders in both realms. 1553, § 11. The treaty above referred to enacted that if any Englishman violently kill a Scot, the English Warden with all diligence shall try to arrest him and bring him to the day of Truce. And if he be lawfully convicted there then the English Warden shall deliver him to the Scots Warden to be punished by death. The same applied, *mutatis mutandis*, when a Scot murdered an Englishman. 1551, § 9

An addition was made in 1556 that 'All the moveable goods of the cōmittor or cōmittors of any slaughter or slaughters in tyme comying' shall be taken by the murderer's officer and delivered to his opposite 'to the use and profit of the wife and children of him that is slain, and in default of the wife and children to the next of his or their bloods that happeneth to be slaine'.[1] This law was left untouched in 1563, but it did not work. Murderers caught red-handed might be executed at once, but this often led to trouble with their countrymen.[2] In 1582, for instance, Cesford, backed by his prince, tried to get Scroope to hold a Truce for redress of goods while slaughters were referred to the princes or commissioners 'according to the auncient custome'.[3] Elizabeth and

---

[1] 1556 (4); Bell, 87. [2] C.B.P. ii, 103, 374, and p. 495. [3] C.B.P. i, 129; C.S.P. vi, 107, 135.

Elsdon Rectory

Embleton Vicarage

XII. FORTIFIED PARSONAGES

Scroope persevered in trying to get the law kept, its neglect being 'the cause of the greateste disorders upon the Borders, and the greateste incouradgement to offenders'.[1] But they met with no success, the law having been so long in abeyance that it could not be put in practice,[2] though Hunsdon alleged that the Scots statement that in Lord Rutland's time it was agreed that slaughters and burnings should be referred to Lieutenants was mere dissimulation.[3] So time buried the words of the treaty in forgetfulness, and Scots Wardens and Keepers committed murders in England,[4] but in 1597 the law was strengthened.

2. *Unlawfully wounding a subject of the opposite realm.*

If 'any hereafter of the subjects of either of the said Realmes shall unlawfullie bodylie hurt or wound any of the subjects of the other Realme, the person or persons so hurt or wounded shall make bill of complaint upon the person that so offended them at the day of trewes'. The offender shall be arrested to answer the bill and compelled to do so 'after like manner as is used of robbers, theaves, or spoylers, and suchlike proofe and trial to be had in everie behaulfe untill the bill be either acquitt or filed'. If the bill is 'fyled', the damage is to be estimated 'by six gentlemen of worship and good fame of Scotland to be named by the Warden of England, and other six of England to be named by the Warden of Scotland, and by the discretion of both the Wardens or their deputies then being present. And the damage so being sett and esteamed to be two tymes doubled as in the case of theft and spoile is used, and deliverance to be maid to the Warden of the Marches where the partie greaved inhabits to be kept with him untill redresse be maid thereof accordinglie.' If the wounded party be 'mutylate and maymed' the offender's Warden must do his uttermost 'without fraud favoure or deception' to apprehend the offender and deliver him to the opposite Warden 'to be punished by

---

[1] C.B.P. i, 130, 164–5. [2] C.S.P. v, p. 193; vi, no. 603. [3] C.B.P. i, 557. [4] C.B.P. ii, 485.

him in streight prison by the space of six months for the said offence'.[1]

This law was quite new, and hitherto there had been no remedy.[2] It was never altered.[3]

3. *Raising fire, &c., in the opposite realm.*

Committers of 'attemptates' such as 'burning or spoyling of goods' are to 'make redresse of the principall with the two doubles to the partie complaynant', and to forfeit all the rest of their movable goods to their own prince.[4] By the treaty of 1553, § 13, the payment of 'double and sawfie' together with six months' imprisonment had been the penalty. 'Double' meant twofold restitution in value, 'sawfie' onefold restitution for expenses incurred in inquiring.[5] The substitution of a heavier fine and confiscation for imprisonment must imply that it had been impossible to carry out the latter. This law, the most important of the Border laws, was never altered again, but in 1578 the Scots Council proclaimed that Scots riding in England in future shall 'not onlie be delivert for dowbill and safer and compellit to mak redress according to the rigoure, but salbe execut to the death'.[6] Nevertheless, the law was not kept, and in 1584 Burghley, feeling that process by law would lead to nothing, thought that Forster should be allowed to avenge a bad Liddisdale raid in kind, but in such a way that it should seem to come from the injured parties.[7] The Wardens, with reference to this law as to others, sometimes made special agreements, e.g. that 'the hurte doune by the fier' should be estimated on oath by four gentlemen, the Scots being chosen by Englishmen and vice versa.[8]

4. *Hunting, &c., in the opposite realm.*

No one of either realm shall enter 'terras, boscos, nemora, forrestas, warrenas, loca dominia quaecunque' of any subject of the opposite realm for the sake of hunting,

---

[1] 1553, § 12.   [2] R.T. iv, 2.   [3] But cf. 1597, § 12.   [4] 1556, § 3.
[5] R.T. iv (2), 13–14.   [6] R.P.C.S. iii, 2.   [7] C.S.P. vii, 346.   [8] C.B.P. i, 531, 633.

fishing, hawking, 'disportum sive solacium in eisdem exercendi', or for any other reason without the owner's consent.[1] This law was never altered, nor did it have much effect in Elizabeth's time. In 1576 the Scots Council in a proclamation stated that the king's deer on the West March 'are not only daily slain by guns with Scotsmen but also by the hunting of Englishmen brought there by Scots without licence', and two years later it repeated the proclamation almost word for word.[2] Again in 1598 Sir R. Carey wrote that the Scots gave as excuse for an armed entry into England that their intention was to hunt such venison as the country afforded. In his opinion they knew it was unlawful, but expected it would be endured as hitherto. The English, however, pursued them and killed four or five besides taking sixteen of the best prisoners.[3] When the Warden of the Scots Middle March tried them, it was declared that they were only doing what was customary on both sides.[4] Carey retorted to the English Council that the Scots had long been used to hunt without licence, but so had they been used to rob and spoil.[5]

5. *Pasturing cattle in the opposite realm.*

Cattle are to be fed within the limits of the owner's realm. If they are fed 'willinglie or customablie' in the opposite realm, the owner of the ground, or his Warden in his default, may have the cattle impounded and kept till the owner shall pay for the first offence 'for everie cattell or nolt a penny and for everie sheape a penny Scotts'. On repetition of the offence the cattle may be impounded and kept till 'double parcage' be paid, and so on till it be two shillings sterling for each cattle or nolt and sixpence sterling for each sheep, and no higher, but that to stand till New Year's Day (January 1) after the first 'parcage'. After New Year's Day the rate is to be one penny sterling and one penny Scots respectively, and then double again till two shillings sterling and sixpence sterling be reached, and no higher till January 1 next. This is

[1] 1464, § 16. Re-enacted verbatim by 1486, § 12.   [2] R.P.C.S. ii, 506; iii, 106–7.   [3] C.B.P. ii, 974.   [4] C.B.P. ii, 992.   [5] C.B.P. ii, 1020.

to go on till the offender by the 'greate and greavous parcage' be forced to keep his cattle on his own ground.[1] An addition was made to this law in 1563 (§ 20), but it was, like the other laws, often disregarded.

6. 'Fishing within the Water of Tweade.'

If any subjects of either realm 'unlawfullie trouble stoppe or make any impediment to the subjects of the opposite Realm in his fishing within the Water of Tweade', the party grieved may complain to the offender's Warden, who shall cause the offender to be attached to the next day of Truce, and, if the offender be 'fyled' (found guilty), he shall pay 'for everie tide that he makes impediment unto the partie complaynant twentie shillings sterling, and to be delivered therfore to remaine with the partie greaved unto the tyme he be satisfied after the lawes of marches and borders'.[2] Some special cases then pending were decided by the seventh and eighth clauses of the treaty. The law was never altered, but fishing disputes lasted till the end of the period. The custom, by which the Tweed was 'common for the fishing to both nations, so as where there is a convenient landing place for the nett on eyther side, they may draw the same over the whole river in compass, landing only on theyr owne grownd', was bound to cause disputes.[3]

7. 'Baughling and reproving.'[4]

As this 'gives great occasion of further and great inconvenience' when done at days of Truce, it is agreed that no one of either realm 'at any daies of truice or other convencōn or assembly betwene th'officers of both the said realms beare, shawe or declare any signe or token of reproofe or baughling against any of the subjects of th' opposite Realme unless he be thereunto licenced by the Wardens of both the Realmes'. If any try to do, or do the contrary of this, he shall be 'attached' by his Warden, and 'delivered' to the opposite Warden 'to be punished by

[1] 1553, § 7.   [2] 1553, § 10.   [3] C.B.P. ii, 1484; i, p. 31.   [4] Bell miswrites 'approving'.

imprisonment at his discretion by the space of one month'. The offender shall also lose his 'cause and matter' and the other party be 'acquited and discharged for ever'.[1]

The word 'baughling', which also appears as 'baughill', 'bawghles', and 'bawghling',[2] meant, according to Bowes,[3] the bearing of a glove or picture (by the offended party) of one who had broken his bond concerning ransom, entry of prisoners, or any other just cause, and the giving out by blast of a horn, or cry, to the whole assembly that such a person was untrue. At other times the party reproved could not honestly be refused a duel if he asked for it. Leslie in his history says that the Scots borderers were wont 'to put a glove upon the point of a spear in exprobation or shame of him who "crakit his creddence" (broke his word) riding of such a manner through all the people showing it'.[4] A flaw in this clause was corrected in 1563.[5]

8. *Perjury at days of truce.*

Perjury being most commonly 'the roote and the ground of the hinderance and perverting of all Justice, occasion and cause of all discord upon the said borders', it is agreed that if any subject of either realm 'acquite himself by his oath taken in force of Lawe before the Wardens or their deputies and afterward be tryed or found foule or guiltie of the said bill', and so 'appeare perjured to both the said Wardens', then 'over and above the just redresse and recompense of the partie greaved', the perjurer 'shalbe attached' by his Warden and delivered to the opposite Warden 'to be punished as a greavous offendor by streyte imprisonment during the space of three moneths', and at the next day of Truce after the said three months he shall be brought before the Wardens, or their deputies, 'to be denounced and proclaymed a perjured man, after which tyme he shall not be reputed a person able to give further faith or testimonie in any cause or matter'.[6] Bowes in his report of 1551[7] made strong remarks about Scots perjury, saying that the increase of

---

[1] 1553, § 14. [2] N.D. xxiii; Bell, 1563, § 22. [3] R.T. iv (2) 10.
[4] 101, modernized. [5] vide p. 115 infra. [6] 1553, § 15. [7] R.T. iv, 2.

theft was not likely to be reformed unless perjury was provided for. As a commissioner he had a hand in the making of the above law, which was left untouched until 1597. The comprehensive oath of the defendant is given below under the 'Form and order of a day of Truce'.[1]

9. *Gross overswearing of the value of stolen or damaged goods.*

If any person of either realm 'unmeasurablie and out-ragiouslie . . . sweare the number and value of his goods to be more or greater then of truth they bee, to the greate losse and damage of the adverse partie', both Wardens or their deputies present 'without any hinderance, stay, or delay of Justice in anywise shall make take unto them twelve of the most worshipfull and credible persons of both the Realmes then being present', six Scots named by the English Warden present, and six Englishmen by the Scots Warden present. Then the Wardens, their deputies, and the said twelve 'shall have powre by vertue hereof to moderate, qualifie or diminish the number or price of the goods or cattels so oversworne as is afore rehearsed'.[2]

Bowes in his report of 1551, cited above, says that there were certain fixed values, e. g. ox, 13s. 4d., cow, 10s., &c., but that horses, swine, household stuff, &c., were not specially rated, the values thereof being declared 'by the oath of the party complainant, or his servant that had custody thereof'. Trouble, however, might arise from the fact that a good ox might be worth 40s. Apparently Bowes was able to get fixed values replaced by sworn values subject to the above method of correction. Fixed values were restored by the next treaty.[3]

10. *Cutting down trees.*

No subject of either prince living in any March or in the debatable ground or elsewhere shall cut down or carry away any trees or wood whatsoever, out of the Marches of either prince by any means or colour, except with the owner's consent. If this law be broken the case shall be

---

[1] Vide p. 143 infra.   [2] 1553, § 16.   [3] 1563, § 16.

reformed 'arboribus caesis aut abductis domini juramento aestimandis'. 1551, § 11.

The Latin is from Rymer's *Foedera*.[1] Bell has 'arboribus cesis et abductis domini juramenti estimans'. Bowes, who was a commissioner, says double and sawfie was to be paid, the value being assessed by the oath of the owner, or of his servant, keeper of the said wood.[2] The law was never altered. Sir R. Carey noted in 1598 that it was the Scots custom to bring in a hundred men and cut and carry away wood, and that thus they had wasted 'one of the goodlyest woodes' in the Middle March. He stopped the practice.[3]

11. *Taking justice into one's own hands.*

If any subject of either prince has been robbed or spoiled by any subject of the other, and 'propria authoritate sua' has made, in revenge for the same, other robberies or spoils, or taken distress of men or goods, he shall lose his cause, and yet nevertheless be punished according to the desert of his trespass.[4]

This law was never altered, but the English doctors asserted in 1597 that a reprisal made by Scroope, after he had vainly used all means of getting justice, was justifiable by civil law.[5] Even Burghley once decided in favour of a secret reprisal.[6]

12. *Recovery of stolen goods.*

If any subject of either prince has stolen or attempted anything within the opposite Marches and fled to his own March, the owner of the property may within six days after the fault, without any safe-conduct, follow the offender and in so doing enter the land whither he has gone, provided that as soon as he has entered it he go to 'aliquem virum bonae famae et opinionis illaesae', living there, and tell him the cause of his entry and declare what goods he has lost, and further that he shall require the

---

[1] xvi, 533.   [2] R.T. iv (2), 15–16.   [3] C.B.P. ii, 974.   [4] 1551, § 13.
[5] C.B.P. ii, 515, 549.   [6] C.S.P. vii, 346.

man to accompany him to testify of his behaviour so long as he shall continue the search.[1]

Bowes in his 1551 Report quotes a similar law. The pursuer might take a sleuth hound with him, but must ask for help at the first house in the opposite realm. Any one hindering the pursuer became liable for the bill of goods taken, together with double and sawfie.[2] This right was preserved, and further provisions made for the recovery of stolen goods in the treaty of 1563.[3]

13. *Fugitives.*

'All manslayers fugitives rebells theaves and other evil doers whatsoever, subjects of eyther princes, recett . . . shalbe avoyded the Realme where they are recett, or delivered to their owne native prince . . . ymediately after this proclamacōn.' If any of the said menslayers, &c., be 'recett' within the opposite realm, the 'receptor', on complaint of the Warden, shall answer at the next day of Truce, and if the 'recettor' is delivered, he shall be 'punished as the fugitive, mansleyere, . . . should have been, and shall alsoe make redresse of his other goods . . . to the partie complainant'. The rest of the 'recettors' goods are forfeited to his prince.[4]

This severe punishment of the 'recettor' was quite new, and the subject was treated again, together with that of stolen goods, in 1563.

14. *Capture of fortalices.*

If any one of either realm take, in time of peace, 'aliquod fortalicium', the owner thereof shall be able to recover it 'per viam facti vel aliter prout melius poterit', and may even punish the malefactor according to the exigency of the case. The 'conservatores' of the country whose subject took the fortress shall be bound to aid the owner to recover it as soon as possible, or, if he prefers, the owner can require the 'conservatores' and the king to see that the fortress is restored to him and the malefactor delivered, and they are bound to fulfil his desires.[5]

[1] 1551, § 10.   [2] R.T. iv (2), 18.   [3] 1563, §§ 6, 19.   [4] 1556, § 1.
[5] 1464, § 10.

Bell has 'facti' here and at 1449, § 12. Nicolson has 'viam pacti' here, and 'vim pacti' at 1449, § 12. This law was never altered, but no case covered by it arose in Elizabeth's reign.

15. *Oath to keep the peace.*

All Wardens of the Marches present and to come, and all notable men near the said Marches from Newcastle and Penrith in England to Edinburgh and Dumfries in Scotland shall swear on the Holy Gospels to keep the present peace in every article, and make others observe it. This oath is to be taken within the next thirty days.[1]

This law was unaltered, but the treaty of 1563 made enactments on the subject of the Warden's oath to do justice[2] and for the publication of treaties.[3]

16. *Unlawful prisoners.*

If any complain that they have wrongfully been taken prisoners in peace time, the Wardens shall hold an inquiry by an assize or otherwise, and proclaim any unlawful prisoners quit at a day of truce, after which proclamation no one may claim a ransom of them. Offenders ought to make redress to the party wrongfully imprisoned.[4]

This seems to have been a custom rather than a law, but proclamations, as above, were sometimes made at a Truce. The law was never changed, though prisoners were taken in peace time not only by private men, but even by officers. Scroope in 1584, by order of the English Privy Council, took the laird of Mangerton prisoner in Scotland, and great quiet resulted.[5] Sir R. Carey did a similar thing on his own authority in 1602, and got redress thereby.[6] ·

17. *Liability to military service on the Marches.*

All men between 'Toytnais' in England and 'Cathnes' in Scotland may, according to the customs of the said realms, be rightly called to the Marches to wage war, except the kings of the said realms and the bishops of St. Andrews and Dunkeld 'personis propriis'.[7]

[1] 1464, § 22.   [2] § 4.   [3] § 23.   [4] 1551, Bowes in R.T. iv (2), 20.
[5] C.S.P. vii, p. 142.   [6] C.H.M. xii, 127–8.   [7] 1249, § 2.

Bell has 'Dunkeld', but a better reading is 'Duresme'.[1]
This curious law, forged or genuine, was never altered,
but troops usually came from between the Trent and
Forth in Elizabeth's time.

18. *Denizens.*

'Fugitivi Scotie qui devenerunt ligei regis Anglie
debent ligari ex parte Anglorum ad conservandum arti-
culos praesentis tractatus . . . Attemptata per eos super
subditos reginae Scotie debent eodem modo conformari
quo reformabuntur attemptata per originales subditos regis
Anglie.' And the converse.[2] This law was never altered.

19. *Matters of great difficulty and importance.*

If such arise between the Wardens 'the same shall be
gently and without opprobrious words compromitted',
put in writing and referred to their sovereigns or their
councils, when as many matters as may be have been
determined for that day of truce.[3]

This again was custom rather than law, and in the
matter of slaughters the English Wardens denied its force.
The 'murder' of Russell in 1585 was brought before a
special commission; but that was no ordinary matter.[4]

20. *Witnesses to the guilt of a subject of the opposite realm.*

'Nullus de Regno Angliae potest probare aliquem de
regno Scotiae per testes (nec e converso) nisi tantummodo
per probacionem corporis hominis.[5]

The clause in the Bell MS. is lost, and the above quotation is from the Acts of Parliament.[6] Nicolson inserts
'reum' after 'aliquem,' and has 'corpus' for 'probacionem
corporis'. The law from 'nisi' to the end was a dead letter,
but the first part lived. The meaning is not clear. 'Probare' may mean 'test'. The sense seems to be that an
English witness was no good for convicting a Scots
defendant and vice versa. According to Bowes in 1551
the Scots Assize would not find a true bill against a Scot
on an English complaint unless the Englishman could get

---

[1] A.P.S. i, 84*.   [2] 1551, § 12.   [3] 1551, Bowes in R.T. iv (2).
[4] C.B.P. i, 345–6, 355, 358.   [5] 1249, § 12.   [6] A.P.S. i, 86*.

a Scotsman to avow the deed, even though the matter were notoriously known in England.[1]

21. Neglect of justice.

Whenever either king feels that either he or his subjects is, or are, 'aggravatum vel aggravatos' contrary to the Truce owing to neglect of justice by the other side, he shall send a herald to tell the other king, who, on information, shall send two or three of his Council twice, or at least once a year, being lovers of peace and justice, to a convenient place near the Marches to meet similar men sent by the complainant king, with power not only to punish delinquents, but to inquire whether the conservators, Wardens or deputies, have been remiss in executing justice, and to punish and reform them if they have. Likewise any one robbed or injured contrary to the abstinence may pursue his injury before any competent judges in any part of the said realms whenever he sees fit, and get justice.[2]

There was no further legislation on the subject. Elizabeth usually proceeded through her ambassador, who was often resident in Edinburgh. The results were occasional abortive commissions to one or more Marches, or more or less effective 'rodes' by the king or lieutenant on the 'broken men'. It is hard to see how the last part of the clause could be effective.

Addendum to code.

It is well to state that the treaties, &c., from which the above code is taken include also three other kinds of law which have been omitted. There are laws which applied to the whole realms, and not to the Borders alone, such as those dealing with interference in the affairs of the opposite realm in time of peace.[3] There are laws or agreements which were temporary or referred to special cases,[4] and lastly there are laws which were already obsolete, such as that relating to the division of the Debatable Lands,[5] which were divided by commissioners in 1552.[6]

[1] R.T. iv (2), 17.   [2] 1486, § 13.   [3] 1533, §§ 2, 3.   [4] e.g. 1534, §§ 14, 22.   [5] 1551, § 2.   [6] C.B.P. ii, 1543.

PART VII

THE COMMISSIONS OF 1563, 1588 AND 1597

THE first few years of Elizabeth's reign were too fully occupied to allow steps to be taken for the meeting of commissioners to settle Border causes. It is true that a commission met at Carlisle in August 1561, but its energies were devoted to the West Marches only.[1] On August 4, 1563, however, a commission was given to Scroope, Forster, Gargrave, John Roxeby, and a member of the Council of the North to meet with Scots Commissioners on Border matters.[2] They were warned not to treat the Scots as enemies, not to stick at trifles, and to make the sittings as short as possible to save expense.[3] The Scots Commissioners were Sir John Maxwell of Terregles and Sir John Ballendine. The two commissions met at Carlisle on September 11, and then sat at Dumfries till September 23, their work being the redress of Border grievances, the incorporation of several Border treaties, the appointment of Wardens, the constitution of their courts, the continuance of ancient customs, the punishment of offenders, the manner of holding assemblies upon the Borders, &c.[4] The treaty they made was printed by Nicolson, and by Rymer, and is also in the Bell MS.[5] Bell's text seems the best. Nicolson misread September 6 for September 11 in the date.

The Treaty began with two temporary clauses as follows: 'Old attemptates to be redressed as by the book signed appeareth,'[6] and offences done before September 10, 1563, and not 'conteyned in the foresaid rowles, writings and bills subscribed and mutuallie amongst us interchanged ... to be put to perpetuall silence and oblivion.'[7]

---

[1] Bell, 89–90. [2] C.S.P. ii, 20; For. vi, 1103. [3] C.S.P. ii, 21.
[4] C.S.P. ii, 31; For. vi, 1238. [5] Leges, 84–103; Rymer, xv, 631 ff. from a Scots text; Bell, 91 ff. [6] 1563, § 1, Bell's marginal note. [7] 1563, § 2.

The next three clauses concern the holding of days of Truce, and are treated hereafter under that heading.[1] There was one other temporary clause to the effect that, in order to avoid all controversies as to the Debatable Lands between the East and Middle Marches of the two realms, the commissioners had made suit to their sovereigns to appoint commissioners to divide them and to set up 'perpetual marches, bounds and meites'. Bell's and Rymer's texts read that this should be done 'amicably'. Nicolson prints 'immediately'.[2] It was never done.

The laws numbered 1–4, 6, 8, 10, 11, and 14–21 above were not mentioned and therefore remained unchanged. The changes and new enactments were as follows, and in setting them out adherence has been made to the numbers given in the above code, and new laws have received new numbers.

5. *Pasturing cattle in the opposite realm.*

The following addition was made to the law of 1553:[3] If the cattle or sheep of one realm be 'staffehoorded'[4] and remain depasturing in the other for six hours in one day, the owner of the ground, or his warden, may take them 'as forfeyt and lost to his owne use without any redresse to be maide thereof'. And to prevent controversy, in so doing 'he shall take with him of his owne countrie foure or moe honest men and credible persons unsuspected, to be present with him to see that the execution be duelie maide'. If the cattle stay for less than six hours the late treaty shall apply, with this addition, that if the keepers of the cattle 'will not permitt the owner of the ground or the warden to use the order of parcage or of pounding established in the said Indentures, but will make lett', the cattle 'shalbe thereby lawfully forfeited'. And for proof of the regularity of the seizure the case shall be tried 'by the oath of the Warden or his deputy, or by the apprehendor thereof together with six other honest men of that

---

[1] 1563, §§ 3–5, infra, pp. 138, 140, 141.   [2] 1563, § 24.   [3] § 7.
[4] Staffherd means to depasture sheep in charge of a shepherd upon common or forest land.—N.E.D.

realm to be declared upon their faith and honors and those
six to be named by the opposite Warden'.[1]

Nicolson misread 'it rating' for 'iterating', though his
reading of the 1553 clause was correct. This law remained
unaltered to the end, and for a time its breach was tole-
rated. One of the complaints against Forster in 1571 was
that he allowed the Scots to build 'sheldes' and depasture
in his March.[2] The Grames of the English West March
were apparently allowed by the Scots to depasture their
beasts in the Scots West March for thirteen or fourteen
years before 1576, when suddenly Lord Maxwell's brother
seized them without warning, and the Grames induced
the English Council to complain.[3] After this the Scots
Council ordered the enforcement of the law, curiously
enough quoting the Treaty of 1553.[4] Forster in 1595
was again accused of allowing at least 10,000 Scots sheep
to feed in England, summer and winter, and cattle also,
and of delivering any Englishman who interfered with
them.[5] Lord Eure, his successor, carried out the law,
whereupon the Scots complained to their King.[6]

7. *'Bawghling and reproving.'*

This is forbidden in the Treaty of 1553, and 'sylence
thereby is put to the complaynant and noe remidie provided to doe justice upon his complainte'. Therefore it is
now agreed that, when any one of either realm complains
of any one in any opposite Wardenry that he will not re-
enter himself as promised or pay ransom, &c., the complainant shall give his bill to the offender's Warden, who
shall cause him to be arrested 'to answeare [sic] next day of
Truice and to doe Justice upon his complainte by giving
of sentence according to Lawe, equitie and reason'.[7]

It was possible to obtain a licence to 'bawchl' a person,
from the Prince or Warden.[8]

---

[1] 1563, §20.   [2] C.S.P. iv, 32.   [3] C.S.P. v, 222.   [4] R.P.C.S. ii,
253.   [5] C.B.P. ii, 129.   [6] C.B.P. ii, 239, 255.   [7] 1563, §22.
[8] C.B.P. ii, 1310.

9. *Gross overswearing of the value of stolen or damaged goods.*

In 1553 Bowes had been able to get fixed values replaced by sworn values, subject to certain qualifications, but this led to more perjury, to avoid which, prices after September 10, 1563, were fixed as follows: 'The single value otherwise the principall' to be for every ox over four years old forty shillings sterling, and so on down to every young goat two shillings sterling.[1]

Bell's price list corresponds with that printed by Nicolson,[2] but ends with the words 'and everie double to be valued after the rate of the single'. Nicolson, who must have used a corrupt text, inserts the ghost-word 'Toope' after the word 'double', and has been copied by Mr. Howard Pease without comment.[3] It seems likely that some copyist wrote 'to pay' and did not properly cross it out before writing 'to be valued'. The next copyist must have coined the word 'Toope', or mistaken it for 'Toope', meaning a ram. This law remained unaltered, but it did not prevent gross overswearing on both sides, and in some cases the owners refused to accept the redelivery of their own cattle, and claimed the high prices they had sworn to instead.[4] According to Scroope in 1596, it was the custom of the Borderers to make their bill for redress twenty times the value of the goods they had lost.[5]

12. *Recovery of stolen goods.*

Two clauses of the new treaty are devoted to this subject, which had been dealt with in 1551.[6] The first says that, though each Warden is ordered 'to proceade upon all complaintes or attemptates by spirring filing and delivering upon his honor together with six other honest and famous men of that wardenrie adjoyned to him for the trial thereof, to be named by th'opposite warden', yet old customs are not thereby abolished. Such customs were 'lawful trodd with hound and horne, with hue and

---

[1] 1563, § 16.   [2] Leges, 94.   [3] The Wardens of the Northern Marches, 98.   [4] C.S.P. v, 228; For. xi, 843.   [5] C.B.P. ii, 369.   [6] § 10.

crye and all other accustomed manner of fresh pursuite for the recovery of there goods spoiled', and 'the order and triall of one Lawfull assise and inquest, adding of lawful proof to be used at the election and choice of the complanant'.[1]

'Trodd' was either 'hote troade, viz., fresh pursuit when the goodes are stollen', or 'cold troade, viz., at any other time after'.[2]

The other clause says that 'for the more spedie furtherance of the true man to recover his goods from the robber spoyler or recettor thereof', it is agreed that, 'if it shall happen th'inhabitants of any of the marches to committ any attemptate within the lymitts of any other marche and so file the other march It shalbe lawfull for the partie greaved to bill the offence either before the Warden of the March where the offender dwelleth, or where the goods remayneth or before the Warden of the March fyled . . . and both the said Wardens shalbe bound to make him lawfull answere and redresse upon his complainte.'[3]

Nicolson obscures the sense by omitting the word 'fyled'. This law gave rise to endless trouble. In June 1578 the Scots ambassador asserted that the peaceful Scots of the Middle March dare not follow 'tread' for fear of deadly feud. This was partly due to the Reedswyre fray.[4] In September 1582 Humfrey Musgrave, Deputy Warden of the West Marches, pursued some Scots thieves into Scotland 'following the troade as the manner is', and was set upon by the thieves and their neighbours. The English, smarting under many unredressed injuries, 'nor knowing well how to comme to any remedy', seized certain 'nolt' and sheep near, 'which were all put to havocke, nutshawed as they term it'. The Scots, who lost their goods, threatened revenge.[5] In 1596 matters came to such a pass that Scroope authorized the Musgraves to recover stolen goods with 'extraordynarie' forces which the Scots estimated at 2,000.[6] This subject is hardly divisible from that of the treatment of fugitives which follows.

[1] 1563, § 6.   [2] C.B.P. ii, p. 724.   [3] 1563, § 19.   [4] C.S.P. v, 356
[5] C.B.P. i, 133.   [6] C.B.P. ii, 346, 354.

13. *Fugitives*.

In 1556[1] the law had been made very severe against the 'recettor' of a fugitive. This clause was now re-enacted with the addition that the opposite warden, when the culprit fled the realm, was to make proclamation 'throughout his wardenrie by the space of six days after the said fugitive', and to tell his brother wardens to do likewise, so that none could plead ignorance.[2] The Warden was encouraged to do justice by the next clause, which says that, if a fugitive carry his goods into the opposite realm, the Warden of it, if he deliver him, 'shall receive the goods to his owne use for his labour'. If no delivery is made the goods must be restored to the fugitive's Warden, 'and to be goods redressed as goods unlawfully recetted against the treaty of peace'.[3]

These laws were broken not only by thieves in favour of thieves, but also by Wardens in favour of opposite gentlemen of consequence. In January 1572/3 Forster complained that the English rebels were daily recet by the Scots and lay on the Borders and made daily spoil on the same. He had written to the Regent, but had received no answer.[4] In August 1583 it was noted that the last part of the law of 1556 about the recettor's goods being forfeited to his prince had not been kept.[5] A few months later Scroope, with Elizabeth's cognizance, 'recetted' the Laird of Carmichael and his son,[6] and in January 1596/7 the Scots Commissioners complained of certain notorious Scots outlaws 'now avowedlie receitt within England . . . in dalie companye with the Lord Evers and his deputies, expresse against the treatyis and last league', and asked for their speedy delivery.[7]

There remains the question of pursuit to which five clauses are devoted. If the fugitives of both realms 'joyne or keape together', or if either Warden shall require all or any of the opposite Wardens to take or ride upon them, then the Wardens so required shall do so with convenient

[1] 1556, §1.   [2] 1563, §9.   [3] 1563, §10.   [4] C.S.P. iv, 473.
[5] C.S.P. vi, 603.   [6] C.B.P. i, 295.   [7] C.B.P. ii, 487.

power at such places and times as they agree upon.[1] And if any person warn a fugitive of the coming of the said Wardens whereby he escape, the offender shall be delivered to the Warden complaining, to be imprisoned for a year, and to pay a fine to the value of all his goods, and to be executed if the Wardens deem it expedient.[2] If a Warden of either realm pursue an offender to the frontier and the offender cross it, the Warden may 'pursue the chaise in hote trodd' till the offender be taken, and bring him back for punishment without let from any inhabitants of the opposite realm. If any such resist him he shall be billed for and delivered to the offended Warden to be punished at discretion. The only limit to the pursuit is that the pursuer at the first town, or to the first person he meets, must give knowledge of the cause of the chase and require them to go with and assist him.[3] But if any of the Warden's company, or the Warden himself, do unlawful harm to the opposite realm while there, the offender shall be delivered to the opposite Warden and punished at his discretion and that of twelve persons of his realm nominated by the opposite Warden.[4] To prevent escape, offenders filed and delivered to the opposite Warden at a day of Truce 'shall quietlie passe and remaine with the partie there [they are] delivered unto during all the time of the said assemblie and two houres after'. If they do not 'they shalbe punished to death or otherwise at discretion of the Wardens as a breaker of th'assurance'. Offenders delivered for execution must be straitly kept till justice is done on them.[5]

The futility of these laws in times of stress was manifest in 1569, when the Scots Borderers practised to the full their custom of succouring fugitives. Elizabeth was strong enough to take revenge on the 'recetters', who had acted without consulting their Regent. When Scots nobles took refuge in England, on the other hand, they were usually 'recetted' with Elizabeth's connivance, and the Scots government was powerless.

---

[1] 1563, § 11.   [2] 1563, § 12.   [3] 1563, § 14.   [4] 1563, § 15.   [5] 1563, § 21.

22. '*Punishment of the complaynant not having cause to com-
    plaine.*'

The new system of 'speiring', filing and delivering
upon the Warden's honour has led to the Wardens being
troubled by bills for goods lost when none have been
really lost. As a punishment for this new offence the
offender shall be delivered to the Warden whom he hath
so troubled, to be punished, imprisoned and fined for his
offence.[1]

Bell's reading 'wholly so troubled' is obviously corrupt.
The title is his marginal note. This law was never altered,
and there is no evidence as to whether it was effective or
not.

23. '*The lord or officer to answer for the tenant.*'

Every lord, &c., is to do his best to make his tenant
appear and answer before the Warden to any complaint.
If the lord be negligent his Warden may make him
answerable for his tenant's offence, always provided that
he shall not suffer death.[2]

This law, which was difficult to enforce, was untouched
by future commissions, but in 1579 the Scots Council,
finding it neglected, ordered landlords to eject fugitive
and outlawed tenants, or their families, without warning,
and without the landlord being liable to legal proceedings.[3]
The title is Bell's marginal note.

24. *Hindering the opposite Warden in his own Wardenry.*

If any shall go into the opposite realm 'to make shoute
or raise fray, beare armour or with force make any impediment to' the Warden of that realm in the execution of his
office, 'he shalbe reputed a publique offender against the
treatie of peace', so that, if slain or hurt or taken by that
Warden, 'he shalbe ordered as a subject of that realm'. If
he return to his own country, the offended Warden may
'bill for him', and 'being found foule' he shall be delivered
to be punished as a subject of the offended realm.[4]

[1] 1563, §7.   [2] 1563, §8.   [3] R.P.C.S. iii, 169.   [4] 1563, §13.

This new law was never altered. The English commissioners in 1597 tried to make out that it covered Sir R. Kerr's case, and that he ought therefore to be delivered. The Scots replied that there was no precedent for it.[1]

25. '*Redresse of corne sowne in th'opposite realme.*'

If any 'shall manure and occupy or sowe with corne any ground within th'opposite Realme,' the owner of the ground, or the Warden, may destroy the same if he thinks convenient, or else make a complaint to the opposite Warden. If the party be filed he shall forfeit his corn to the complainant, pay four times the value of the corn sown, and suffer three months' imprisonment.[2]

The title is Bell's marginal note. This law as applying to all the Marches was new, but a very similar law applying to the West only was made in August 1561.[3] Bell's text is corrupt at the end of that clause, but this new law was certainly more severe. The law remained unchanged, but was not obeyed. In 1576 the Scots Council ordered the Wardens to make open proclamation for the keeping of this law, as daily harm and inconvenience were caused by its being neglected.[4] In 1580 the Scots complained that the Grames bought lands in the Scots West Marches, planted themselves there, and sowed corn and inhabited the lands against the laws.[5]

26. '*Punishment for them that shall thrice committ attemptates.*'

Redress 'by payment of principall with two doubles' having failed, the penalty for the third fault shall be 'the paine of death as a common offender against the Lawes of the Marches'. Beyond the aforesaid redress, therefore, the offender's Warden shall do his best to take and bring him to the next day of Truce and deliver him to the opposite Warden for execution 'so that by this example all others shall take feare to offend or violate the amitie'. Provided always that the second offence be committed

[1] C.B.P. ii, 493.   [2] 1563, §17.   [3] Bell, 89-90.   [4] R.P.C.S. ii, 523.   [5] C.R.B. xxvi.

after the man has been found foul of the first, and the same with the third and second.[1]

The title of this new law, which was never altered, is Bell's marginal note. Forster was accused in 1595/6 of not executing such thieves when delivered to him.[2]

27. *'For publishing the treaties once in a year.'*

Negligence of officers in not giving knowledge to the subjects by continual exercise of justice how to behave having been the cause of great enormities, it is agreed 'that all and everie of the Wardens of both Realms shall incorporate and joyne together in one booke' all treaties and indentures made 'during this last amitie and perpetuall peace'. When the Wardens have taken their oaths,[3] the book, 'or at least so many articles and heades thereof as tend to the preservacōn of the amity', shall be publicly read once a year at the next meeting of the Wardens after midsummer.[4]

The title of this new law, which was never altered, is Bell's marginal note. Nicolson, by a misreading of a perhaps corrupt text, produced the curious ghost-word 'Pennrye', the correct reading being '& everye'.

28. *'One redresse and order of redresse to be used of all the Marches.'*

Every Warden having had a 'different forme and manner of proceeding from the other', it is agreed that every Warden shall execute his office according to these and other articles heretofore passed, and use one form of judgement and execution of justice 'according to the said laudable lawes, and to the custome of the Marches heretofore used'.[5]

The title of this new law, which was never changed, is Bell's marginal note.

For twenty-five years the international Border Laws remained as the Treaty of 1563 left them. They can hardly be described as a success, though they had not led

---

[1] 1563, § 18.   [2] C.B.P. ii, 211.   [3] See 1563, § 4.   [4] 1563, § 23.
[5] 1563, § 25.

to war, for days of truce had become rare, and an immense number of unredressed bills had accumulated. After the war clouds of December 1587, when the Scots had been expected to invade England with Spanish aid,[1] had passed away, James VI appointed Carmichael, Hume of Hutton Hall, and George Young commissioners to treat for the adjustment of Border controversies.[2] They met Hunsdon, Forster, John Selbie, and Richard Lowther at Foulden on January 18, and their resolutions are to be found in the Bell MS.[3] and among the unprinted Border Papers.[4] They began by dealing with cases which had happened since 'haulden rigg', or Hadden rigg, the scene of a fray in 1540, five miles east-north-east of Kelso, earlier cases being set aside 'to lye over to the further orders of the princes and their counsells upon new motion to be maide by either of them to others in that behalf'. They picked out important bills and remitted the rest 'to the ordinarie meetings of Wardens and their deputies to be appointed ymediatelie after our dissolving'. They dealt in all with fourscore bills and arranged for pledges 'to be entered reciprocally to remaine till the bills be filed'. Thus in all their proceedings up to January 25 there are nothing but temporary arrangements and agreements as to their own methods of procedure. The remnants of the bills were remitted to the Wardens, 'beginning with the latest first', fresh arrangements were made about pledges, and the sittings closed on February 24, no addition having been made to the Border laws except on two points which follow.

29. *Denial of justice.*

'That if in anytyme hereafter it fall out that in the order [of] metings of the wardens justice be refused to any of them of any one particular complaint, the said refusall shalbe to him that is denied justice of that bill no cause to give up further meting, but he shall still be holden to give and take redresse for other bills leaving the order taking with the said bill refused to the princes and their counsells.'[5]

---

[1] C.B.P. i, 565, 569.   [2] C.B.P. i, 585.   [3] 102 ff.   [4] C.B.P. i, 593–4.   [5] Bell, 105.

This law remained unchanged, but further legislation on the same subject was made in 1597.[1]

30. *Pledges.*

On January 30 it was agreed 'That for the greater terror to theives and malefactors and suretie of deliverance for sick bills as sall happen to be fyled', the Scots King shall enter to England one gentleman for each March, and two for 'Liddesdell'. The English shall likewise enter five Englishmen. These pledges shall remain till the bills be filed and the offenders entered, and shall 'lye on eyther side', till all unlawful bands be discharged.[2] On February 24 it was agreed that for the performance of the treaty each realm shall enter 'four gentlemen of honest birth and reputation' to be responsible for bills filed and to stay in the opposite realm till the bills were satisfied and unlawful bands and prisoners 'discharged and put to libertie'.[3]

These provisions were expected to be temporary, but as they failed, and led to more strict precautions being taken in 1597, it is well to give them.

For ten years nothing more was done, and it was found that the Laws of the Marches, devised by our ancestors from the 'auntiant accustomed lawes of a camp', had become neglected or forgotten by the people.[4] English commissioners, Tobie Matthew, Bishop of Durham, Sir William Bowes, Francis Slyngesby, and Clement Colmer, D.C.L., were appointed on October 2, 1596, to decide all Border questions with Scots commissioners.[5] The Bishop wished to meet the Scots on November 13 at Berwick,[6] but by October 29 he had given up all hope of doing so,[7] and on November 11 James VI excused the Scots because of 'the notorious seiknes and infirmitie of the Lord of New-bottle, quha wes to be first in commission', and because the Warden of the Scots Middle Marches and the Keeper of Liddisdale 'for certane reasonable causs excusit thame selfiss'.[8] The Bishop doubted the Scots desire and inten-

---

[1] § 10.   [2] Bell, 103–4.   [3] Bell, 106.   [4] C.B.P. ii, 469.   [5] C.B.P. ii, 400.   [6] C.B.P. ii, 415.   [7] C.B.P. ii, 425.   [8] C.B.P. ii, 440.

tion to meet the English,[1] but on November 27 James VI
ordered them to do so at Foulden Kirk on January 12
next.[2] They actually met on January 14 and agreed to sit
at Berwick,[3] and by January 24 had agreed upon articles
for their proceedings in the treaty.[4] There was still trouble
owing to the episode of Will of Kinmont, and to Sir R.
Kerr's invasion,[5] which were finally reserved to the princes,[6]
but by February 19 the greater part of the East and
Middle March bills since the last commission had been
filed and the rest remitted to the Wardens. The commissioners adjourned, having agreed to meet on the West on
March 10,[7] but James VI postponed the meeting for a
month on 'a sodaine'.[8] Finally the commissioners met at
'Gretney Kirk' on April 12, and went to Carlisle,[9] and after
arranging for the redress of West March bills and for
pledges, made the Treaty of May 5, 1597. Nicolson's text
reads May 5, 1597, though he heads it 1596. Both texts
in the Public Record Office are dated May 5. Bell's text
gives May 1.

The English commissioners have been named, the
Scots were the Bishop of Dunkeld, George Houme,
Knight, and Andrew Kerr of Fawdonsyd. Nicolson adds
a fourth, namely George Young, whom the Bell MS. and
Border Papers omit. James VI had authorized any three
to sign.[10] The English commissioners had asked for and
apparently failed to get the assistance of one learned not
only in the civil law, as Colmer was, but also in ordinary
practice and in the *jus gentium*.[11]

'The last treaties betwene Elizabeth Queene of England
and James King of Scotts' contains 36 clauses which are
printed fully by Nicolson, except part of clause 33, and
are contained in the Bell MS. There are English and
Scots Texts in the *Border Papers*, vol. xxxiv, 163–8,
170–5. Of the 36 clauses, numbers 3, 4, and 5 concern the
details of days of Truce and are given under that heading.[12]

[1] C.B.P. ii, 442.   [2] C.B.P. ii, 447.   [3] C.B.P. ii, 476.   [4] C.B.P.
ii, 481.   [5] C.B.P. ii, 491, 493.   [6] C.B.P. ii, 515.   [7] C.B.P. ii,
519.   [8] C.B.P. ii, 564.   [9] C.B.P. ii, 588.   [10] C.B.P. ii, 622–3, 646.
[11] C.B.P. ii, 567.   [12] Vide infra, p. 140.

One, number 25, concerning unordered complaints, is temporary, and to the effect that if any such remain all Wardens shall interchange rolls with their opposites before June 10 next, and within eight days, either in person or by deputy, return them at the usual meeting places 'filed or cleaned upon their honors under the pain of paying the bills themselves'. This arrangement was not to prejudice the complainant's right to use an avower and so claim 'double and sawfie'. This interchanging of rolls was not done, and its omission made the Bishop of Durham apprehensive for the whole treaty.[1] Fifteen clauses are additions to or alterations of old laws, viz. no. 9, Slaughters; no. 10, Denial of Justice; no. 16, Perjury; no. 12, Recovery of Stolen Property; no. 24, Fugitives; and nos. 26–35, Pledges. These are treated first under the numbers given in the code and in the Treaties of 1563 and 1587, and the remaining seventeen, which are new, are numbered consecutively thereafter.

1. *Slaughters.*

Former treaties are 'to stand in full effect and force with this addition'. The Wardens shall do justice within fifteen days after their opposites require it of them, under pain of paying £10 sterling to the plaintiff for every month's delay 'without prejudice of further following of th'offender, according to the treaties in that behaulfe provided'.[2]

Nicolson obscures the sense by omitting the words 'without prejudice'. This is the first Elizabethan law on the subject, the former treaties referred to being those of 1551,[3] 1553,[4] and 1556.[5] The English commissioners were not satisfied with the clause,[6] they would probably have preferred the addition of a statement that slaughters were not to be referred to the princes.

8. *Perjury.*

'For eschewing of perjurie . . . It is ordeyned that everie partie sweare his owne bill or otherwise to have no deliverie for the same.'[7]

---

[1] C.B.P. ii, 659.   [2] 1597, §9.   [3] §9.   [4] §11.   [5] §4.
[6] C.B.P. ii, 626.   [7] 1597, §16.

12. *Recovery of stolen property.*

'For maisterful and violent theft and reafe by night or day and for secreate stealing wherewith is joyned either bodilie hurt of men, women, or children or violent resistance against the followers in hote and fresh pursuite of their goods,' besides ordinary redress of the goods, any offender chosen by the plaintiff shall be delivered to the opposite officer to be punished by his discretion according to the offence.[1]

The question of the recovery of stolen property was much debated in 1596. Scroope, alleging that lawful 'trodes' had been much troubled by Scots ambushments, authorized the Musgraves to enter Scotland with 'extraordynarie' forces. Buccleugh alleged that with 2,000 men they attacked 'a hous of reasonable strenthe', were beaten off, and 'farraged' most of the bounds of the Debatable Land, driving away 200 nolt. The raid was repeated eight days later, and at least twice thereafter. This law against resistance seems to show that the English commissioners had persuaded the Scots that Scroope had suffered great provocation.[2]

13. *Fugitives.*

The Wardens, before June 30, shall make a list of persons of their March exiled for theft, and send it to their opposites with a request to see that those 'recetted' within their bounds are taken and delivered. The opposite Warden shall do this, or, if he cannot, shall declare them fugitives in all Marches of his realm, and their houses and 'sheilds' to be destroyed and themselves not to be 'recetted'. If he do not, he shall be responsible for deeds done by them in the meantime.[3]

29. *Denial of justice.*

Any 'warden or keeper' who has two opposites may do justice with the one though the other refuse it, 'leving the refuser to be ordered by the princes and their counsells'.[4]

This would really apply to every such officer. The

[1] 1597, § 12.   [2] C.B.P. ii, 346, 354.   [3] 1597, § 24.   [4] 1597, § 10.

Scots West Marches bordered only on the English West March, but this did not prevent raids on them by the English Middle March.

30. *Pledges.*[1]

Two or more of every surname of broken men on either side and of equal rank shall be named in a bill by the opposite realm and entered to the opposite officer as pledges.[2] For such Borderers as are of no known clan each Warden shall enter a gentleman to remain till the bills be satisfied.[3] Entry shall be between now and July 1 next.[4] The princes shall be entreated to appoint commissioners to see this carried into effect.[5] Pledges shall be kept by indifferent men at their own expense and not handed to any with whom they are at feud.[6] Pledges shall not remain in the opposite realm after the bills filed are redressed.[7] If a pledge die, the opposite officer shall choose another of his surname to be entered.[8] If the bills filed be not redressed within a year and a day after this indenture, the prince or officer holding them may keep them or take their lives. 'Provided that if the said prince or officer opposite dispose upon their lives after th'aforesaid yeare and day, he may call for and shall receive from his opposite as many of the like quallitie to lie another yeare upon the like condicōn and so from yeare to yeare as aforesaid.' The part in inverted commas is entirely omitted by Nicolson.[9] 'This entrie shall in no wise be extended to the redresse for slaughters, but so far foorth as the commissioners shall agree and appointe in this treatie thereupon.'[10] Pledges shall lie for all attempts filed upon their surnames unredressed and for future offences till their liberty.[11]

These laws, like those of 1588 on the same subject, were meant to be temporary, but the fact that they did not work prolonged their existence. The English commissioners wrote that in the delivery of pledges, about which there was much trouble, 'the very life of this whole service

---

[1] For bills filed in this treaty and in that of 1588.   [2] 1597, §26.   [3] 1597, §27.   [4] 1597, §28.   [5] 1597, §29.   [6] 1597, §30.   [7] 1597, §31.   [8] 1597, §32.   [9] 1597, §33.   [10] 1597, §34.   [11] 1597, §35.

will consist.'[1] Sir William Bowes stuck to his opinion and declared, in September 1599, that the pledge system had hitherto been the only means to surcease violence, ordinary justice having been little done since on the West and Middle Marches.[2] The Wardens thought otherwise. On March 18, 1597/8, Sir R. Kerr stated that the pledge system was useless, as, though punishment might make them know their faults, poverty compelled them again to wickedness.[3] Two years later Wyllughby remained convinced that the security of the Borders was not much dependent on pledges of base quality, but rather on the vigilance of the Wardens.[4]

31. Churches and ministers.

The commissioners agreed to entreat their princes 'to cause God's ministers of the Word to be planted at every border Church to enforme that lawlesse people of their dutie . . . and that to this effect order may be tymelie taken for reparacōn of the decayed churches within the borders'. The chief inhabitants are to protect the parsons.[5]

It was rather late in the day, but this agreement marked a real advance. Much had been heard about the various and only right methods of obtaining salvation, much attention had been paid to the loaves and fishes, but here were eight commissioners, the majority of them laymen, publishing their belief that religion might have an effect on the lives of 'lawlesse people'. A Bernard Gilpin in every Border church might have solved most of the problems of the Marches, but such men are rare. The suggestion probably came from Lord Eure, who had written to Elizabeth on April 17, 1596, that one of the most grievous causes of decay was 'want of knowledge of God', whereby the better sort forgot oath and duty, let malefactors go, against the evidence, and favoured a 'partie' belonging to themselves or their friends. The churches, he added, were mostly ruined to the ground, and the ministers and preachers 'comforthles to com and remaine where such

---

[1] C.B.P. ii, 626.   [2] C.B.P. ii, 1101.   [3] C.H.M. viii, 87.   [4] C.H.M. x, 78–9.   [5] 1597, § 1.

heathenish people are', so that there were neither teachers nor taught.[1] The matter may also be viewed from the standpoint of the Church as policeman, but anyhow the clause came too late to be of any effect before the death of Elizabeth.

32. *A Border Council.*

'For the better prevention of such great enormities and mischeeves as have of laite yeares undone the border and disquieted the peace betwene the Realmes', the commissioners agreed to entreat their princes 'to choose and establish a counsell in everie march of the most sufficient and discreate borderers inhabiting the bounds thereof', this council to meet twice a year.[2]

This recommendation (it cannot be called a law) was apparently neglected by the princes.

32. *Warden 'rodes'.*

No Warden or keeper shall ride in person or cause any to ride in hostile manner within the opposite realm without special command under the seal and hand of his prince, 'under the paine to be accounted a publique enimie of the peace'. Any persons accompanying such a 'rode' shall lose redress for any offence done to them before that 'rode', and shall nevertheless satisfy the party grieved for 'skaith and damage according to the Lawes of Marches'.[3]

This law, which was obviously directed against such exploits as the rescue of Will of Kinmont and the raids of Sir R. Kerr, seems to have been effective.

34. *A black list of thieves.*

The 'border counsell' shall make at their meetings 'diligent enquirie and triall of all notorious theaves and robbers within their wardenrie' and make a list of them and send it to their Warden, who shall, at the first attempt, 'trulie tried and filed upon any of them hereafter', put him immediately to death, or, if he be fugitive, proclaim him such and demolish his house at once.[4]

---

[1] C.B.P. ii, 255.   [2] 1597, § 2.   [3] 1597, § 6.   [4] 1597, § 7.

This new and drastic law was apparently never enforced.

35. 'Deadlie fead.'

If any one bear 'deadlie fead' against any of the opposite realm 'for executing of any theofe by justice or killing him with read hand', the Warden, on being told, shall take the offender, and either make him at once renounce the feud in writing, or deliver him to the opposite Warden till he has done so and found surety to the satisfaction of the plaintiff. This law shall be retrospective.[1]

It is strange that the first legislation on this important subject should be found in the very last treaty. In July 1596 deadly feud was defined as follows: 'Deadly foed, the word of enmitye in the Borders, implacable without the whole blood and family distroied.'[2] Combats between the inhabitants of opposite Marches had apparently been allowed, if licensed, but unlicensed meetings had been forbidden as likely to cause feuds to arise.[3] The Scots, when they suffered from even the smallest theft, were said to threaten blood revenge by the clan,[4] and the fear of incurring such feuds, wrote Eure in 1597, was one reason why the common people were loath to attend before the commissioners at Carlisle and Dumfries.[5]

36. Delivery of an officer upon a bill filed.

If a Warden deliver an officer upon a bill filed 'and afterwards borrow him againe upon his word as the use is, If in the meantyme the partie so filed depart this life by whatsoever way or meanes', the Warden shall pay the bill and seek his remedy from 'the heirs and executors of the defunct as he may best'.[6]

37. Idle persons.

'That none of the broken borderers be suffered to keape in their companies any idle persons not imployed in some honest service or trade.' 'That no idle person be suffered

---

[1] 1597, § 8.   [2] C.B.P. ii, 323.   [3] R.P.C.S. iv, 81.   [4] C.B.P. ii, 103.   [5] C.B.P. ii, 582.   [6] 1597, § 11.

to remane in border villages or ale houses.' Those who 'recett' the same 'shall be billable for their so doing as if they had actuallie recetted the goods by them stolne'.[1]

38. *Malicious arrest.*

Any one maliciously causing another 'to be arrested to daies of truice without just cause', shall be made by his Warden to pay damages to the complainant. And, for the better trial thereof, the complainant must swear that he is persuaded that he has just cause to pursue that bill against the person he has caused to be arrested.[2]

39. *Bona fide possession of stolen goods.*

If the possessor of stolen goods be not sued within a year and a day, the goods shall be his for ever. If, however, he be sued within that time, he shall give sufficient proof of his innocence before the Wardens or their deputies 'and he shall render the goods which he received onlie and shall give up and nominate a responsible debtor of whome he had the said goods'. This is to excuse 'none that are privie to the theft'.[3]

The words 'and he shall render the goods which he received onlie' are omitted by Nicolson. The text in the Public Record Office agrees with the Bell MS.

40. *Backbilling.*

If any one unjustly 'offend another in word or dead hereafter for filing any bill against them he shall never be heard to backbill against the Avower', and yet shall be punished at the Warden's discretion.[4] To avoid delays it is ordained that any one backbilling against an avower 'shall do it within fortie days after the fyling, or otherwise to be excluded from that remedie for ever'. To this effect every Warden must hold Warden Courts and do justice within twenty days after he shall be required by the party, or pay the bill himself.[5]

This law, which was really domestic, was new in Eng-

---

[1] 1597, § 13.　　[2] 1597, § 14.　　[3] 1597, § 15.　　[4] 1597, § 17.　　[5] 1597, § 18.

land, but in Scotland there had been customs governing backbilling.[1] Backbilling apparently means bringing an accusation against some one who had testified to your own guilt on a former charge. Malice was naturally suspected.

41. 'Causing and commanding.'

'Causing and commanding being billed in any complainte shal be no less criminall than having stealing and recetting.'[2]

By 1563, § 8, a lord who neglected to make his tenant appear might be answerable for his tenant's offence, but could not suffer death. By this law he could, if he had caused or commanded the crime.

42. Bonds are to bind heirs.

If any borderer procure any of the opposite nation 'to be bound for him by word or writing and releave him not in due tyme of the same bond whereby the suretie shal be compelled to pay the summe for which he gave his bond, or in case he die', his heirs shall have to pay though there be no mention of heirs in the bond. Proof shall be the 'bond in writing', or a 'lawfull avower of th'opposite nation'. Similarly if the binder die his heirs shall reap the benefit of the bond.[3]

It was not quite clear to the English Council in 1591 whether it was the usage of the Borders to charge an heir with things for which he was not personally responsible. Bothwell alleged that it was.[4]

43. Actions of debt.

Unless both parties, or at least the defendant, live within the March, 'actions of debt shall not be tried before the Wardens but before the ordinarie judges'. The Marches are defined as from Newcastle and 'Peareth' (Penrith) to Edinburgh and Dumfries 'exclusively'.[5]

[1] R.P.C.S. iii, 621.   [2] 1597, § 19.   [3] 1597, § 20.   [4] A.P.C. xxi, 30–1.   [5] 1597, § 21.

44. *Comprehensive bills of complaint.*

'Where divers offences are billed for in one and the same complainte, the partie defendant, upon his appearance, shall be filed of noe moe crimes therein conteyned then shall be speciallie recorded upon the mergent of his bill by the opposites hand.'[1]

45. *Interlined bills.*

In bills filed and found 'at the time of deliverie or swearing to be interlined in any materiall point or name the words or names so interlined shalbe of no effect or force but taken as unwritten', unless inserted by us or future commissioners.[2]

46. *Place of next meeting.*

The Scots commissioners having 'willinglie consented both to beginne and prosequute this treatie within England', the next commission shall meet in Scotland, unless the princes or their commissioners shall agree otherwise. The Scots King shall give a sufficient safe conduct.[3]

The Treaty of 1597 had added fifty per cent. to the amount of Border law, but many of the clauses concerned but small points, though they did remedy old defects. The English commissioners were not sanguine in their hopes for its success, especially when Johnstone alone of the Scots Wardens made any attempt to obey the order to attend and deliver all persons billed for offences since the commissioners first met at Berwick. Divers insolent broken Borderers were credibly reported as combining to defeat the treaty and openly saying the pledges 'will not enter for King nor Keiser'.[4] Two and a half years later Sir W. Bowes acknowledged that the expected fruits of the commission had not yet appeared,[5] though the commissioners had filed more bills than any four commissions then extant, and had concluded a treaty more 'behoofeful' for the good of England than ever before written or practised.[6] Wyllughby, on the other hand, in December 1599,

---

[1] 1597, § 22.   [2] 1597, § 23.   [3] 1597, § 36.   [4] C.B.P. ii, 626.
[5] C.B.P. ii, 1023.   [6] C.B.P. ii, 1101.

complained that the work of the commission had been badly done, and that 'because of theis knottes', which he saw 'nobody goe about to untye', he could not do good service as Warden.[1] In spite of his opinion, it seems clear that the treaty was a great improvement on its predecessors. Its success depended partly on the carrying out of such suggestions as those about churches, ministers, and a border council, and the six years of Border history that remain would not furnish enough evidence for judgement, even if those suggestions had been put in force at once, which they were not. The second thing which would determine its success or failure was the way in which it was administered by the Wardens, and it is to the administration of international Border Law that we now turn.

[1] C.B.P. ii, 1137.

PART VIII

A DAY OF TRUCE

THE best authorities for this are Sir Robert Bowes's *Form and Order of a Day of Truce*, written in 1551,[1] which refers to the East and Middle Marches, and Richard Bell's *Manner of holding a day of truce*, which was afterwards printed by Nicolson and Burn in modernized spelling and with some mistakes hereafter noted. It refers to the West Marches.[2] There seems to be no Scots version extant.

For the sake of clearness in exposition the course of procedure has been here divided into some score of divisions to which numbers are affixed, and, where possible, notes. Bell's account was written down over fifty years after Bowes's. They agree pretty closely, and, where they differ, their names have been appended to their statements. The procedure was as follows:

1. The opposite Wardens agreed upon a day and place of meeting.[3] The usual places were on the March confines or within Scotland,[4] though some Scots maintained that they should always be in Scotland.[5] In 1579 the Scots Warden was allowed to go to Carlisle, and the English Warden went to Dumfries, as it was difficult to meet on the frontier during the short winter days.[6] The whole thing was really a matter of convenience, as was shown when Forster, after nearly forty years' experience, wrote 'somtime I went to him into Scotland, somtime he to me as the conveniencie of the place served: in winter if the weather served not, somtime I sent my deputie to Yatam (Yetholm), somtime he went to Kirkneuton, ther to determine of causes'.[7] The most usual East March meeting-

---

[1] N.D. xxii ff.; R.T. iv (2).   [2] Op. cit. I, xxiii ff.; Bell, 142 ff. Other evidence will be found in C.B.P. i, 343; S.P. Borders, xli, 238–40, and A.A. ii, 296 (1832).   [3] Bowes.   [4] Bowes.   [5] C.B.P. ii, 1134. [6] R.P.C.S. iii, 84.   [7] C.B.P. ii, 1003.

places were Foulden-rig, the West ford at Norham, near Wark castle, at Carham, or at the Riding Burn: on the Middle Marches, Cocklaw, Stawford, and the Reedswyre, and, on the West, Kershopefoot, Rockcliffe, or Gretna Kirk. There was no fixed place for any March. Sometimes after a meeting the Wardens cast lots and rode into the realm of the winner to do justice, say, at Kelso, afterwards returning to continue it in the loser's realm, say, at Alnwick.[1]

2. Then notice was given throughout the Wardenry for bills of complaints to be prepared.[2]

3. Copies of these bills were sent to the Scots Warden whose business was to get the offenders arrested and to secure the attendance of those offenders who had been filed before.[3] If, however, specially poor men made complaints between the days of Truce, both Wardens were accustomed to send the bill to their opposites requiring redress without delay, and if redress had been given and accepted before the day of Truce the offender was discharged.[4]

4. Proclamation was made and letters sent in the Queen's name for all lords, knights, gentry, &c., with a convenient number of their charge and tenants, to repair the night before and give their attendance to the Warden defensibly arrayed the day following with their best horses and nags.[5] The Treaty of 1563 (§ 3) says Wardens 'must keape their daies of Marche often and in proper person so farre as may be and not by deputies without just and great occasion'. Scots were sometimes put to horn for nonattendance.[6]

5. As the parties approached the appointed meetingplace they waited while the English Warden sent a deputy or meet person[7] to crave or demand assurance until sunrise of the next day. This was if they met for one day only. According to Eure, days of Truce were not limited 'from sonne to sonne', unless the Wardens specially agreed upon it. This has an important bearing on the case of Will of Kinmont.[8] Bowes says that four or six ancient, discreet,

[1] C.B.P. i, 421.   [2] Bowes.   [3] Bowes; see also Laws, 1553, § 1.
[4] Bowes.   [5] Bell.   [6] R.P.C.S. ii, 357.   [7] Bell.   [8] C.B.P. ii, 283.

and well reputed Borderers were sent to get assurance.
The Scots Warden was accustomed to grant this by holding up his hand; which done, the deputation returned to
report to their own Warden.

6. The Scots sent to crave, or demand, and get assurance likewise.

7. Each Warden then proclaimed among his own company, in his prince's and his own name, the keeping of the
assurance upon pain of death. Bowes notes that if any had
an old or a new feud made unto them they were to complain to their Warden and not break the assurance.

8. Bowes says that a further proclamation was made
that if any had borne 'Bawghles' or 'reproaches' unto any of
the opposite party, for faith broken, after the custom of
the Borders, they were to lay it aside during the assurance.
Bowes thought it convenient that before any began to bear
'baughill' he should hand the cause of quarrel in writing
to both Wardens, who should either by themselves or by
the assizes of both realms settle the bill by justice. The
question was covered by the laws of 1553 (§ 14) and 1563
(§ 22).

9. Then, says Bell, the Warden of England 'with his
company entreth into Scotland riding to the place where
the Lord Warden of Scotland lighting off horseback stands
still untill his coming, then and there in all friendlie and
orderly manner mutually embracing the one the other'.
Though the English is clumsy the sense is clear, and
directly opposite to that given by Nicolson and Burn.
Bowes merely says that they met with salutations in gentle
manner.

10. Then, according to Bowes, they proceeded to justice, beginning by naming the assize, the English Warden
appointing the Scots, and vice versa. Bowes notes that it
was best to put on assize such as had notice of the offences
to be tried and would tell truth, the very best being those
who had cases coming on later, and so desired expedition.
In all Marches the jury was composed of six Englishmen
and six Scots. Bell adds that the cases might be tried
by the Warden's honour, by the jury, or by a 'vower

publique', i.e. a countryman of the accused agreed upon
by both parties. He adds, though Nicolson and Burn omit
it, 'which order being answered It is of late altered to the
stipulacōn and hands of the parties billd, and such or four
other hands as the partie greaved will appointe for to
excuse him or them billed'.[1] The Treaty of 1563 laid down
that each Warden, in the presence of his opposite and of
the inhabitants of both the Marches, must swear yearly
at the first meeting after midsummer to exercise his office
'without respect of person, malice, favour or affection
diligently and undelayedlie', to 'doe justice upon all complaintes presented unto him upon every person compleyned upon under his rule', to 'search and enquire and
redresse . . . at his uttermost powre . . . any complaint
referred to him to speire file and deliver upon his honour'.
If in so doing he acquitted any of the defendants, nevertheless, if he found the real offender, he must make redress
and delivery even if the true offender were not named in
the bill.[2] 'Speire' means 'to enquire', 'file' to avow the
truth of a bill.[3] In 1597 it was settled that the truce must
be held within four[4] days of midsummer, at which the
Wardens had to interchange their commissions.[5] The
Treaty of 1597 also laid down that each Warden should 'be
bound by his foresaid oath to speere out' any attempt
done by his March exceeding five persons, and to 'file the
same upon his honour and deliver therfore within fiftene
daies' or pay the bill himself, provided the complaint was
made within forty-eight hours of the attempt.[6] In filing
thus, the Warden had to set down in the margin of every
bill filed or cleared 'foule, or cleare, as I am verilie perswaded upon my conscience and honor'. Any bills signi-
fied within forty-eight hours and not filed or cleared in
fifteen days were to be foul[7] on the Wardens themselves
for their neglect.[8]

The jury system did not work; the Scots were only to
find offences done by Scots, and the English those by

---

[1] Bell, 143 (back), last five lines.   [2] 1563, §4.   [3] C.B.P. ii, 1310.
[4] Bell says five.   [5] 1597, §3; C.B.P. ii, 622.   [6] 1597, §4.   [7] Bell
miswrote 'fall'.   [8] 1597, §5.

Englishmen, and so from favour to friends, countrymen, and kinsmen, and specially from fear of deadly feud, little or no good could be done that way. This was the conclusion of the Redeswyre commission of 1575.[1]

In the Russell case of 1585 the futility of the avower and of the Warden's honour was apparent. These were then 'the ordinarie and onlie waies of triall', and, as the Warden would not acknowledge the fact and no avower could be found, the delinquent was 'quitt by lawes of the Borders'. The English, however, stood by the opinion that the Scots Warden was 'fowle', 'ex notarietate facti'.[2] Avowers could but rarely be got in Scotland for fear of feud, and in England it was probably the same, and the Warden could not be expected to do much unless his prince gave him some pension to prevent his consenting to evil or supporting 'badd persons'. Even then Lord Eure was doubtful, and told Burghley that to expect justice for conscience' sake would be too much.[3] Sometimes, moreover, as in the case of Buccleugh, the Scots officer had 'not only bene an actor, but also a speciall procurer of those invasions, day forries, most crewell slaughters', &c., so his word of honour was useless.[4] Another condition that could not always be fulfilled was the interchange of commissions. In the very month of the Treaty of 1597 Sir R. Carey had none to show.[5] Again, in the following year, Wyllughby found that most of the Wardens had no patents, and so the meetings were frustrate 'and our attendance subject to scorne'.[6]

11. Then, says Bowes, the English Warden, or his clerk, gave the oath to the Scots jurors, and the Scots Warden, or clerk, to the English. This was later enjoined by the fifth clause of the Treaty of 1563. The oath given by Bell is as follows: 'Yow shall cleare noe bills worthie to be filed, yow shall fyle noe bill worthie to be cleared, but shall doe that which appeareth with a truth for the maintenance of peace and suppressing of

[1] C.S.P. v, p. 193 (for an example of a feud in 1597 see C.B.P. ii, 498).
[2] C.B.P. i, 343, cf. ii, 383.   [3] C.B.P. ii, 187, 343, 410.   [4] C.B.P. ii, 601.   [5] C.B.P. ii, 643.   [6] C.B.P. ii, 944.

attempts. So helpe you God, &c.' 'Fyle', from the same root as 'foul', means 'make foul' or 'culpable';[1] 'cleare' means 'to declare innocent'.[2]

12. This done, and a warden-sergeant of either party appointed to keep the jurors, the Wardens drew apart to some quiet place to confer upon their matters.[3]

13. The Wardens, having withdrawn themselves as above, interchangeably called their rolls and bills in the presence of the gentlemen of the best sorts of both countries.[4] Bowes says that they chose out eight or ten, more or less, bills that they would have answered that day, or the whole roll of both sides if there was time. It was their custom 'to begin at the last done matter first and so to proceed backwards'.[5] By the third clause of the Treaty of 1563 the Wardens were to keep on sitting till 'all former attemptates compleyned upon be ordered and fullie answered'. They were not to 'make redresse of value for value, or bill for bill but for all offences compleyned upon to them'. In 1584/5 Scroope found that the restitution under the treaty without respect of value for value, though true in strict law, was unequal, taking effect on us here where we are 'somewhat afore hand', and not in Liddisdale, where by delay of redress 'we are greatlye behynd hand'.[6]

14. The bills were tried by the articles of the last treaty, and if the case was not provided for therein there was no remedy.[7] He must mean by the last treaty containing a clause on the subject: for example, there had been no law about hunting since 1486.

15. The usual form of trial, as above, was that of English bills by the Scots inquest, and vice versa.[8] Before the plaintiff gave evidence he had to take 'The Oath of swearing bills filed', as follows: 'Yee shall leile price make and truth say what your goods were worth at the tyme of their taking to have been sold in a market taken all at one tyme and that you knowe no other recoverie but this. So God, &c.'[9] The defendant, if innocent or given to perjury took

---

[1] R.P.C.S. II, xii.   [2] C.B.P. ii, 1310.   [3] Bowes.   [4] Bell.
[5] Bowes.   [6] C.B.P. i, 293.   [7] Bowes.   [8] Bowes.   [9] Bell.

the 'Ancient Oath for excusing bills' as follows: 'You shall sweare by heaven above you, hell beneath you, by your part of paradice, by all that God maide in six daies and seaven nights, and by God himself yee are whart out sacklesse of art, part, way, witting, ridd, kenning, having, taking or recetting of any of the goods and cattells named in this bill, so helpe yow God, &c.'[1] 'Whart out' seems to mean 'entirely' or 'absolutely';[2] 'sacklesse' means 'innocent', 'ridd' means, perhaps, removing or clearing away.

16. When the Wardens had finished calling, fouling, and making delivery of bills, a proclamation was made in the name of both princes of the good order that had been taken. Bowes adds that the next day of Truce was fixed within eight, fourteen, or twenty days at furthest, and all were charged to keep good order meanwhile. The third clause of the Treaty of 1563 said Truces must be kept monthly or oftener on every March, and appointed days must not be slipped. But they were not held anything like monthly, and there were sometimes intervals of a year or more.[3] Moreover, appointed days were often 'shott', or when meetings did take place justice was denied.[4] Of course there were exceptions when justice was done, as, for instance, when Hunsdon first became Warden and got delivery for bills valued at nearly £15,000 in three months. But this unusual state of affairs was really due to the pressure of the Regent Moray.[5]

17. Then 'leave being taken by the Wardens in all kindlie sort',[6] or 'gentle and loving countenance' being showed between the Wardens,[7] they went home. Bowes notes that thieves lay in wait to see whether they could by any word or countenance make grief between the Wardens, deputies, or chief Borderers, and so take occasion to commit unlawful crimes. The classic instance was at the Redeswyre in 1575. Sometimes a raid followed almost at once, as in 1600.[8]

18. Bowes says that the Wardens, after their departure

---

[1] Bell.   [2] C.B.P. ii, 1344.   [3] e.g. C.B.P. i, 676, 972.   [4] e.g. C.B.P. ii, 495.   [5] C.S.P. v, 540.   [6] Bell.   [7] Bowes.   [8] C.B.P. ii, 1198.

to their own realm, proclaimed good rule and threatened offenders. Bell says that the Warden called the gentry together and inquired their opinions of the day's proceedings before dismissing them with thanks. A few details can be added from the treaties, &c.

1. In 1473 it was agreed that men should come to Truces 'in peaceable wise, without harness, axe, bill, spear or bow, and without any other fencible weapon (save sword and knife) under pain of escheating of their weapons', and being delivered to the other party for punishment. The numbers were not to exceed a thousand for Wardens, five hundred for lieutenants, and two hundred for deputies.[1] Hunsdon notes that on September 21, 1568, he met Cesford with two thousand a side.[2]

2. The Warden of the complainant shall receive the complaint and send the roll to the opposite Warden, who shall do his best to inquire into it and get his sergeant to arrest the accused 'presently without delay' (Nicolson adds 'if they be present'). If absent they are to be arrested to answer at the next Truce. Then and there the Warden and Assize shall either file the bill or give another lawful answer (Nicolson adds 'at their next meeting'). Six of the twelve sizers are to be chosen by each Warden.[3]

3. When a bill has been filed and no lawful deliverance or recompense made for it, the offender's Warden, if he lacks an offender, shall deliver such other person by the assent of the opposite Warden as he will undertake to be sufficient for the bill. The person so delivered is to stay with the offended party till he be fully satisfied by March Law. When both Wardens have answered an equal number of bills the overplus shall none the less be answered without fellows.[4]

4. A new method of answering bills, i.e. by the Warden's honour, was started in 1553 with reference to offences since 1551. If the Warden in ignorance acquitted a foul bill the complainant might pursue a new bill 'on better informacion' to the same Warden or his successor.[5]

---

[1] Rymer, xi, 789.   [2] For. viii, 2542.   [3] Bell, 1553, § 1.   [4] 1553, § 2.
[5] 1553, §§ 4, 5.

This method, which was meant to be temporary, was extended in 1563.[1]

5. No infamous persons, rebels, fugitives, or thieves of either realm convicted by Assize shall be admitted to office, or offer testimony, but good, loyal, just, trustworthy, and unsuspected persons only.[2]

6. Sizers were to hold office for three months after taking the oath, and eight of the twelve was a quorum.[3]

Enough has been said above to show the difference between the ideal and the real day of Truce. The ideal day was impossible for many reasons, not least of all because bills accumulated so fast that the Wardens could not keep on sitting till they were all settled, even if no one broke the assurance made for the day before the meeting, its duration, and one or two days after.[4] Expert Border opinion in 1598 was agreed that Truces, when held at all, were held in form much as in theory.[5] But the great fact is that possibly about a quarter of the sixteen or seventeen hundred Truces that should have been held in Elizabeth's reign, were held, and that at some of these very little justice was done. No complete list of Truces is extant, nor can one be compiled. The Wardens and their clerks had much else to do; among other things to administer domestic March Law.

[1] 1563, §4.   [2] 1486, §10.   [3] 1556, §5.   [4] Bell, 87 (back).
[5] C.B.P. ii, 1001–3, 1010.

PART IX

ENGLISH DOMESTIC BORDER LAW

THIS had four sources which sometimes overlapped. They were Acts of Parliament, ordinances made by Lieutenants or Wardens, the ancient statutes of such towns as Berwick and Carlisle, and the customary March Treasons appended to the form and order of a Warden Court. About 1580 a statute of March Treasons seems to have been contemplated, but it never became law.[1] The ordinary laws of England such as the 'statute for hews and cryes' ran in the Borders,[2] but some four very important Acts and a number of lesser ones applied to the Borders only. The earliest still in force seems to have been 15 Richard II, c. 16, which forbade the unlicensed export of food or armour to Scotland, and which Forster was warned to keep.[3]

14 Henry VI, c. 3, fixed the Cumberland Assizes and gaol delivery at Carlisle. 31 Henry VI, c. 3, limited the Warden's powers of arrest for offences triable in Warden Courts to the three Border Counties, under penalty of two years' imprisonment and a fine of a hundred shillings. 22 Edward IV, c. 8, was intended to benefit Berwick and increase its population, by forbidding the export of goods to Scotland except through Berwick or Carlisle. The penalty was the forfeiture of the merchandise, and the Act was enforced as late as 1602.[4] 11 Henry VII, c. 18, §§ 2, 3, exempted 'any person holding office and being in service' in Berwick or Carlisle from following the king in war. 2 & 3 Edward VI, c. 34, made the sheriffs of Northumberland, like other sheriffs, enter into recognizances before exercising office.

14 Elizabeth, c. 13, annexed Hexham and Hexham-

---

[1] C.B.P. i, 81.   [2] C.B.P. i, 834, ii, 171; 27 Eliz., c. 13.   [3] A.P.C. xiv, 245.   [4] C.B.P. ii, 1545.

shire to Northumberland owing to their former use as a sanctuary by offenders.[1]

43 Elizabeth, c. 16, dealt with the maintenance and repair of bridges near Carlisle.

The four most important laws were as follows:

23 Henry VIII, c. 16, had dealt with the sale of horses, geldings, and mares into Scotland without the king's licence. It was felony for the seller, exchanger, deliverer, and also the man dealing with him. Wardens in their Warden courts, and Justices of the Peace in their Quarter Sessions might try the cases, and any Englishman might lawfully arrest any Scot leading or conveying any horse, &c., into Scotland from England, and should have half the value of the horse, the king taking the rest. This law had been repealed by some general words in the Acts of Edward VI and Mary, and was re-enacted by 1 Elizabeth, c. 7.[2] It did not apply to horses brought, for example, from Norway, if the ship put into Berwick.[3] Horse-selling against this law seems to have been very common about 1579–80, and efforts were made to stop it.[4] The sellers occasionally included gentry such as Sir Cuthbert Colling-wood.[5] James VI was involved in the traffic, and was greatly annoyed when his English agent, Ashfield, was made drunk by the English ambassador and conveyed to England in 1599.[6] But, in spite of the occasional energy of the English government, William Selby estimated in 1601 that three out of every four horses in Scotland between the two seas were English, and the price in England had therefore become so high that none save gentry could afford to pay it. The selling was done partly with the Warden's connivance and partly by the use of 'Plac-quettes' granted for no definite time, and used sometimes for twenty years and for the sale of sixty horses instead of two.[7] The Scots horses were according to Fynes Moryson 'full of spirit and patient of labour but very little'.[8] Hence the Scots desire for English geldings. There seems, how-

---

[1] D'Ewes, 103, 134, 200.   [2] D'Ewes, 22.   [3] A.P.C. x, 76.   [4] A.P.C. xi, 131–2; C.B.P. i, 75, 104.   [5] C.B.P. i, 601.   [6] Spotswood, iii, 79–80.   [7] C.B.P. ii, 1368.   [8] Travellers, 86.

ever, to have been some unlicensed export from Scotland to France.[1]

The other three Acts dealt with Border fortification and government. 2 & 3 Philip and Mary, c. 1, was an Act for the rebuilding of castles and forts, and for the enclosing of grounds from the Borders towards and against Scotland. It referred to the three Border counties and to the Bishopric. After December 1, 1555, it legalized commissions to inquire into decays of castles, fortresses and 'Fortelettes villageis', houses and habitations, and the causes and remedies thereof, and into the number and place of new castles, &c., to be built, and into the parts most apt for enclosure and for conversion to tillage. Order might then be taken for the same, and tenants taxed to provide money, and bound to sell wood and lend oxen at reasonable prices. It applied to places within twenty miles of Scotland. The commissioners might make and repeal by-laws, and their decrees assigning the lands of owners, who refused to pay the tax, to others who would pay, were to bind all persons in perpetuity when certified into Chancery with the royal assent. No decree should be binding unless certified, and Parliament alone should alter the decrees, which might even extend to Crown Lands. Penalties exacted under the Act were to be used for carrying out its objects, and the Act was to last for ten years and to the end of the next Parliament then following. Elizabeth thought that the non-observance of this Act was the prime cause of decays,[2] and in 1580–1 it was revived and strengthened by an Act for the fortifying of Borders towards Scotland,[3] which applied to the three Border counties and to the Bishopric. This Act states that owing to decays commissioners may be appointed to inquire by the oaths of twelve men or more, or otherwise, into the decays of houses since 27 Henry VIII, and the causes thereof, and to give orders for reform. Commissioners may order owners to rebuild decayed houses, take measures to see that tenants are properly furnished and have them evicted if through their own fault they are not, and make sub-

[1] R.P.C.S. i, 561.   [2] For. viii, 2453–4; C.S.P. ii, 778.   [3] 23 Eliz., c. 4.

tenants contribute towards the principal tenant's furniture if the tenement is too small to maintain a man furnished. Absentee landlords and tenants who do not appear on the commissioners' summons may be fined. Commissioners shall not interfere with lessees or copyholders unless their lands seem to have been liable to service. Future lessees shall be resident on their lands, or else somewhere within the Borders and put in a meet person. Farmers who leave the Borders are to forfeit their lands within twelve months, and the lord shall put in a resident tenant.

There was some controversy between the two Houses over this Bill, and the Lords finally yielded,[1] but the Act was not enforced at once.[2] This was possibly owing to Border complaints, the chief objections being the danger of curtailing the power of the lords in dealing with their tenants, thus rendering the former discontented, and the fact that most of the tenants being bondmen and by nature insolent through barbarous education opposed all burdens laid upon them by their lords. There was also said to be danger, as proved in later years, in devising remedies whereby multitudes had cause to complain and general revolt was fostered.[3] When a commission was appointed it did so little that the gentry thereafter continued laying towns waste to make 'demaynes' thereof for their own private commodity to the decay of the Border and hindrance of the Queen's service. This is Forster's statement.[4]

Nothing seems to have been done towards carrying the Act out fully, but at the very end of the reign a further Act, 43 Elizabeth, c. 13, was passed for the more peaceable government of the Border counties and of the Bishopric. After reciting the evil state of the Borders, it enacts that any who take or detain people prisoners for ransom, or spoil their goods upon deadly feud or otherwise, and any who aid them or assent, and any who take blackmail or give it, or wilfully burn any barn or stack of corn or grain in the said counties, and are convicted before the Justices of Assize, the Justice of Gaol Delivery, the Justices of Oyer

---

[1] D'Ewes, 273.   [2] A.P.C. xiii, 349.   [3] C.B.P. i, 82.   [4] C.B.P. i, 787.

and Terminer, or Justices of the Peace, shall be felons, and suffer death without clergy, and forfeit as in the case of felony. To prevent outlaws attending fairs, lists shall be sent by the clerks of the peace to the sheriffs who shall proclaim them in the County courts and in thirteen named towns, and monthly at future County courts. Mayors shall proclaim them at fairs, and once in six weeks at markets. Any one wittingly and willingly having intercourse with outlaws and not doing his best to arrest them shall be imprisoned for six months and till he can find two sureties for his good behaviour for one year after. Justices of Assize, &c., shall try and punish sheriffs and mayors for offences under this Act. The Act shall not abridge the Warden's power. This is noted by Camden as a good law,[1] but it was passed too late to have any effect.

The second type of English domestic Border law is the ordinances made by certain Lieutenants and Wardens, of which the Bell MS. contains three examples, the first being those made by Lord Wharton at Newcastle in 1552. They consist of ten heads regarding watches, rising at and following fray, recetting fugitives, informing officers about thieves and fugitives, practising with rebels, attendance at and keeping of March days, residence of gentry and officers, speaking with Scots, the furnishing of tenants and servants, and the publication of these ordinances. The ordinances were signed by Wharton, his three deputies, and thirty-eight others, including the Marshal of Berwick and the Sheriff of Northumberland.[2] The second, which has not been printed, is given in full below from the Bell MS.[3] with notes. It is as follows:

'Articles accorded by the Right hono^rll Thomas Earle of Sussex, Viscount fitzwater Lo. Egremont and Burwell, captain of the Queenes Maties gentlemen pencōners and gent at arms, knight of the most hono^rll order of the Garter, Chief Justice and Justice of Oyer of all her Maties forrests, parkes, chaises and warraines by South Trent, Lo. president of her Maties councell established in the North partes, and her highnes Leiuetenant generall of all her said

---

[1] Camden, 635.   [2] Bell, 177–9; Leges, 143–7.   [3] 180–2.

North parts.   At Anwick the xiith of November 1570.

| 'Keaping of watches.' | 1. | That the night watches for townes and fourds shalbe kept presentlie in the townes and at the fourds fit to be watched, and th'other foords dampned, and that day watches shalbe also kept in places accustomed, and the setters, searchers and overseers appointed as they were in former watches, And if any be deade other to supplie by th'appointment of the wardens; and gent. And that diligent watch be maid by the watches for apprehending of such as passe into Scotland, or out of Scotland with lettres or messages.' |

Bell's clauses are not numbered, but I have numbered them for purposes of reference. This clause corresponds with the first of Lord Wharton's clauses, *ut supra*.

| 'following of fray.' | 2. | 'Itm̄ that everie man upon the fray raysed by night or day shall follow the fray upon paine of imprisonment for vii days and losse of iiis. iiijd.' |

This clause corresponds with Lord Wharton's second clause, except that fine and imprisonment replace the penalty of death. In 1592 it is noted that on the English West Marches ordinary watches were not observed as in former times, and hue and cry was disused as no one dare follow it.[1]

| 'Those that faile in following to answeare the goods stolne | 3. | 'Itm̄ that the persons that shall faile in answering or following of the fray shall answeare the value of the goods lost if any be lost and the persons that reskewe the goods shall upon a manifest desert, by adventure, have for their travell, in peace tyme if it be within England grownd after the raite of xiid. in the pound. And |
| For reskewe of cattell xiid. in England: for Scotland iis. in the pound.' | | if it be within Scotland grownd after the rate of iis. in the pound of the goods reskewed, and the owner to have his goods presentlie, the reskewer to have his porcōn of the owner, and if the owner refuse to deliver it the Warden to compell him.' |

This clause was new.

---

[1] Dom. Add. iii, 334–5, no. 39.

4. 'Itm̄ if there be any Scottsman that shall come into England and shall take and carry away by stelth or otherwise unlawfully any goods belonging to any Englishman, and the said Scotts man shall (either going to the fact or returning from the fact) be received by any Englishman or Scottsman dwelling in England, the partie so receiving shall answere the goods lost and be compelled thereto by the Warden of the M̄ches where the goods were lost, and if the partie that lost the goods and the receiver dwell both in severall wardenries then both the Wardens shall joyne to see due execution of this article.'

'the receyver of a Scottsman to answere the goods.'

Clauses 3 and 4 of Lord Wharton's articles refer to recett of fugitives, but the penalty is death.

'Everie castle to give warning by fire when any fray ys.'

5. 'Itm̄ That everie man that hath a castle or a towre shall upon every fray raysed in the night give warning to the countrie by fire in the topps of the castle or towre in such sort as he shalbe directed from his warning castle upon paine of iiis. iiijd.'

This clause was new.

'Places to be appointed for discrying of fire.'

6. 'Itm̄ That two or three or moe speciall places be appointed in everie wardenrie as warning places where watch shalbe nightlie kept, to the end that upon fire discryed to be given to other Castles, there may be alse fire given to warne the whole countrie and that the place be knowne to the people that they may knowe the cause of the fire in those places to be onelie upon the rasing of the fray and not for such other causes as other Beacons com̄onlie be fired, and that the countrie be devided into partes whereby the Castles of everie parte shall knowe how to receive the warning.'

This clause was new.

7. 'Itm̄ that everie one that shall have any goods stolne or taken, within x daies after the stealing thereof, deliver to the Warden or deputie of the M̄che where the goods were stolne a bill of

'To deliver notes of goods stolen within x daies.' the goods lost and if he knowe the names of the partie that took them to the end that the Warden may at everie moneths end make up his book of the hurts done in his Wardenrie that moneth, and by whome it may be knowne whereby he shall understand the staite of his office everie moneth and a perfect booke thereof which for many reasons is very necessarie.'

This clause was new.

'to keape horse.' 8. 'Itm̄ that all gent and freholders shall keape horse, armour and weapon for themselves and their familie, and cause their tenents to keape horse armor and weapons according to the auncient use and custome of the borders.'

This obligation was old, but the clause new.

'landlords to appoint tenents sufficient ground for finding of horses.' 9. 'Itm̄ That everie landslord [sic] shall appointe sufficient ground to everie of his tenents where upon he may finde horse, armour and weapons according to the custome of the borders.'

This clause was a partial addition to Lord Wharton's ninth article.

'not fitt yt land for manuring be waiste.' 10. 'Itm̄ that no lands lord shall permit to suffer any part of his land that is fit to be manured to be waist without a tenent or occupyer longer then of necessitie he shalbe forced.'

This clause was new.

'for enclosers upon the borders.' 11. 'Itm̄ that lands lords upon the borders shall consider what they and their tenents shalbe able to doe to enclose their townes upon the borders, and the whole countrie shall joyne in aide to helpe them with that they cannot of themselves doe so as they may enclose this yeare certaine townes upon the Ring [sic] of the borders with ditch and quicksett, and others the next yeare, and so yearlie untill all be enclosed neare the ringe whereby the uttermost partes being strengthened the people of England with their goods may lie in safetie and the Scotts entring

> England come in perill, and when the border towne be enclosed the borderers shall aid the inland men to enclose also their borders.'

This clause was new. 2 & 3 Philip and Mary, c. 1, had lapsed by this time and was not revived till 23 Elizabeth, c. 4.

'No man to take a Scotts- man in service without the Wardens li- cence.'

12. 'Itm̄ That no man receive any Scottsman to be his servant without licence of the Warden of the M̂ches under his hand writing, and that everie man within one moneth make certificate to the Warden of the names of all such Scottsmen as be his tenents at this present, which of them be denizens, which not, and that everie man that hath any Scottsman to his servant shall deliver his name to the Warden within one moneth and everie man that shall hereafter take any Scotts- man to his servant shall before he receive him into his service, give his name to the Warden, and that everie man that hath or hereafter shall have any Scottsman to his servant shall bring foorth his servant to answere or shall answere for him during his abode with him.'

'Scottsmen being servants to be brought before the Warden.'

13. 'Itm̄ That noe man shall put away Scottsman [*sic*] from his service before he first bring him to the Warden to offer him to answere all mat- ters wherewith he shalbe charged, to the end everie Warden may make a perfect booke there- of and thereby have knowledge of all the Scotts- men within his charge from tyme to tyme.'

'To apprehend seditious persons.'

14. 'Itm̄ That good order be given to apprehend all such persons as shall report any seditious, lewde or slanderous tailes or rumors touching the Queenes Ma^tte or any of her highnes counsell or any of the nobilitie or principall officers of the Realme or that shalbe derogative directlie or indirectlie to the peace and quiet of the Realme.'

The last three clauses are new.
The document is unsigned in Bell's text.
The third example is some articles made by Huntyngdon with the consent of Scroope, his deputy, Sir R. Carey, and

others after a meeting at Newcastle, soon after Scroope took office, in September 1593. They refer to the West Marches and are given in the Bell MS.[1] Certain 'Heades to be considered upon' were given by Scroope to the gentry of his March and the articles seem to have been drawn up with the aid of their answers, unless Bell's date of the latter, December 10, 1593, is correct, which seems very unlikely as Scroope enclosed them in his letter to Burghley on May 12, 1593.[2] They are styled laws by Bell.[3] The first three clauses concern pledges to be given by 'principalls and chiefes' for their 'dependers', and the punishment of chiefs who refuse, and of those who 'recet' them. The offender's goods are to be seized and his wife and family evicted. The next two, about escheats and compounding with thieves, are left to the Warden's 'wiser consideration'. To avoid deadly feuds all future murders in the West Wardenry shall be punished with death and loss of goods. The Warden shall try to appease former feuds, and ward and bind those who refuse to agree. Persons threatening others may be bound over and fined. No Scots prisoner shall ride a mile beyond his prison, or his keeper shall be imprisoned. Imprisonment, besides punishment by March Law, shall be the fate of 'recettors' of Scots felons or murderers. Payers of 'black maile' shall be fined £6, and English brokers and takers shall be punished at the Warden's discretion. Compounding with English thieves without the Warden's licence shall lead to punishment as an accessory. Defaults in watches shall be punished by fines, forfeitures, and 'corporall punishment'. Rewards shall be given to informers about breaches of these and other orders. Recognizances shall be kept in a book, and forfeitures paid to the treasurer of the 'countrie'. Fines shall be collected and spent as ordered on 'hurt soldiers and marriners'. Lastly Sussex's laws about fray and furniture are revived. The ten signatories include Sir R. Carey and William Musgrave the Sheriff of Cumberland. Other examples of this type of law exist.[4]

---

[1] 151–4.   [2] Bell, 146–50; C.B.P. i, pp. 457–9.   [3] 152.   [4] C.S.P. iv, 32; For. ix, 2108.

The third class of domestic English Border Law comprises town statutes such as those of Berwick[1] and Carlisle. The latter contained by-laws about watches, Scots, apprentices, &c.[2] The former include fifty 'auntient statutes', and about ten 'newe orders' made to last till the new fortifications were finished. They are too long for more than passing reference in a general history.

The last class is that of March Treasons, a subject which has never been dealt with fully. The Bell MS.[3] under the heading 'The charge of the Warden Court' gives a list of seventeen sets of circumstances and fourteen 'additionalls' into which the jury had to inquire. Nicolson printed fourteen in *Leges Marchiarum*.[4] Sir R. Bowes in 1551 gave seven, but did not pretend that his list was complete.[5] Nicolson and Burn print twenty-two and a half all lumped together. One of their omissions is in *Leges Marchiarum*. Here Bell's list is given shortly, except those omitted by Nicolson and Burn, which are given in full.

1. March treason, i. e. trysting with a Scot and bringing him into England to slaughter, burn, rob, steal, &c. This was common.[6]

2. Aiding, recetting, or riding with a Scot who came to do the above.

3. Harbouring, recetting, or conveying a Scot after he had done the above.

4. Putting forth or supporting any Scot in peace or war 'with any armor or artillerie belonging to warre' without the Warden's licence.

5. Selling or putting forth 'any manner of victualls' or warlike stores without the Warden's licence. Bell adds in the margin 'Tempore guerrae'.

6. Selling horses to Scots without the Warden's licence.[7]

7. Selling 'of intent and purpose' a horse to an Englishman to sell to a Scot.

8. Doing anything to break the truce made by the Commissioners, as in killing, assaulting, forraying, or

---

[1] Scott, 447–56; see also For. iii, 594–5; C.B.P. i, p. 269, no. 230 (4), nos. 822, 896, ii, nos. 949, 966, 1470.   [2] Creighton, 119.   [3] 166–70.
[4] 127 ff.   [5] R.T. iv, 2.   [6] C.B.P. ii, 129.   [7] Cf. 1 Eliz. c. 7.

robbing any Scot in Scotland. The mention of the Scots Queen in this clause dates it as before 1587.

9. Murdering, assaulting, affraying, or robbing any Scot who entered England with a proper safe-conduct.

10. Giving knowledge of any intended 'inrode' in time of war.

11. Marrying a 'Scotts woman or confederate in friendship' without the Warden's licence.[1]

12. Selling or sending timber into Scotland for house-building.

13. Conveying gold or silver coin then current, plate, or bullion into Scotland above forty shillings at a time.

14. Bewraying the plan of any Englishman to annoy Scotland in war time.

15. 'Also if any Englishman and Scotts within this Wardenrie enterprise to coyne any money either of the Queenes Majesties coyne or the coyne of any other foreyne realme and uttered the same.' Nicolson and Burn omit this. *Leges Marchiarum* gives 'of' vice 'and', and 'realm' vice 'wardenrie'.

16. Trysting and intercommuning with Scots without the Warden's licence, or with it to the hurt of the realm. The jury had also to inquire 'what hurt cometh thereby from tyme to tyme'. The Privy Council in 1592 described unlicensed trysting as 'one of the meanest of March Treasons that maie be'.[2]

17. Receiving or putting forth 'any Scottsman pilgrime or other', and keeping and 'recetting' them with their writings and money without the Warden's licence 'or otherwise then is accustomed by order of the Lawes of Marches'. This is the last of the cases given in *Leges Marchiarum*. Bell gives the following under the heading 'Additionalls', of which numbers 18, 19, 22–5, 30, and part of 31 are omitted by Nicolson and Burn.

18. 'Itm ye shall enquire if any Englishman have contrarie his dutie of allegeance entred into any unlawfull assurance, rebellious promisse, condition or bond with any Scottsman.'

[1] See Dom. Add. iii, 334–5, no. 39; C.B.P. ii, p. 392.   [2] A.P.C. xxii, 552.

19. 'Also if any Englishmen have into his or their companies receyved, lodged or comforted any other Englishman or forreyner, malefactors and offendors against her Majesties Lawes; and the same openlie or privatelie have conveyed or put over into the Realme of Scotland.'

20. Not keeping watches ordained by the Wardens against Scots and English riders 'obedientlie and well'.

21. Not rising and riding 'at any commandment warning cry or fray' raised by the Warden, deputy or searchers or watchers 'so oft as hurt or prejudice hath bene likelie to ensue unto this realme or m̃ches or to any subject within the same'.

22. 'Also if any person within the west wardenrie haith not at all tymes bene obedient in assisting ayding and supporting the Lo. Warden or his deputie in doing and executing of all and everie thing apperteyning to his authoritie after the lawes and customes of the m̃ches.'

23. 'Also if any person haith made any reskewe of any of the Lo. Wardens servants in doing or executing of any thing by the direction and commandment of the Lo. Warden, after the Lawes and Customes of the m̃ches.'

24. 'Also if any Englishman hath unlawfully taken away a Scottsman prisoner or his goods and the same deteyneth wilfully contrary to the Lo. Wardens commandment and custome of the borders.'

25. 'Also yow shall enquire if any Englishman without licence haith called for entrie of any Scottsman unlawfully taken prisoner at any tyme, and haith kept him or them without knowledge of the Lo. Warden or contrarie his commandment.'

26. Receiving any Scots fugitive or rebel or his goods against the laws or proclamation.

27. Unjustly filing a Scots bill on an Englishman for profit or of malice.

28. Hindering the 'trodds' of any Englishman pursuing his stolen goods which had been carried into Scotland.

29. Setting at liberty any Scot 'taken Read hand and with the manner' without the Warden's special licence.

30. 'Also if any Englishman haith mett, compounded and agreed with any Scottsman for his goods stolne from him without the Lo. Wardens licence.'

31. 'Also if any Englishman haith payed any black-maile either to Englishmen or Scotts. Th'offenders therein is [*sic*] to be fined v^{ll} str. and the brokers and takers of any such blackmaile being Englishmen are to be punished at the Lo. Wardens discretion.' Nicolson and Burn omit the penalty and substitute 'or any Englishman hath taken or received any such blackmaile'.

There are many instances of such payments,[1] but inquiry was difficult as witnesses were often overawed by the blackmailer.[2] The payment of blackmail by an Englishman to an Englishman was in 1595 stated to be new.[3] This bribing was said to be called 'Blackmeale' because the reason of its being taken was 'fowle and dishonest', and because it was paid 'In meale corne or victuall'.[4] Scroope stated in 1600 that if the taker of blackmail shared it with a Scot, as the custom was, it was March Treason, and punishable by death.[5] This raises the whole question, which is seemingly unsolvable, as to how many of the above thirty-one offences were March Treason and punishable by death.

There seems to have been no definite rule as to the administration of domestic justice on the Borders. The ordinary laws of the realm of course applied there and also the special laws mentioned above. The usual course of justice like sessions of the peace, punishment of felons, &c., sheriff's accountings and the like had very little place on the Borders, partly because of the power of the Warden 'crossing' it, and partly because private men took liberties and protected 'falters' to strengthen themselves.[6] It is clear that the Warden Court was the most important Law Court, and there is sufficient evidence of the way in which it was held. Sir Robert Bowes gave an account of the method used in the East and Middle Marches in 1551,[7]

[1] For. viii, 1973; C.B.P. ii, 129, 276, 431, 613, 1531.   [2] A.P.C. xxv, 384–5.   [3] A.P.C. xxv, 255.   [4] C.B.P. ii, p. 164.   [5] C.B.P. ii, 1192. [6] C.B.P. ii, 171, 184.   [7] R.T. iv (2).

and 'Th'ordre to keipe a Wardens Court', &c., in the time
of Henry, Lord Scroope, is given in *Leges Marchiarum*.[1]
In the Bell MS.[2] is a document headed 'To Keape a Warden Court', which was printed by Nicolson and Burn, but
chopped and changed about and interspersed with pieces
from the version in *Leges Marchiarum*. For instance, they
end up with a quotation from the latter as if it were from
Bell.[3] From the above three sources the following account
has been made, and the sources are noted unless all three
authorities agree.

Bowes in a short introduction states that proclamation
ought to be made, for about fourteen days before each
court, in all markets for 'all gentlemen, freeholders,
officers and headsmen borderers' to attend the court, and
for plaintiffs to cause defendants to be arrested. He adds
that the chief gentlemen fit to pass upon the inquest, and
others whose presence is necessary, ought to be summoned
by special letters from the Warden, and that it is good
policy to attach offenders known to the Warden before
the court is proclaimed. The court itself begins with an
'Oyez', and the reading of the Queen's commission of
Wardenry by the warden sergeant. That done, all gentlemen summoned to serve are called upon to answer their
names. A jury is then empanelled, and Bowes gives its
numbers as twenty-four, or fifteen at the least. The others
do not mention them. The jury is then sworn, first the
foreman and then the rest (four at a time according to
Bell and *Leges Marchiarum*) to inquire truly and make
true presentment to the Warden. This latter, says Bowes,
should be in writing. The jury is then charged to inquire
into various matters or March treasons, and Bowes adds
that they should also settle complaints made to the Warden about booty, prisoners, ransoms, &c. Then, according
to Bell and *Leges Marchiarum*, the jury go apart. (Here
Bowes almost fails us, and the rest depends upon the other
two sources unless otherwise stated.) Then, after another
'Oyez', men who have any complaints or bills triable in the
court bring them forward, and recognizances are called

[1] 120 ff.   [2] 166 ff.; cf. S.P. Borders, xli, 241 ff.   [3] N. & B. i, pp. xxvi ff.

and sureties taken. Then there must be a lull till the jury are ready with their verdict. They are then called by name, the bills taken, and the prisoners brought to the bar, charged and made to plead. If any plead not guilty, a jury of gentlemen is called, the prisoner being allowed to challenge any, and when the jury is full it swears to make true delivery according to the evidence, and is charged to inquire into the prisoner's guilt, and, if it finds him guilty of March Treason, to inquire also into the lands he holds and their value. (Bowes says a man 'arrayned' for March Treason 'can have no challenges to any of the inquest that passe upon his deliverance neither yet can he have his clergy'. His lands also are forfeit. Yet the officer should take care not to put 'his extreame enemyes' upon the inquest.)[1] Then an 'Oyez' is made for witnesses against the prisoner, and they are heard. The jury then retires and returns when it has agreed on the verdict. Bell here ends his account of the proceedings of the court with the words 'and after judgement given by my Lord adjourne the court to a new day of warning'. The manuscript copied in *Leges Marchiarum*, however, adds an instruction to the executioner to behead the man, and an exhortation which the Warden might make to the prisoner if he pleased. All this is printed by Nicolson and Burn as if it were part of the Bell MS.

Warden Courts were held well inside the frontier at such places as Hexham, Alnwick, or Morpeth. Arrests could only be made by the Border officers within the Border counties. Both English and Scots prisoners were tried, and, if guilty of March Treason, beheaded. For instance, fifteen Liddesdale men were convicted of spoiling a poor man's house in Tynedale, having been taken in the attempt, and executed.[2] It was sometimes as hard to convict an English prisoner at a Warden Court as it was to convict a Scot at a day of Truce. Eure notes in 1596 that of about sixty prisoners only three were found guilty. One of them, a notable March breaker, was 'so befrinded by

---

[1] R.T. iv (2), 35.   [2] C.B.P. i, 508, ii, 567, 569, 596; For. viii, 917; 31 Henry VI, c. 3.

the jurie, that that daie and night, and the next daye att night, noe verdicte would be given', and so, says Eure, 'for saifitie of the gentlemens health I was inforced to drawe the prisonner from them, and receave there half verdicte of those theie had agreed on. The jurie rested withoute meate and drinke accordinge the custome in like case, almost to there undoeinge'. This breach of the common law by the Warden was done by the advice of the Queen's learned 'councell'.[1] Sometimes the gentry of the Border tried to call a man's life in question for March Treason, as a means of getting revenge, and in such cases the Privy Council, if petitioned, might interfere and order the Warden not to proceed till the Queen's pleasure was known.[2]

Apart from the Warden Courts, which dealt mainly with matters peculiar to the Marches, there was some attempt to carry out the ordinary laws of the realm on the Borders, and naturally there were conflicts of jurisdiction, as in 1600.[3] There being no definite rule for every case, the Privy Council used its discretion when necessary.[4] It sometimes recommended torture.[5] There were coroners' inquests,[6] and the Justices of the Peace held Sessions whereat execution was administered to offenders and order taken for the Marches. The Warden sometimes presided at these.[7] These J.P.s were sometimes old and slack.[8] Justices of 'oier and terminer' held jail deliveries sometimes extending in length to three days, as at Hexham in 1596, where fifty-nine prisoners were tried; two escaped, six pleaded clergy successfully, and only nine were executed.[9] The ordinary County Assizes were held too,[10] not always without hindrance, as for instance at Carlisle in 1597, when on the second day at 4 a.m. the jailer's house was attacked, two prisoners rescued and horsed, and their pursuit prevented by men with 'gunnes and dagges'.[11] It is not surprising then that the attempts

---

[1] C.B.P. ii, 249.   [2] A.P.C. xxii, 552.   [3] C.B.P. ii, 1250.   [4] A.P.C. xiii, 316–17.   [5] A.P.C. vii, 222.   [6] C.B.P. i, 232, 252.   [7] For. x, 603; C.B.P. ii, 249.   [8] C.B.P. ii, 1470.   [9] C.B.P. ii, 248.   [10] Dom. Add. iii, 252, no. 106; A.P.C. ix, 291; C.B.P. i, 721.   [11] C.B.P. ii, 682.

to enforce the ordinary laws were somewhat intermittent.[1]
There were also local courts like those at Carlisle and
Berwick. At Carlisle the Mayor held a court, but if he
did wrong the Privy Council might call upon the Warden
to interfere. This was one of the English courts at which
a Scot might sue.[2] In Berwick there was a conflict between
the Mayor's and the Marshal's Court. The Mayor had
to hold four quarter sessions a year for trial of titles of
lands and for administration of justice upon felons and
malefactors in that liberty. He also held courts every
fourteen days for the trial, by a jury of twelve sufficient
burgesses, of debts and trespasses. The Marshal claimed
that his court had been established by the Privy Council
in King Edward's time; but the Mayor denied this, and
said the Marshal had only held one court in the two years
ending June 1584, and that no justice had been done
therein. Finally the Marshal was ordered to hold a court
once a quarter. A burgess who had an action against a
soldier had to proceed there, while a soldier had to sue
a burgess in the Mayor's Court. Thus the burgesses
failed to get their desired complete jurisdiction over all
persons in pay.[3] Berwick also claimed to be exempt from
the sheriff's jurisdiction and from that of the warden-
sergeant, saying that he could make no arrest within its
liberties but only 'commend' them to the Marshal's
officers in the Town.[4]

Above all these courts stood the Council of the North,[5]
which had considerable Border jurisdiction. Among its
members were such experienced Border officials as Henry,
Lord Scroope, Hunsdon, Forster, and Sir William Drury,
who were not, of course, bound to attend continually. It
held four sessions a year, lasting a month, three at York,
and the fourth for twenty days at Newcastle or somewhere
in the Bishopric or Northumberland, and then for eight or
more days at Carlisle or somewhere in the West Marches.
Its business was, however, only partly judicial, for it had

---

[1] Creighton, 85; A.P.C. xi, 195.   [2] A.P.C. xiv, 251-2.   [3] C.B.P. i,
240.   [4] C.B.P. ii, 494.   [5] The whole subject has been excellently
treated in Miss R. R. Reid's *The King's Council in the North*.

to supervise the work of the Wardens and to see Acts like
2 & 3 Philip and Mary, c. 1, carried out. Its judicial
work was with notable offenders.[1] Occasionally there were
attempts to get the Privy Council to call cases up to
London, but the Privy Council showed little inclination
to do so.[2] It rather discouraged appeals to the Central
Courts, as the bringing up of the gentry as witnesses was
costly and led to the unfurnishing of the country. Moreover, the loose Borderers were bolder in the absence of the
gentlemen.[3]

[1] Dom. Add. ii, 462–6, no. 59.   [2] A.P.C. x, 105.   [3] A.P.C. xiii, 193–4.

PART X

SCOTS DOMESTIC BORDER LAW

IF existing evidence is to be trusted, Scots domestic
Border Law was limited to Acts of Parliament and Convention, occasional orders by the Privy Council, and 'the
poyntis belangand to the Wardane court', but it is probable that the Wardens and keepers, like their opposites,
made and published ordinances which have been temporarily or permanently lost.

The first Act of any importance seems to be that of
October 13, 1455,[1] which forbids Scots giving warning of
Scots riding in England, passing into England in war
time, trysting with Englishmen or taking unlicensed
assurances with them, carrying off goods taken at a Warden 'rode' before they had been divided, and supplying
victuals to Berwick. All these things were treason. Englishmen entering Scotland unlicensed were declared lawful prisoners, and armed men were to be ready to follow
the Warden when required. Other Acts of the same
century governed the Warden's duties and powers.[2] The
Act of 1535, no. 22, 'For bigging of strenthis on ye Bordouris' seems to have been the only other important Act
before 1567.

During our period there was an Act 'anent' warnings in
the King's causes in places 'ubi non patet tutus accessus',[3]
and an Act for furthering criminal justice all over the
realm[4] which applied especially to the Borders; an Act
'anent' the disorders in the West Marches[5] and one
'anent' pledges.[6]

Besides these there were four very important Acts as
follows:

1. 1567, no. 27. 'Anent thift, and resset of thift, taken

---

[1] A.P.S. ii, 44–5.   [2] See A.P.S. ii, 35, no. 4, 92, no. 3, 144, nos. 4–6, 165,
no. 4, 214, no. 6, and 220, no. 9.   [3] A.P.S. iii, 456.   [4] A.P.S. iii, 459.
[5] A.P.S. iv, 22.   [6] A.P.S. iv, 179, 236.

of presonaris be thevis, or bands for ransounis, and punichement of the samin.' For remedy of the daily thefts and murders taking place, and the payment of blackmail by inland people, the 'reset' or helping of thieves may be proceeded against as 'airt and pairt of thair thifteous deidis'. The trial shall be by Assize. No thief shall take any Scot prisoner, and bands already given are voided, and it is treason for the thieves to try to get them fulfilled. No one shall take assurance of thieves or pay them blackmail. When thieves try to steal in the incountry the inhabitants shall raise the fray against them, or be held partakers with them.[1] This Act was not effective enough, and sterner methods were used in 1572, when the Council ordered three Borderers 'to birne the houssis, cornes and gudes of the persons underwritten', take the owners and bring them to the Regent, and not let their wives and bairns occupy their lands.[2] Troubles in the inward parts of the realm continued to prevent its enforcement and it was proclaimed again in September 1573.[3] In July 1600 it was again stated to be neglected and therefore proclaimed anew.[4]

2. 1587, no. 59. 'For the quieting and keeping in obedience of the disordered subjects inhabitants of the borders, highlands and isles.' The Privy Council shall sit on the first of each month to hear complaints, and a register shall be kept. Landlords shall find caution to present their men when accused and to satisfy the injured party. Non-resident landlords shall have thieves arrested. Chieftains of clans shall enter pledges. Notorious thieves born in Liddesdale, Ewesdale, Eskdale, Annandale, and the Debatable Lands shall be sent back to their birthplaces. Registers of pledges and of landlords shall be kept. The heirs of cautioners for good rule shall be bound, and sureties made by landlords shall not supersede those of chieftains. When stolen goods are carried to and 'resset' by another clan, the plaintiff shall pursue the chief of that clan. Persons seeking pardons for thieves shall be liable

---

[1] A.P.S. iii, 31–2.   [2] R.P.C.S. ii, 127.   [3] R.P.C.S. ii, 275–6.
[4] R.P.C.S. vi, 137.

as thieves. The Justice Clerk shall pursue the takers and payers of blackmail, and send 'close valentines'[1] to masters of notable thieves to present them for trial, twice a year. No one shall marry an English Border woman under pain of death. The Wardens shall inquire as to Englishmen occupying Scots ground in pasturage or tillage. Pledges for Borderers shall be placed north of the Forth. Fugitives and their families shall have no action against their landlords for burning or ejection. Mediate persons who sell goods for thieves shall suffer banishment and loss of movables.[2]

3. 1594, no. 37. An Act for the punishment of 'thift, reif, oppressioun and sorning'. This was directed against the Highlands and Borders. A list of suspected robbers shall be made and landlords shall find surety to make their tenants answerable. All suspected persons shall be 'given in valentines' to their masters to make them appear before the judges. Householders who do not appear shall be denounced rebels and fugitives. The last clause is as follows: 'It shall be lawful to true and honest men to concur and join themselves in counsels and actions for defence of the lives and goods of themselves and their tenants against thieves and sorners and to follow and pursue them' . . . and to take them and imprison or execute them.[3]

4. 1600, no. 35. An Act anent Border 'thiftis'. The cause of disorders being their impunity, no Warden shall take redress of goods as satisfaction of the party injured 'but shall cause execute with all rigour the laws and acts of parliament against thieves and their recetters, and cause them to be punished to the death conform to their deserving'. If any one be fugitive for crime, the Warden, &c., 'shall cause burn his house, put his wife and bairns forth of the same' and proclaim his disobedience at the market cross to prevent 'recet'. This Act was originally made at the meeting at Falkland and confirmed a year later. It also applied to the Highlands.[4] The increasing severity

---

[1] 'Close valentines' means 'sealed letters sent by royal authority'.   [2] A.P.S. iii, 461–5.   [3] A.P.S. iv, 71–3.   [4] A.P.S. iv, 181–2, 237.

of these Acts shows increase of disorders and the impotence of the government.

One example of what may be called Orders in Council must suffice. In November 1582 the Council decreed that Borderers accused of 'thift, stowth, fyre-rasing, oppin rubbereis, oppressions, and utheris capitall crymes quhatsumevir' should be henceforth tried in the Tolbooth at Edinburgh.[1]

Finally 'Thir are the poyntis belangand to the Wardane court'. There are about a dozen of them, and in England they would have been called March Treasons. The only list extant dates from the fifteenth century and its chief points are warning Englishmen of 'Scottishmenis oistis', warning Englishmen to come into Scotland, stealing Scots goods and putting them in England, 'recetting' stolen goods or horses 'in Scotis hostis', supplying victualls, goods, or arms to the English Marches, trysting without licence with Englishmen, helping English prisoners to escape, &c.[2]

The administration of domestic justice on the Scots Borders is a very tangled subject. Warden Courts are not to be distinguished from what were called Justice Courts, or even from the Steward Courts of such places as Annandale. An account of the last is printed in *Leges Marchiarum*,[3] and says that besides 'all actions concerning Chancellarie' it dealt with 'all criminal causes sic as assisters with England', as well as 'murders, fire, ravishing of women, stouth and sic like'. It was supposed to meet 'in the Tolbuith of Lochmaben ouklie, every Thursday, beginning at eight hours in the morning, and remaining while three hours afternoon', but there seems to have been no tolbooth, so that it actually met in Loughmaben Kirk, which was 'verie unseemelie and unfitting'.[4] William Ker of Cesford, when Warden, held justice courts at Jedburgh,[5] and there seem to have been ordinary magistrates in the Borders, as there were in England, at Dumfries for example,[6] and commissions

---

[1] R.P.C.S. iii, 528–9.   [2] A.P.S. i, 714.   [3] 130–3.   [4] Mar and Kellie, 130.   [5] R.P.C.S. iv, 45.   [6] R.P.C.S. iv, 520–1.

of justiciary were given to men who were not Border officials.[1]

It does not, however, seem that any of these courts fulfilled a really useful purpose, but there were two other methods of dealing with Border cases. The first was to have them tried before the High Court of Justiciary at Edinburgh. Sometimes the criminals gave surety to appear before the next 'aire' of their county, sometimes the cases were finished at Edinburgh and the criminals hanged or fined there.[2] In 1590 Commissioners were appointed to sit at Edinburgh and to hear and determine Border causes every Monday in the year at 7 a.m. in summer and 8 a.m. in winter. All other commissions of justiciary were meanwhile suspended.[3]

A more effective method of punishment was a raid by the Regent or the King and the more or less summary execution of such thieves as were caught. The Regent Morton especially favoured this method. But when all things are considered it must be concluded that Melvill was right when he said in his Autobiography[4] that 'Heiland or Bordour thift' was a thing of which the 'remead falles amang impossibilities'.

[1] R.P.C.S. ii, 614–15.   [2] Pitcairn, ii, 405*–6*, 432*, 434*, 476*, 487*.
[3] C.B.P. i, 674–5.   [4] 190.

PART XI

'DECAY'

THE word 'decay' is often used in Border papers with no exactly defined meaning. Sometimes it refers to the gradual falling into ruin of castles, sometimes to the decrease of horse or foot for Border service, sometimes to the laying waste of villages by riders, and sometimes to the decrease of land under tillage. It may therefore, not without justification, be taken as a whole to mean that 'something' which was 'rotten in the state of' the Borders.

That the Borders of both realms were in decay in 1558 and remained so is indisputable, and the causes are obviously divisible into two, the hostility of the opposite nation and domestic mismanagement. This hostility was old. In 1307 died Edward I, whose life's work had resulted in the stirring up of hatred which survived the Union of the Crowns, and even for a time the Union of the Parliaments. Scotland was driven into the arms of France, and the unwise efforts of Henry VIII and Protector Somerset made her (or rather part of her, for she was not a united nation) cling still more closely to France. Thus the Borderers had an outlet for their predatory habits which not only did not cease when the realms were officially at peace but even continued when the Marches had become officially known as the Middle Shires. Overpopulation in places like Redesdale, Tynedale, Teviotdale, and Liddesdale was the main reason why young men took to stealing for a livelihood,[1] and it was chiefly from their inroads that feuds between surnames like the Irvings and the Grames arose, whereby lands were 'spoilt and heried' and thereby 'decaied and ympoverished'.[2] The country people dared not kill thieves for fear of incurring fresh feuds,[3] for if a thief killed were of surname 'as a Davyson,

[1] C. J. Bates, *Hist. of Northumb.* 217; Hodgson, I, i, 70; C.H.M. iii, 540.
[2] C.B.P. i, 127, 158. [3] C.B.P. ii, 371.

a Younge, a Burne, a Pringle or Hall or anie thei make accompt of', then the slayer was likely 'dearly to buy it', for the thief's surname would take his life, or that of two of his kinsmen, in revenge. Sir Cuthbert Collingwood had seventeen of his tenants slain for honestly killing a Burne in defence of Prince and Country. Scots Wardens like Sir Robert Kerr, Baron Roxburgh, took part in feuds,[1] but their opposites, who were seldom Borderers, kept pretty clear of them. There were also internal feuds in both realms, and when these were healed there was more danger to the opposite Border.

The whole system of Border Laws was devised for the prevention of feuds and thefts, or, in default, for the redress of injuries, but for various reasons it was often a failure. One government did not trust the other, and with reason. Elizabeth's word was not always worth its face value, and James VI acknowledged that he sometimes encouraged the raiders.[2] But even under trustful and trustworthy governments there would have been difficulties. Elizabeth's position on her throne did not always seem secure, but was security itself when compared with the Scots government of that period. Burghley's record for long service was not approached in Scotland, and Sir Simon Musgrave was quite right in attributing Border offences to 'the uncerten and tickle governement of Scotland which hath continued of a long time there' and 'hathe incouradged and imboldenede the evill disposede persons of the borders there to comit murders and spoiles'.[3] He wrote in 1583, and four years later the strife of the Scots lords in Parliament prevented the appointment of a lieutenant for the Borders.[4] Elizabeth was strong enough to remove an unreliable Warden, and her writs could be executed anywhere in her realm, but James and his regents had to take large armed levies to the Borders when they wished to hold Justice Courts. The Scots Wardenries were often vacant or in dispute, so that justice was hard to get. An occasional English deputy like R. Lowther might find himself unable to command his

[1] C.B.P. ii, 373.　　[2] Laing, i, 81.　　[3] C.B.P. i, 165.　　[4] C.B.P. i, 523.

March,[1] and a Warden like Lord Eure might be unpopular and not very successful, but no English Wardenry
was ever so disturbed as the Scots West March,[2] no part
of any English March could defy the Warden, as Liddesdale defied the Scots Warden,[3] and no English Warden
had to depend on men like Fernieherst and Buccleugh for
justice in the greater part of his office.[4] Thus the Scots
Wardens were often unable to give redress even if they
wished, and as a result were mistrusted in England and
mistrusted the English in return. They were usually
'border-bredd persons', in whose 'unapnes' to bear office
Sir W. Bowes thought most of the Border troubles had
their origin.[5] Their 'often exchange' hindered redress as
they would seldom be responsible for past offences, their
object being, in English eyes, 'to defer justice and delay
time'.[6] It is true that men like Buccleugh and Sir R. Kerr
grounded their apologies on 'the unskillful inconstancie'
of their opposites,[7] and that James VI accused Thomas,
Lord Scroope, of deferring meetings,[8] but, when men like
Hunsdon, Henry, Lord Scroope, and Wyllughby are
compared with men like Buccleugh and any one of the
Cesfords, it is clear that we are dealing with two different
stages of civilization. It is true that in Ireland English
officials could descend below the level of the untutored
Irish, but no English Warden, or Keeper, acted as Sir
R. Kerr and Buccleugh acted before the marvellous reformation which followed their warding in England.
James VI, on one occasion, admitted the 'oversight' of his
officer and removed him,[9] but there was no such happen-
ing in England, Forster being removed for sins against
his own people rather than against the Scots. Neither is
there any English parallel to the licence given by James VI
to Sir R. Carey in 1601 to pursue with fire and sword
such men as had committed outrage on the English Borders and slain their own officer.[10] It was an open confession
of inability to do justice in the ordinary way. Generally,

---

[1] C.B.P. ii, 1170.　　[2] C.B.P. i, 291.　　[3] C.B.P. i, 399.　　[4] C.B.P.
ii, 171.　　[5] C.B.P. ii, 499.　　[6] C.B.P. ii, 1040.　　[7] C.B.P. ii, 909.
[8] C.B.P. ii, 1419.　　[9] C.B.P. i, 265.　　[10] C.B.P. ii, 1348.

however, no such confession was made, and distrust arose, which, with other motives, led both sides at various times to refuse to keep 'trews',[1] and to refuse redress even when 'trews' were held, to the great encouragement of the evil men on both sides.[2] The stereotyped remedy was an international commission, the last of which met in 1597. The death of Elizabeth in 1603 was too early for the failure of the last to be quite clear, but the others failed, and other remedies were adopted from time to time. The most popular was force, which was used by Sussex and Scroope in 1570 and 1584 with effect,[3] and by Forster in 1584,[4] without any licence from James or his regents. This remedy was often advised,[5] but not to an extent which would cause war.[6] Underhand dealing was also suggested, as in 1596 when Eure urged that the feud between Cesford and Buccleugh should be renewed, and one of them caused 'to wrecke the other'.[7] There were also from time to time private indents between Wardens, like that between Scroope and Johnstone in July 1602.[8] But the most popular remedy, except reprisals, was a bond, or assurance taken with Scots surnames. These were illegal, but were tried, for example, by Forster in 1580[9] and urged upon Walsyngham by Scroope and Forster in 1583,[10] and carried out by the latter in 1584.[11] Yet, in spite of all this, external raids coupled with domestic mismanagement resulted in the Borders, though they had improved, being the most unquiet place in England in 1603, and vying with the Highlands for that undesirable title in Scotland.

There had been a general inquiry into the state of the Borders in 1541,[12] but for evidence of internal mismanagement in the early part of Elizabeth's reign we have to rely on the opinions of the experienced Sir Rafe Sadler,[13] isolated complaints by Sir Thomas Dacre and Valentine Browne,[14] and the more detailed inquiries of Hunsdon and Knollys in 1568.[15] A little later there were charges made

---

[1] C.B.P. i, 234, 241, 245, 972.   [2] C.B.P. i, 885 (1).   [3] C.B.P. i, 198.
[4] C.B.P. i, 258.   [5] C.B.P. i, 171, 191, 555; ii, 312, 692.   [6] C.B.P. ii, 632.   [7] C.B.P. ii, 347.   [8] C.B.P. ii, 1472.   [9] C.B.P. i, 64.
[10] C.B.P. i, 175.   [11] C.B.P. i, 278.   [12] Bates, i, 38–41.   [13] Sadler, ii, 282–8.   [14] For. vi, 34.   [15] C.H.M. i, 1269; For. viii, 2534, ix, 736.

against Forster in 1571, and in 1575 a statement was made by him and the gentry of his party.[1] After 1579 the evidence is fuller. There are the muster rolls of 1580 in which the excuses of the unfurnished are set down,[2] and in 1583–4 there was a special commission of inquiry, during which Walsyngham went down to the Borders and conferred with Forster and Scroope.[3] In 1586–7 there were further complaints against Forster, which led to two separate inquiries by Huntyngdon and by Hunsdon.[4] There was an inquiry in the West March in 1593 when Thomas, Lord Scroope, took office,[5] and a more general inquiry by commissioners in the same year.[6] Finally we have the inquiry made by the commissioners of 1597, various notes by the Wardens, and an undated list of causes, probably written in 1579.[7]

From these it is possible to draw up a list of the causes of 'decay', most of which were economic and domestic, though of course Scots raids reacted on the situation in England.

One of the chief economic causes was the smallness of tenements. Forster and his friends alleged in 1571 that a tenement scant enough to provide one man would be divided among his sons, however many he had. In 1580 men who came to the musters unfurnished urged as an excuse the smallness of their holdings, some of them being worth but 8s. or 10s. The commissioners of 1584 confirmed this view, and the survey of 1604 confirms it in the district round Harbottle.[8] The tenants, whatever the size of their holdings, had to pay excessive 'grassums', or 'greshoms', i.e. fines for leases. Forster's friends in 1571 stated that the fine was sometimes nine or ten years' rent; the unfurnished men of 1580 alleged this, and oppression by their masters, as a cause of their defects, and Forster considered it the chief cause. The commissioners of 1584 included it in their reports and added the fact of the

---

[1] C.S.P. iv, 32; For. xi, 167.   [2] C.B.P. i, 47, 50.   [3] C.B.P. i, 175; Dom. Add. iii, 92–4, 123, 127–8.   [4] C.B.P. i, 451, 453–5, 515, 534, 541, 546–7, 554, 556.   [5] C.B.P. i, 834.   [6] Dom. Add. iii, 352–4, 357, 358–60.   [7] S.P. Borders, xx, 80.   [8] R.P.S. 85.

Queen's holding land in minorities. Excessive fines on his Northumberland tenants was one of the charges against Lord Eure in 1597.[1] Enclosures and the turning of land from tillage to pasture formed another excuse. According to Scroope and the Bishop of Carlisle in 1571 the Earl of Northumberland's West March enclosures had so impoverished two hundred men that they could not keep horse or armour.[2] At the musters of 1580 men said that much ground had been turned to pasture, and the commissioners of 1584 complained of that and of the taking of towns into demesne. At the end of the period, in 1597, the Dean of Durham said private men had dispeopled whole villages, and could and should be made to repair them, the increase of tillage being the needful thing.[3] On the other hand the long peace was stated to have made men turn to tillage and keep cattle rather than horses,[4] and the commissioners of 1584 complained of the letting of tenements to ploughmen. A paper peace there had been, but the Borders had not been quiet enough for some people. Thus it was that non-residence of nobles like the Earl of Northumberland, who lived at Tynemouth while he held Norham,[5] of gentry, who dwelt sixteen, twenty, or forty miles from the Borders, and even in London itself,[6] of Border officers,[7] and of Berwick Captains[8] was reported throughout the period. And to this non-residence and the parsimony of the government was due the decay of castles.[9] Yet in spite of non-residence there was overpopulation in some parts and many bastard children whose fathers could not maintain them. Most of the above causes might have been remedied, but dearth and plague were then hardly preventible.[10] One further economic cause which was still operative, at least as an excuse in 'Tynmouthshire' in 1580, was the suppression of the monasteries, the men of Benwell and Elswick alleging that they could not serve as they did before the abbey was

[1] C.B.P. ii, 652.   [2] Dom. Add. ii, 367.   [3] Dom. iv, 542–3.   [4] C.B.P. i, 41.   [5] C.B.P. ii, 881; C.S.P. v, 643, vi, 100.   [6] C.H.M. i, 1269; For. ix, 736; C.B.P. i, 41.   [7] C.B.P. ii, 1407.   [8] C.B.P. ii, 1515. [9] C.H.M. i, 1269, vii, 451–3; C.B.P. ii, 955.   [10] C.B.P. i, 507, 514, ii, 255, 364, 377, 1095.

suppressed, a charge against Tudor landlords which rings
true.

Another important cause of decay was unappreciated
kindness shown to Scots. There was apparently no restric-
tion in practice on the immigration of alien Scots, and
lands were let to them, and they paid higher rents than
Englishmen could afford, because they could live in England with more security than the English.[1] Hunsdon in
1569 estimated that in his Wardenry there were 2,500
Scots, and few or none of them denizens,[2] and Randolph in
1586 said every third man within ten miles of the frontier
was a Scots tenant or servant to an Englishman, and that
English owners were ready to turn out Englishmen in
favour of Scots. He spoke of Northumberland.[3] On the
West Marches there were few Scots farmers or servants,
but thousands of Scots 'roges' at the end of the period.[4]
Hunsdon found that owing to the numbers of Scots
'planted within Northumberland, especially uppon the
verie Borders . . . no exploit or purpose can be so secretly
resolved uppon, but uppon the gathering of the men together, the Scottes have straight warning'. He wished to
expel all the Scots, except those who were necessary as
colliers, fishers, or shepherds.[5] Scots residents were said to
act as guides to Scots robbers, and Tobie Matthew, in 1597,
suggested a statute against demising lands or tenements
to Scots, or taking them into service.[6] These Scots, of
course, in spite of the law, intermarried with English folk,[7]
and statutes against intermarriages or even meetings with
Scots were suggested by Tobie Matthew. 'Trysting', as
this was called, was common, though illegal, and in the
January of 1603 Sir J. Carey complained of the too great
familiarity and intercourse between English and Scots.
The gentry feasted together, and the thieves planned
robberies together.[8] To favour Scots robbers, and even
to pay 'blackmeale' to them, was a common practice of
long standing, and the poor who could not pay it were

---

[1] For. viii, 2534; C.S.P. v, 634, vi, 100.   [2] C.H.M. i, 1269.   [3] C.B.P.
i, 453.   [4] C.B.P. ii, 613.   [5] C.B.P. i, 571.   [6] C.H.M. vii, 451-3.
[7] For. xi, 291; C.B.P. i, 834, ii, 253, 1435.   [8] C.B.P. ii, 1537.

spoiled.[1] Private bonds were also taken with Scots prisoners, whereby the private gentleman was secure while the rest of the March was spoiled.[2] Again, in spite of statute law and the scarcity of horses in England, there was a continual sale of horses into Scotland with or without licence. Tobie Matthew wished to make licences illegal.[3]

Though some of the English seem to have agreed very well with Scots, they did not agree among themselves, and their own litigiousness, and that of their lords, caused trifling matters to be carried up to the courts at London, to the impoverishment of the country.[4] Furthermore, there were private quarrels or feuds between families, involving other houses, which would rather overthrow each other than face the enemy.[5] This fact was noticed by the commission of 1584, but feuds continued till the end of the period, though they were never as great as those in the Scots West March. A good instance was the Selby-Collingwood feud which began in November 1586.[6] These feuds sometimes took the form of factions against a Warden. Lord Eure wrote 'they have erected a faction of the Woddringtons against me, crossing my government secretly, openly reviling, publishing libels against me, which your lordship knoweth in time will withdrawe hearts from service',[7] and R. Lowther, when deputy, wrote that the gentlemen 'of the factyon' would not obey him.[8] There were also the irresponsible surnames like the Grames of the West March, but these men were less numerous in England than in Scotland.[9] Against these factions the Warden sometimes lacked the support of the central government, and in other matters too. Thomas, Lord Scroope, suffered from the Grames, the Carletons, and the Lowthers,[10] and got no real help. Wyllughby got some support in his differences with his council,[11] but Sir R. Carey received more than one command 'to leave this course of peremptorie writing . . . and doo as you

---

[1] C.B.P. ii, 119, 1020.   [2] C.B.P. ii, 255.   [3] C.B.P. ii, 1368.
[4] C.B.P. i, 118.   [5] C.B.P. i, 41.   [6] Dom. Add. iii, 213–14.   [7] C.B.P. ii, 441.   [8] C.B.P. ii, 1183.   [9] C.B.P. ii, 1241–2, 1245.   [10] C.B.P. ii, 456, 479, 491, 553, 625, 735, 741–2, 1008, 1010–11.   [11] C.B.P. ii, 1343.

ought',[1] and was for some time unable to get the government to allow him to 'enlarge' his two efficient deputies in spite of the Bishop of Durham's letters on their behalf.[2]

The central government was also very reluctant to supply the Wardens with extra forces when they said they were necessary.[3] Wardens were also hindered by the unwillingness of the gentry and of the country, and by the untrustworthiness of the Borderers.[4] For instance, Forster's friends, during his sequestration from office, did their best, by refraining from resisting the Scots, to make it said that the Border was 'spoyled rather more than less by his remove'.[5] It was also hard to make the gentry answerable for their tenants and servants.[6] Sometimes one Warden took offence at the acts of another, and was hard to pacify.[7] Then there were unsuitable Wardens. Sadler succeeded in getting Northumberland removed, but Forster, though he held office for the greater part of this period and was whitewashed by Hunsdon,[8] can hardly be regarded as satisfactory, and Eure, though apparently well meaning, was not a success.[9] Hunsdon, a successful Warden, was for a long time non-resident, and the lack of an absolute Warden at Berwick seems to have been an important cause of decay.[10] Similar causes on a smaller scale were unsuitable deputies, peculating captains, unfit keepers of castles, and remiss officers,[11] and to them and to the Wardens were due things like the neglect or negligent holding of musters,[12] the neglect of watches,[13] the failure to dam up fords,[14] the non-observance of the Border Laws as a whole,[15] and of special statutes like that of 'hews and cryes'[16] and Philip and Mary's statute for enclosures.[17] If the Borders had been enclosed as they are now, the driving of a prey of cattle might have been so hazardous as to

[1] C.B.P. ii, 651.   [2] C.B.P. ii, 1025, 1028.   [3] C.B.P. ii, 611, 628, 707, 1254.   [4] C.B.P. ii, 452, 683, 1206.   [5] C.B.P. ii, 563.   [6] Sadler, ii, 282–8; C.B.P. i, 834.   [7] C.B.P. ii, 452, 483, 530, 646.   [8] C.B.P. i, 556.   [9] C.B.P. ii, 670, 672, 680–1, 756, 758, 881.   [10] C.B.P. ii, 404, 586, 590, 593, 643, 697, 725, 815.   [11] Sadler, ii, 282–8; C.B.P. i, 4, 834.   [12] C.B.P. ii, 956.   [13] C.B.P. i, 834; ii, 831.   [14] C.B.P. ii, 980, 993.   [15] C.B.P. ii, 171.   [16] C.B.P. i, 834.   [17] C.S.P. ii, 778.

become unprofitable. Smaller causes, which were not repeated, were the spoils during the rising of 1569, alleged in 1584, and the losses by the Dunkirkers at the end of the reign.[1] During the last ten years of the reign there was a growing idea that the lack of 'true religion' and education were important causes of the decay.

The remedies tried were chiefly legislative and have been mentioned, but it was one thing to make laws and another thing to get people to carry them out, generally at their own expense. The government occasionally lent fifty or more men from Berwick garrison to protect some March, or made the Warden an extra allowance for the pay of troops. But much of the work had to be done by the Wardens on their own initiative, and often at their own expense. Wyllughby made himself unpopular in this way, and hastened his death by his efforts to suppress piracy. In 1593 John Carey banished all the Scots servants and some of the Scots inhabitants, apparently only from Berwick, and did his best to pacify quarrels, thus rendering feuds unlikely.[2] But on the whole little was done, and the Borders did not improve in Elizabeth's time, except in international redress. It is hard to estimate the rate of internal decay or its amount, but between 1553 and 1580 the light horse of the West March showed a decrease of 180 or about 25 per cent., and the commission of 1584 found in the East March 767 decayed tenements and 216 unfurnished, besides 27 ruined castles, and 39 tenements turned from tillage to pasture. In the Middle March 216 tenements had been converted to demesne, 226 wasted by the Scots, and 8 towns decayed by enhanced rents or huge fines, 14 towns wholly decayed by the Scots and 4 castles decayed. In the west 417 tenements, 383 horsemen, and 164 footmen were decayed, and in Westmorland 126 tenements had been divided and 67 were uninhabited.[3]

There is much less evidence about Scots decay and its causes, and it comes mainly from English sources. These

---

[1] C.B.P. i, 47, 50; ii, 1601.   [2] C.B.P. i, 826, 838.   [3] C.B.P. i, 54; Dom. Add. iii, 127–8.

are not untrustworthy, neither is the lack of Scots evidence
any reason for supposing that there was little decay in the
Scots Marches. The Middle and West Marches were
continuously troubled by 'greate feedes and slawghters'
among the surnames, and by great disobedience. This
disobedience was at its very worst in the West. In 1582–3,
for instance, Lord Maxwell, alias Morton, forbade all his
adherents, tenants, and dependers to make Johnstone any
answer or service as Warden, so that Johnstone found
it hard to sustain himself in office, three or four hundred
of his Wardenry being at disobedience, riding on him,
burning his house, spoiling his friends, slaying his relations, and taking them prisoners. Almost eighty houses
were burnt at one time, and three hundred at another, so
that Johnstone had to ask for royal aid.[1] Maxwell, when
he took office, had similar troubles, and the surnames
became at last involved in private war on a large scale, in
which there were battles like that at Dryfe Sands. More
than one Warden met a violent death while in office. The
office was undesirable, but no one wished his rival to hold
it.[2] The rivalry between Cesford and Fernyhurst in the
Middle March was of the same kind, but on a smaller
scale,[3] and in the East there was no such rivalry. Again
there were frequent changes of Wardens,[4] and the Wardens were often inefficient, cherishing favourites and
supporting factions.[5] Sometimes there was no Warden,[6]
and at others all three Wardens were absent at the same
time.[7] Scots thieves seem to have been more impartial
than English thieves in their depredations, and often
spoiled in their own realm.[8] Impunity is said to have
caused an increase in theft, but victuals were so scanty and
over-population in Liddesdale so great, that it is doubtful
whether fear of punishment ever kept any one from robbing.[9] Sometimes domestic strife in the central plain
prevented the government from dealing, or attempting to

---

[1] C.S.P. vii, 304; C.H.M. iv, 175; R.P.C.S. iv, 98; C.B.P. i, 120, 153, 291,
293, 303, 308, 316–17.   [2] C.B.P. i, 771, 778, 792, 918; Birrel 49.
[3] C.B.P. i, 258.   [4] C.B.P. ii, 1143.   [5] C.B.P. ii, 171.   [6] C.B.P.
i, 341.   [7] R.P.C.S. iii, 567–8.   [8] C.B.P. i, 270, ii, 1211.   [9] C.B.P.
ii, 1491–2; C.H.M. iii, 540.

deal, with the Border outlaws. Regents, like Moray, and later James VI, made journeys to the Borders at the head of a levy, and hanged thieves, but the impression made seldom lasted long. The Council took 'bands' from various unruly surnames, ordered the Wardens to reside permanently in their offices, and once decided to send to Dumfries 'one hundreth hieland men to be interteyned upon the expenssis of the said outlawis rentiss and leving',[1] but there is no evidence that the Highlanders went. Church-building, as in England, was not suggested as a remedy till the end of the period, and was never tried.[2] At last, in October 1602, James's Council sat at Dumfries, and a general 'Band' was made against thieves, murderers, and oppressors, and subscribed by the Border landlords. It was pretty comprehensive, guarding as it did against neglect of pursuit, warning thieves, 'reset', trysting with thieves, freeing captured thieves before presentation, &c., and the penalty in some cases was the acceptation of the crime of the reaver.[3] But it was impossible to enforce it. There is no evidence about the increase of decay in Scotland, but much of the damage could be repaired in a few hours, even when a big raid like that of 1570 had taken place.

It remains to attempt an estimate of the damage done by one country to the other, and the evidence is insufficient and its credibility doubtful. In some cases it might be well to divide the sums sworn by twenty.[4] The bills were kept in a slovenly way, the offenders' names and the dates were sometimes omitted, and the lists are incomplete, as many 'stoulths' were not reported.[5] Illustrations must therefore suffice, and it is unwise to draw strong conclusions from them. The commissioners of 1597 filed bills for the last ten years in the West Marches, the damage done by England being assessed at £13,007 10s., and that done by Scotland £11,978 18s.[6] Eure alleged that the principal loss unredressed of his own March for the same period was between £16,000 and £20,000 'without duble

---

[1] R.P.C.S. vi, 32.   [2] Autobiog. 100.   [3] R.P.C.S. vi, 828-9.   [4] C.B.P. ii, 369.   [5] C.B.P. ii, 295.   [6] C.B.P. ii, 606-7.

or saphie'.[1] It is impossible to state the average loss per annum. For example, during Scroope's journey to London in 1601 the Scots did damage estimated at £5,040 in less than six months, and the bills against England for that time and the previous six months came to £312 only.[2]

[1] C.B.P. ii, 410.   [2] C.B.P. ii, 1410.

PART XII

THE ANNALS OF THE BORDERS
1558—1603

I. THE BORDERS IN TIME OF WAR
(November 1558 to July 1560)

IN 1556 Spain and the Empire resumed their war against France, a war in which England and Scotland were soon involved, and which continued after the death of Mary.

1558 Nov. Elizabeth needed peace; her treasury was worse than empty, her title open to dispute, and her religious views unwelcome to many of her subjects. One of her first acts, therefore, was the nomination of commissioners to treat with representatives of the King and Queen of Scots,[1] and at the same time she took precautions against the continuance of the war by ordering simultaneous Border musters, the fortification of Berwick, the recalling of absentee captains and soldiers, the keeping of fords and watches, and the maintenance of spies in Scotland.[2] Vigour was necessary, for the Scots were riding as far as Morpeth as quietly as in Teviotdale, and their rank riders were going in tens and twelves from town to town calling on men to rise, saying that the Scots were coming, and offering to save their horses and cattle if they would be their prisoners. Bigger forces numbering as many as seven hundred Scots and French had entered England, and the only recorded retaliation on the East Marches was a raid by Lord Evers to burn the mill of Eyemouth.[3] On the West there were also some reprisals, and the Scots were less dangerous.[4] The whole state of the Borders was most distressing, and particularly dangerous in view of

---

[1] C.S.P. i, 439. [2] For. i, 52, 59, 72, 104, 168–9; A.P.C. vii, 10, 15–16.
[3] For. i, 139. [4] A.P.C. vii, 41; For. i, 167.

the religious changes which were in the making, for the feudal nobles of the Borders as well as their tenants were in favour of the old religion, as Lord Wharton's vote showed in the following April,[1] and it had yet to be proved whether hatred of the old enemy would outweigh hatred of the new doctrines. The Earl of Northumberland, however, was for the moment loyal, and was thanked for his diligence and secrecy.[2]

1559. Early in the New Year fresh musters were ordered, and a thousand men, 'mere countrymen and no borderers', were to be raised in Durham and Yorkshire to aid the earl.[3] The Scots, however, also had difficulties: the nobility desired peace, and the horsemen refused to serve unpaid, while their French allies desired peace too, lest Elizabeth should be driven to side with Philip of Spain. Negotiations, therefore, proceeded apace, the Scots only making one unimportant raid, and, an abstinence having been made for March and April, as many of the English troops as possible were discharged.[4] On April 4 the Treaty of Cateau-Cambrésis was concluded[5] and more men were discharged, though the task was made difficult by the lack of money wherewith to pay them.[6] The Treaty was not made without reference to Border conditions, for the fortifications at Eyemouth were to be demolished within fifteen days, and the English were to destroy such fortifications as they had made contrary to treaty.[7] However, as the commissioners were ignorant of Border affairs, 'certain Articles concerning the granting of Safe-conducts to Homicides, Thieves, Rankriders upon the Marches and Fugitives' were left to be settled by others with local knowledge.[8] These met at Ladykirk, and negotiations took some time as the Scots desired clauses that they might pass through England without safe-conducts, and that a certain cattle-dyke in the Bounds might be pulled down, to be inserted in the Treaty. At length,

---

[1] D'Ewes, 30.   [2] A.P.C. vii, 39.   [3] Dom. Add. i, 487–8; A.P.C. vii, 41; For. i, 230, 581.   [4] For. i, 269, 311, 465, 581; C.H.M. i, 570; A.P.C. vii, 73–4.   [5] Rymer, xv, 509.   [6] For. i, 493, 586; A.P.C. vii, 86.   [7] Rymer, xv, 509 ff.   [8] C.S.P. i, 448, 456; Camden, 25.

however, peace was proclaimed at Norham on July 16, and the last war between England and Scotland was over.[1]

War with France, however, and the French party in Scotland, soon began again. Six days before the Treaty of Upsettlington was completed Mary Stuart became Queen of France, and in consequence the Guises became more powerful, and sought control of Scots affairs. Elizabeth wished to maintain the peace, but kept a watchful eye on the troublous state of Scotland considering how she might best thwart the French, if, as seemed probable, they should turn their designs from Italy to Scotland. The fort at Eyemouth was reluctantly dismantled,[2] but Border justice was not satisfactorily renewed,[3] and the situation of the Scots Protestants was not secure enough to warrant a decrease of the English Border troops, though Knox was optimistic.[4] Moreover, a French fleet was said to be in readiness.[5] Thus, when Knox came to Holy Island to press for English intervention,[6] Elizabeth's reluctance to treat with another queen's rebels was overcome by the quartering of the arms of England by Francis and Mary, and so, under cover of meeting Scots commissioners for reforming unredressed Border offences and of attending to Berwick fortifications, Sadler was sent north with a secret licence to confer or practise 'with any maner of person of Scotland either in Scotland or England' for 'certen speciall service', and given £3,000 in gold wherewith to comfort them secretly without impairing the treaties.[7] Negotiations for Border redress were carried on with the Regent, simultaneously with the 'secrete affaire',[8] and the commissioners had sundry meetings, the Scots in the end hastening an agreement, being 'lyke to have moche comber amongst themselffs at home'. They agreed on certain orders for the Warden's proceedings at days of Trews, and about prisoners and bonds, agreements which Bothwell, the Scots lieutenant, soon broke.[9] The 'secrete

[1] Rymer, xv, 520–7; C.S.P. i, 463, 467. [2] C.S.P. i, 487, 497, 510.
[3] For. i, 978, 991, 1051, 1054; C.S.P. i, 501. [4] C.S.P. i, 448, 510; For.
i, 979. [5] C.S.P. i, 508. [6] C.S.P. i, 511. [7] Sadler, i, 388–92;
C.S.P. i, 517, 520. [8] Sadler, i, 395–405, 407–8, 414–15, 422–3, 427, 429,
436, 439–41, 447–51; C.S.P. i, 518, 532. [9] Sadler, i, 457–9, ii, 2–4, 34.

affaire' is not Border history, but the coming of Arran to England and his intrigues there made the Regent prohibit Scots intercourse with Berwick. The Scots, however, came as usual,[1] but the Regent was more successful with her counter-intrigues, for it is clear that she practised with Lord Dacre to allow the English Grames to ride on Maxwell, whom she did not recognize as Warden, in order to keep him from aiding the Lords of the Congregation. The Scots commissioners made no protest, but the Lords did, and Elizabeth had to disavow Dacre.[2]

Sadler must have worked hard, for, apart from his intrigues, he reported on the new works at Berwick[3] and also on the general state of the Borders. 'It is more than xx years ago', he wrote, 'syns I had som understanding of this frontier, and yet dyd I never know it in such disorder; for now the officer spoyleth the thefe without bringing forth his person to tryall by the aw; and the thefe robbeth the trew man, and the trew men take assurance of the theves that they shall not robbe them, and give them yerely rent and tribute for the same'. He attributed all this to the lack of 'stoute and wise officers'.[4] Northumberland, he thought, 'a very unmete man for that charge which is comytted unto him here',[5] and Dacre was guilty of 'great necligence', owing to which his Wardenry was in much disorder.[6] At the end of September, at Cecil's request, Sadler suggested the names of suitable Wardens, one of whom, Lord Wharton, was not likely to be acceptable.[7] As a result Northumberland went up to court, and Sadler unwillingly took over his Wardenries in November.[8] He was not burdened for long, as in December Norfolk was made Lieutenant of all England North of the Trent,[9] and Lord Grey de Wilton relieved him of the Wardenries.[10] They were sent because Elizabeth saw that it might be necessary for her to intervene forcibly in Scots affairs, and that her Borders, Papist as they were, might be dangerous

---

[1] Thorpe, 118.   [2] C.S.P. i, 538; Sadler, i, 447–53, 461–3, ii, 5–8, 13. [3] Sadler, i, 406–7.   [4] Sadler, ii, 441–4.   [5] Sadler, i, 409–10.   [6] Sadler, ii, 13–14, 42–3.   [7] Sadler, i, 460, ii, 8–11.   [8] Sadler, ii, 65; For. ii, 213, 274, 349.   [9] For. ii, 435.   [10] For. ii, 497; Grey, 53–8; C.H.M. i, 601.

if her arms were unsuccessful there. Wynter's fleet
was sent to the Forth, and its appearance there
1560.   seems to have decided the Kerrs and Humes,
who, though Papists, were anti-French, to incline
towards the Lords of the Congregation, and thus, perhaps,
make English intervention needless.[1] While Norfolk was
levying troops under difficulties,[2] meetings were held
with the Lords, and resulted, on February 27, in the
Treaty of Berwick, an offensive and defensive alliance
against the French.[3]

As the French did not fulfil their promise to remove
their troops, the English army entered Scotland on
March 30 under Grey, Scroope, and others, but Dacre
was not sent as Norfolk could not trust him. Sadler was
left in charge of Grey's Wardenries, and four hundred
extra Border troops were thought sufficient to keep off the
Scots Borderers, and to furnish convoys, in spite of Hume's
threats, the young lairds of Cesford and Ferniherst having
left the Marches.[4] These three soon joined the Scots
Lords, so Berwick garrison was gradually decreased to
supply reinforcements to Grey, until at one time only a
hundred men were left.[5] The siege of Leith, though Border troops were present in small numbers, was not Border
history, for the French were quite unable to fulfil their
threat 'to make Yorke the bounds of Ingland',[6] but it gave
Cecil an excellent chance of seeing the Borders, as Elizabeth sent him first to Newcastle and then to Edinburgh
to treat with the French.[7] At the twelfth hour the conference was successful, peace was signed, and by July 11
the English army departed for Berwick. The Articles
included no special Border clause except about Eyemouth.[8]

[1] C.H.M. i, 604, 609; C.S.P. i, 630, 697.   [2] For. ii, 274; C.H.M. i, 612,
625; C.S.P. i, 646.   [3] C.S.P. i, 665; Thorpe, 133; Rymer, xv, 569;
C.H.M. i, 626; Spotswood, i, 310–14.   [4] C.H.M. i, 633, 649; For. ii,
933; C.S.P. i, 698; Grey, 39.   [5] C.H.M. i, 689, 702; C.S.P. i, 776.
[6] C.H.M. i, 714.   [7] Thorpe, 151; C.S.P. i, 813; C.H.M. i, 732, 737.
[8] C.H.M. i, 761; Spotswood, i, 325; Rymer, xv, 581, 591–7.

II. MARY'S PEACEFUL BEGINNINGS IN SCOTLAND, 1560–4

AFTER the Treaty of Edinburgh Norfolk prepared to go south, and the usual attempts at economy by discharging troops were made. Cecil had gone before him, but had seen enough and heard enough to be convinced that the Borders must be set in order, especially as Francis and Mary refused to ratify the last treaty. Various people were consulted, including Lord Wharton, who drew up an elaborate memorial, and Cecil compared their reports with those of Henry VIII's and Edward VI's time, and with his own observations made on the spot, and summoned Grey to court to give further advice.[1] It had already been decided to remodel the fortifications of Berwick entirely, and new walls were in process of construction. For strategical reasons, or because the town was less prosperous than of old, the new walls were to measure but one and three-quarter miles in circuit, the Edwardian ones having been two and a half. Portinari, some famous Italian, was sent to make suggestions, and the castle was left outside the new walls, which were built with prominent bastions, from the casemates in which guns could sweep the face of the intermediate wall. Outside was a ditch two hundred feet wide, in the midst of which was another twelve feet broad and eight feet deep which was always kept full.[2] The ancient statutes of the castle and town were also reviewed, and new orders made for use while fortifications were being built.[3] The Scots government too, weak as it was, tried to pacify its own West Marches, where the number of thieves had greatly increased during the late troubles, by sending for Maxwell, the Warden, and making him confer with the Lord James Stuart and Randolph.[4] The Scots Protestants had made

[1] C.H.M. i, 787; C.S.P. i, 860; Camden, 47; For. iii, 326, 351, 353, 403, 407–8. [2] For. iii, 375, 379, 400–1, 628. [3] For. iii, 594–5. [4] For. iii, 419, 434 (1), 469 (2).

a meagre attempt to win the Borders to the new faith,[1] and Parker tried to get some bishops appointed in the north.[2]

They were necessary, for the ability of the pastor at Berwick, and other places, to 'say his pater noster truly either in English or in Latin' was doubtful.[3] Maxwell made loud complaints against Dacre for lack of redress, but nothing was done to the latter at present, possibly because of the difficulty of finding a successor,[4] but Forster was given the Middle Marches, and Grey sent back to the East.[5] He found marvellous disorder, but set to work with a reforming will, held musters, arranged 'Trews' with varying success, and received Cecil's thanks for his diligence 'in reformation of Northumberland's disorder'.[6] Arran and Lord James Stuart repaired to Jedburgh and took such good order as had not been taken for many years, by means of sessions, bonds, the pacification of feuds, and arrangements for the maintenance of the new religion.[7] On December 5, while these settlements were in progress, the unexpected death of Francis II had for the time being put an end to the ambitious schemes of the Guises.[8] But the prospect of the return to Scotland of a hostile queen spurred Elizabeth on in her preparations for Border defence.

1561. Grey, though hampered by the lack of most necessaries, was energetic and cautious, and tried to impress the Arran marriage embassy favourably.[9] New bishops were appointed to the Border sees, and Elizabeth sent Mary a fancy picture of Border quietude to show the high standard which she would be expected to maintain if she returned.[10] Things were really very much unsettled. Dacre was refusing justice to Maxwell, Cesford's tenants were nightly robbing the East Marches, Hume was delaying justice, and the open and unredressed forays of the Liddesdale men made Forster ask for leave to do them

[1] Spotswood, i, 325.　　[2] Parker, 123.　　[3] For. iii, 683.　　[4] For. iii, 614; Thorpe, 164.　　[5] For. iii, 663–4; Grey, 40.　　[6] For. iii, 735, 812; C.S.P. i, 921, 928.　　[7] For. iii, 807; C.S.P. i, 934.　　[8] C.S.P. i, 943. [9] Camden, 56; For. iii, 851, 956, 966, iv, 5, 47, 69, 89; C.H.M. i, 820; C.S.P. i, 944.　　[10] For. iii, 932.

displeasure.[1] But Grey's energy got his own Borders into a state which justified his leaving them in June.[2] In August, when the return of Mary was almost certain, a commission of inspection spent two and a half weeks visiting places near the frontier, making a seeming settlement of the Dacre-Maxwell trouble, and sending in a list of reforms needed in the Queen's castles, enclosures, musters, &c.[3]

If Mary had returned to a united country, and thus been able to be hostile to England, the English Borders would have been none too well prepared for resistance. But domestic difficulties in Scotland forced her to bide her time, and thus, within a week of her landing at Leith on August 19, Border proclamations were made for maintaining the amity with England.[4] On Mary's return she found that her own Borderers were 'impatient of all good orders',[5] and Randolph reminded her that the English lacked redress. Her Council therefore decided to send the Lord James Stuart with levies to Jedburgh and Dumfries to 'daunten' the thieves, and asked for the co-operation of the English Wardens against 'recet' in England. Cesford and Fernyhurst were ordered to present thieves for trial, others had to give bonds, and others were ordered to be punished for 'their contemption in not compeering'. The Scots Wardens were confirmed in office.[6] In November Lord James went to Jedburgh with very full powers, and, meeting with the co-operation of the opposite Wardens, was able to fulfil his instructions, though he was disappointed about the Maxwell-Dacre feud. He held courts, met and conferred with Grey and Forster, burnt many houses, hanged over a score of thieves, brought forty or fifty others to Edinburgh for trial, of whom twenty-three were put in the Castle, and took bonds of others. The chiefest of all Border clans came in to him to take such order as the Queen pleased for staying theft in time to come. The results made Randolph quite optimistic, and the enclosure

---

[1] For. iii, 946, 948, 1001, 1039, iv, 14, 16, 19, 60, 262, 309; C.S.P. i, 954, 995; Thorpe, 168.   [2] For. iv, 89, 117.   [3] For. iv, 360, 420, 429–30, 438, 441–2; C.S.P. i, 1007, 1010; Thorpe, 173.   [4] For. iv, 455.   [5] R.P.C.S. i, 164.   [6] R.P.C.S. i, 163–5, 168–9; For. iv, 621; C.S.P. i, 1029, 1033.

of some three thousand acres of the English Borders
       seemed also to promise well.[1] So well indeed that
1562. a meeting between the queens was proposed in
       January, though Mary still delayed the ratification
of the Treaty of Edinburgh.[2] This meeting did not take
place, being indefinitely postponed by Elizabeth, disturb-
ances in France being the excuse. It is more likely, however, that she feared that Mary might see the nakedness of
the Border lands, and encourage by her presence, if in no
other way, the discontented Papists.[3] The amity was not
seriously disturbed by this postponement, nor even by the
disagreements between opposite Wardens, of which the
Dacre-Maxwell dispute was the worst. A meeting at
Gretna on April 29 did little good, and finally Randolph
recommended the removal of Dacre, a course which
Elizabeth carried out early in the next year, Henry, Lord
Scroope, being his successor.[4]

Mary gave further proof of her good intentions by
again sending the Lord James Stuart, now Earl of Mar
and shortly to be Earl of Moray, with Hume, Cesford, and
three thousand horsemen to quiet the thieves of Liddesdale and 'Tivydale'. Leaving Edinburgh on July 1, he
surrounded Hawick about ten next morning and captured
fifty-three thieves, of whom ten were 'quytte by the Assize'.
Twenty-two of the condemned were drowned at once 'for
lack of trees and halters' and six others were hanged at
Edinburgh on July 6. The effects were salutary but insufficient, and in November, after his journey with Mary
to the north, he apparently went again and captured the
same number, some of whom were executed and the rest
'lett upon band'.[5] England had no such great internal
Border troubles, though the Grames of the West were a
law unto themselves, and Sir Henry Percy and others of
his affinity gave trouble to Grey. But it was only by keeping the terrors of the law constantly before the eyes of the

[1] R.P.C.S. i, 184–8; For. iv, 641–2, 656, 679–80, 703 (note), 714; C.S.P. i,
1049, 1051; Herries, 60; Spotswood, ii, 16.   [2] Thorpe, 177.   [3] C.S.P.
i, 1126; For. v, 164, 228–9.   [4] For. iv, 788, 802, 812, 970–1, 995, v, 9,
21–2, 456, 542, 585; C.S.P. i, 1065, 1067, 1071, 1132, 1147, 1152; Bell, 196.
[5] C.S.P. i, 1101, 1121, 1123; For. v, 83, 274, 283; Herries, 63.

Borderers that they became for the most part quiet in spite of a disposition to the contrary.[1] Berwick fortifications progressed, though hindered by the slowness of payment,[2] but the death of Grey in the south on December 15 was a serious loss, and was lamented by many for the good justice he had done on the Borders. Though not a man of great capacity he seems to have been faithful to Elizabeth, and the most serious of the misdeeds alleged against him was that he had not paid his deputy, John Selby, for two years.[3]

1563. In spite of Mary's continued refusal to ratify the Treaty of Edinburgh, and of her attempts to force Elizabeth to acknowledge her as heir, the amity was well maintained, and Mary was 'well obeyed' in Scotland, though the Scots Borderers still desired to break all good order.[4] The international and local Border situation was so peaceable that in March the English government decided to stop some of the works at Berwick, discharge many men and send some of the garrison to serve in Ireland or France. Scroope was appointed Warden in the West in April, but the more important post in the East was not filled up till the appointment of Bedford near the end of the year.[5] Raids and revenges there were and Scots priests had 'cropen' into England to do mischief there, but these had no international effect,[6] and did not hinder the meeting of the commissioners appointed by both sides to examine and redress all attempts since the last peace, and reduce matters to order. The English commissioners, Scroope, Forster, Gargrave, who was Chancellor of York, and John Rokeby, LL.D., also inquired into the state of their own West Marches, which were found much decayed, especially the citadel and castle of Carlisle, owing to Dacre's neglect. They then met the Scots, Sir John Maxwell and John Bellenden, who was Justice Clerk, at Carlisle on September 11, and having moved to Dumfries,

[1] For. iv, 939, 995, 1010, v, 55–6, 61, 111, 137.   [2] For. v, 1342.
[3] For. v, 1355, 1375, vi, 34, 268; C.S.P. i, 1157; Stow, 1104.   [4] C.R.M.
84.   [5] For. vi, 519, 696, 726–7, 1350, 1422; C.B.P. i, 537.   [6] For.
vi, 602, 768, 839, 915; C.S.P. ii, 3, 9, 16.

sat there till September 23. Evidence as to the amount and number of bills redressed seems lacking, but the Treaty is extant and is considered in another part of this work.[1] Apparently the only matters they left unsettled were the compensation for the plunder of a Scots wreck and the division of the debatable lands between the opposite East and Middle Marches. Time was to show the weakness of their legislation, and soon after their separation Cesford felt it beneath his dignity to keep the three 'Trews' they had arranged for him, as there was no English East March Warden for him to meet. Hume took a similar course of action, and the thieves were thereby encouraged.[2]

1564. Throughout 1564, though Mary's marriage proposals were a possible cause of friction, the amity was maintained and good will shown on both sides. The new Warden, Bedford, arrived at Berwick on March 27 to find the place weaker than he had expected, and at once accelerated the building of the various works, which for reasons of economy had been slackened, and set an example of energy by taking part with his household servants in the watches. In planning the works he was aided by the Italian experts Portinari and Concio. His work did not meet with due appreciation at court, though he visited every place in his Wardenry and even found time to survey Holy Island.[3] With Forster he should have met the Scots commissioners to divide the remaining debatable lands, or 'threaplands', but the meeting was postponed and the question remained unsettled till the Union.[4] With Randolph in November he met Moray and Maitland in three days' conference, ostensibly on Border affairs, but really about Mary's marriage, and no agreement was reached.[5] But neither the marriage, nor the 'threaplands', nor the apparent indifference of Cesford to justice, nor the presence on the Borders of Bothwell, 'as naughty a man

[1] pp. 113–22.   [2] For. vi, 861, 872, 1103, 1280, 1406, 1422, 1433, 1481; C.S.P. ii, 20–1, 31; Dom. i, 229; Bell, 91–101; Leges, 84–103.   [3] For. vii, 277–8, 285, 350, 352, 419, 448, 472, 482, 571; C.S.P. ii, 30.   [4] For. vii, 381, 421, 548, 572, 664–5; C.S.P. ii, 86–7.   [5] C.S.P. ii, 103–4, 112, 118.

as liveth', whom Mary, in spite of her outward demeanour, was thought to favour, disturbed the amity. For Mary showed a good disposition to justice and even paid for redress out of her own pocket, while the East and West March Wardens concurred well with each other. Mary also brought pressure to bear on Cesford with good results.[1] Cesford and Maxwell complained of disregard of their authority by their own Borderers, but the subjects of the whole of the north of England were in good obedience, so that 1564 was one of the most peaceful years in domestic and international Border history.[2]

[1] For. vii, 406, 408, 457, 488, 1079; C.S.P. ii, 70–1, 112.   [2] C.S.P. ii, 112; R.P.C.S. i, 300; Dom. Add. i, 550.

III. THE FALL OF MARY, 1565-7

SO far matters were more or less even between the rival queens, but at the end of July Mary made a match, which, to those who were not wise after the event, 1565. seemed a masterstroke. The year opened peaceably and the Scots showed a good inclination to Border justice,[1] while the English went on with Border surveys, though Bedford had to become importunate before he could proceed with Berwick fortifications.[2] The chief cause of his importunity was the presence of Bothwell in the Scots Borders, though Mary assured Randolph that he would never recover favour, and prepared an expedition against him, whereupon he vanished.[3] The Borders of Scotland were very much unsettled: there was a sanguinary feud between the Elwoods and the Scots, which the government failed to stop; Maxwell was fortifying his Marches apparently out of his own pocket; and the Papists began to arouse themselves and the unruly folk in Liddesdale to commit disorders. Moreover, Throckmorton's attempt to stop the Darnley marriage seemed to have failed, and Mary's whole demeanour had changed as if by witchcraft.[4] Some plot against Elizabeth's throne seemed to be on foot, and therefore on June 4, partly as a precaution, and partly in the hope of making Mary give up the Darnley match, the English Council decided to send Bedford back to his charge, to increase the garrison and advance the works at Berwick, to hold musters, to prepare an army, and to put the Borders in a state ready for service at an hour's notice. Incidentally stern measures were to be taken against Scots monks and friars spying in the English Borders, and a watch kept on Darnley's mother.[5] Soon after, repairs at Carlisle and Bewcastle,

[1] For. vii, 918, 928, 969; C.S.P. ii, 133.   [2] Dom. Add. i, 557-8; For. vii, 1031, 1057, 1061-3, 1068, 1086.   [3] For. vii, 1062-3, 1123; C.S.P. ii, 157, 161, 171, 174.   [4] For. vii, 1124, 1140, 1161, 1192, 1202, 1206, 1221; C.S.P. ii, 110, 171, 174-5.   [5] For. vii, 1224.

and the enclosing of the frontier lands with quickset hedges were ordered.[1] None the less at the end of July Mary married Darnley, and the Scots Protestants directly, and Elizabeth indirectly, seemed in a hard case. Much of Mary's strength lay in the Borders, especially the Middle March, and not only Hume but Maxwell, whom the Lords of the Congregation had especially trusted, sided with the queen against their party, though the latter only did so for a time. Elizabeth, partly by aiding the Ellwoods in their feud, managed to keep some of the Borderers at home, but her Wardens continued to hold 'Trews', the name of King Henry being omitted, and she was determined that unless Eyemouth were refortified she would not go the expense of sending troops to take part in the Scots civil war.[2] This war so occupied the attention of both governments that the Border thieves rode not only in England but within eight miles of Edinburgh.[3] On September 6 Moray and his party were at Dumfries asking for English aid, men, money, and munitions. He got £1,000 pounds from the Queen and £500 out of Bedford's own pocket, and three hundred men sent secretly by way of Carlisle. There was no force on the English Border large enough to make him sure of victory, and so, when Mary came to the Borders with Bothwell, the favour shown to whom was already causing 'jarres' between the king and queen, and six thousand men, he took Bedford's advice and prevented a battle by retiring to Carlisle, where he was kindly used.[4] Maxwell made his peace with Mary, who left him and Bothwell with two or four hundred men to guard the Borders.[5] She was now mistress of her own realm again, but its unsettled state had reacted on the Borders, where a Maxwell-Johnstone feud arose, and there were various Scots raids, for one of which Bedford retaliated, but, as neither side wished for war, there was no war.[6]

[1] Dom. Add. i, 566, 568.   [2] For. vii, 1317, 1320–3, 1329, 1352, 1367, 1375, 1379, 1397, 1404; Dom. Add. i, 572.   [3] For. vii, 1461, 1474; C.S.P. ii, 251.   [4] For. vii, 1466, 1479, 1491, 1535, 1548, 1585; C.S.P. ii, 249–50, 256–7, 270, 272, 280–1.   [5] For. vii, 1594–5; C.S.P. ii, 283.   [6] For. vii, 1644, 1720, 1727.

1566. The state of unrest, however, continued, especially in the Scots Borders, and there were rumours of big raids to be made in England, but on March 9 Rizzio was done to death, and the next day Moray entered Edinburgh from exile, having acknowledged Elizabeth's goodness, such as it was, and promised to do his best to requite it. These circumstances made Bedford more hopeful for Border peace.[1] In place of Moray and his party, Morton and Ruthven fled to England, the latter only to die, the former for nine months' exile. Their 'recet' in England coincided with Mary's 'good words' to Shan O'Neil's messenger.[2] Outwardly, however, Mary showed a good inclination to Border justice, and her Council, when she was in childbed, assured Killegrew that she would content him. In July she did order her Wardens to do justice, but her Marches were too disorderly for her command to be obeyed, though not dangerous enough to prevent Berwick harquebusiers being spared for Ireland.[3] Mary actually proclaimed that she would make a Border journey in person on August 12, thinking it hopeless to quiet the 'Incuntre' till the Borders had been reduced to obedience. The very proclamation had some effect, but during the two months for which the journey was postponed there was much riding against England, and internal disorder in the Scots Marches.[4]

In one of these fights in Liddesdale on October 7 Bothwell was so sore wounded that he was carried home on a cart for dead, but recovered. That Mary visited the Borders at this time, and that she went to the Hermitage to visit Bothwell on Tuesday, October 15, rests on the authority of a letter from Scroope to Cecil written on October 17. Scroope and Forster reported that Bothwell was brought to Jedburgh on October 21 in a horse-litter. Forster and Maitland of Lethington reported her serious illness. Forster stated that while she was at Jedburgh she

---

[1] For. viii, 7, 27, 29, 35, 182, 184; C.S.P. ii, 351, 353, 356, 358.   [2] C.S.P. ii, 363-6, 372, 378, 381-2, 392, 395-6; For. viii, 205, 225, 244, 289, 298, 359, 361, 386.   [3] R.P.C.S. i, 456, 462; For. viii, 508, 528, 530, 544-5, 550, 575, 597; Birrel, 5.   [4] R.P.C.S. i, 475-6; For. viii, 604, 618, 624, 736, 747.

did little touching her justice court; no one was executed, but all the offenders were fined. Pitscottie, however, states that 'the puir men war hangit and the rich men war hangit be the purs'.[1] Having promised Forster redress for all his complaints, she left the Borders in quiet except Liddesdale, where not six people were in obedience, and set off towards Hume, purposing to view Eyemouth.[2] It was now mid-November, and as she passed Berwick the soldiers stood armed on the walls and honoured her 'with many schottis of arteillerie'. At the Bound Road she was met by Forster, then in charge of Berwick during Bedford's absence, with Bothwell, Hume, Cesford, and five hundred horse in her company. She discussed Border matters with Forster on Halidon Hill, where her thigh was so much injured by his horse that she had to spend two days in Hume Castle, and then left for Edinburgh by way of Dunbar, having ordered her Wardens to keep good rule.

She left a good impression on the English officers, but, as soon as her back was turned, Bedford, who was on his way to James's christening, found that the Borders were never so much out of order as her leniency had made them. Liddesdale was daily committing spoils in Scotland, and to prevent their continuance Bothwell had to be given two hundred men in wages as Lieutenant of all the Marches.[3]

1567. For the few remaining weeks of Darnley's life the amity was preserved and nothing of note occurred on the Borders except domestic troubles among the Grames, and in Redesdale and Liddesdale.[4] Then, early in the morning of February 10, Darnley met his death, and the resulting turmoil among the various Scots parties soon encouraged the Scots Border thieves, whose exploits reacted on men of their trade in England. Cesford had to keep his house for fear of Scots thieves, and the lives and cattle of Forster and his servants were in danger. The raiders rode within two miles of Morpeth, and, as there were no March Days either appointed or kept, Forster had

[1] For. viii, 749, 760–1, 764, 772–3, 783; C.S.P. ii, 434; Pitscottie, ii, 192.
[2] For. viii, 761, 764, 772, 795.   [3] For. viii, 804, 825–6, 842–3, 850; C.S.P. ii, 447, 451; Melvill, M., 172–3.   [4] For. viii, 905, 912, 917–18, 942, 960–1.

to come to terms with the Scots Border gentry.[1] This Border unrest gave Bothwell an excuse to gather troops for a raid on the thieves of Liddesdale, and he used them to seize Mary on April 24. The marriage could not be stopped, but the English Border forces were mustered and Bedford ordered north to comfort the Scots Lords who opposed Bothwell. Nightly spoils, however, continued, and on May 15 at 4 a.m. Mary and Bothwell became man and wife. Civil war being imminent, Mary set about raising what Border forces she could for use against the Lords, but on June 15, the very day for which the levy had been fixed, the Lords, whose forces included some Borderers under Hume, met her at Carberry Hill. She surrendered, and Bothwell was allowed to retire from the field.

On July 24 her reign ended, and she left the Borders, as she found them, 'impatient of all good orders'.[2]

[1] For. viii, 978, 998, 1003, 1075, 1124, 1169.   [2] Spotswood, ii, 51; For. viii, 1192, 1195, 1199, 1209, 1292; Herries, 93; R.P.C.S. i, 516–17.

IV. FROM CARBERRY HILL TILL
LANGSIDE, 1567–8

FOR a time after Mary's imprisonment in Lochleven
the state of the Borders was 'very tickle'. It seems
that the Scots raids and threats proceeded from the Bothwell faction, and Bedford and Throckmorton thought that
the only way to stop it was to support the Lords. Elizabeth remained undecided, and matters grew worse until
the common people of the English Marches began to
desire war.[1] Such was the state of affairs when on
August 22 Moray was declared Regent in Edinburgh.[2]
He at once showed energy by summoning Herries to
confer with the Lords, and met with a refusal; but many
Borderers 'came in' to the Lords. He got ready to march
against the Hamiltons and Herries, whom Elizabeth
ordered her officers to comfort, and their submission did
not influence Elizabeth, who continued to acknowledge
Mary, a fact which made Bedford welcome his own final
recall.[3] Moray, freed for a time from civil war, decided
to settle the domestic Border question, proclaimed the
usual musters for November 8, and then 'prevented the
day' and, coming secretly and suddenly to Hawick, took
thirty-four thieves, some of whom he had hanged and
others drowned, set five free on caution, and took ten to
Edinburgh. Accounts vary as to numbers, but at least
twenty were executed, and at the same time the entertainment of thieves or paying blackmail to them by the people
of the incountry was made treason.[4] The effects
1568. of this journey were such that the Borders were
quiet, except for one small Liddesdale raid, until
the following April, when he came to the Borders again

[1] For. viii, 1422, 1439–40, 1442, 1477, 1480, 1490–1, 1511–13, 1598, 1600;
C.S.P. ii, 556, 562, 566.   [2] For. viii, 1620; C.S.P. ii, 607.   [3] For. viii,
1667, 1676, 1753, 1790–1; C.S.P. ii, 610.   [4] R.P.C.S. i, 579, 585; Birrel,
12; For. viii, 1808, 1812.

and saw redress done to Drury, such as had not been done for seven years.[1]

Moray's zeal for Border justice was for a time interrupted by the escape of Mary from Lochleven on May 2. The plan was probably known on the Borders, which became suddenly unsettled at the time and provided her with troops led by Herries, Johnstone, and Ferniherst. Many heads of Border clans were uncertain what to do and sought and failed to get advice from England, but Hume and Cesford fought against Mary, who was beaten at Langside. She fled to her West Marches, and at Dundrennan, against the advice of her friends, 'resolved to go to England and throw herself on the mercy of Elizabeth, in hopes by her assistance to be repossessed again in her Kingdom'.[2] The landing of Mary on the evening of Sunday, May 16, in the 'lytle prety fyscher town' of Workington, was a very important event in Border history, but it did not, as has been said, change the policy of Border rule from an element in international diplomacy to an element in peaceful domestic government. Moray may have felt that war against England was impossible, but some of his successors thought otherwise, and therefore made no war of extermination on the thieves, thinking that they might some day be useful in England. On May 17 Mary with her twenty followers, among whom was Herries, went to Cockermouth, where Scroope's deputy, Richard Lowther, met her and took her to Carlisle, where she was lodged in the Castle.[3] The Earl of Northumberland, in whose liberty she had landed, tried in vain to get Lowther to deliver her to him. Knollys and Scroope were sent down to deal with her without having any clear idea of Elizabeth's intentions. The danger of her presence was increased by the repair of the gentry to her, and it was natural that there should be much difference of opinion as to how she ought to be treated.[4] Moray

[1] For. viii, 1946, 2050, 2132; C.H.M. i, 1171.   [2] For. viii, 2147, 2152, 2160, 2171-4, 2206; C.S.P. ii, 650-1; Herries, 102-3; Spotswood, ii, 98; H.J.S. 27.   [3] For. viii, 2199; C.S.P. ii, 658, 661, 664; Herries, 103; Birrel, 16; H.J.S. 28; Leland, ix, 54; R.P.C.S. ii, p. ix.   [4] For. viii, 2219, 2229, 2232, 2247; C.S.P. ii, 669-71, 677-9, 691, 696-7.

saw clearly that his own West March was the chief source of danger, and therefore on June 13 he arrived at Sanquhar with six thousand horse and a thousand foot, including Cesford and Hume. On his way to Dumfries and Annan, where he met Scroope, he had used his heavy ordnance to destroy castles, had burnt steads, and received many submissions. By this means, and with the help of English officers, Mary's Border followers were temporarily cowed, and Drumlanrig was left as Warden. Elizabeth, however, except for moving Mary to Bolton, had hindered Moray, and the results of her tortuous policy were what every Border officer expected, lack of justice, raids, plots, and the encouragement of Mary's Border friends.[1]

In August Elizabeth made her cousin Hunsdon Warden and Governor in Bedford's place, and his letters are full of accounts of Border raids made by the Scots friends of Mary in the hope of causing a war with England, and of help given them by Scots who had settled in England which made Moray's small raid on Jedburgh in September of none effect. Hunsdon showed great energy and suggested many remedies, but the foundation of all the disorders was Elizabeth's lenient treatment of Mary.[2] The trial at York in October seems to have caused a lull in the disorders, but, in Moray's absence, it did not last long, and the Scots Borders were described as 'ready to go by the ears, for they are at catch that catch may'. Raids in England, however, were checked partly by Hunsdon's making an example of some Teviotdale thieves, and partly by the weather which also made Mary's escape almost impossible.[3] So things remained till Moray returned to Scotland in January, about the time 1569. when Mary was moved to Tutbury. He soon made a journey to Jedburgh with two thousand horse, but, as before, the chief thieves had been warned, and so he missed them, but took sixty others, of whom he hanged

[1] C.S.P. ii, 703, 708, 710-12, 716-17, 732-3, 767, 779; For. viii, 2274-5, 2289, 2291-4, 2299-300, 2362, 2387, 2405-6, 2411, 2448-9; Holinshed, S., 509-10; Herries, 105; H.J.S. 39; Dom. Add. ii, 54. [2] C.B.P. i, 537; Birrel, 17; For. viii, 2496, 2524, 2530, 2536, 2542. [3] For. viii, 2602; C.H.M. i, 1221, 1230, 1245; C.S.P. ii, 922.

three. Having received a loan of £5,000 and two hundred
Berwick troops he came to Kelso with four thousand men,
and, having met Forster, went on and burnt Liddesdale
till not a house was left standing in it. Then, after giving
the usual pious instructions to the Wardens, he returned
to Edinburgh.[1] In the middle of September he came
again to Kelso for five or six weeks to suppress the outlaws and settle the Borders. He made delivery to England
for bills valued at £1,200, including principal, double
and 'saffee', and promised delivery for others valued at
£1,000. Then, after taking sureties from many Borderers,
and, assured of English concurrence against 'recet', he set
out for Dumfries, burning on the way and terrifying the
Liddesdale surnames to come before him with pledges.
He could not find any one suitable for Warden of the West
March, but great obedience was shown in all parts which
he visited. His policy had been the extermination or ex-
pulsion of all who would not be law-abiding citizens, and
for once it was English and not Scots domestic affairs which
prevented the results of that policy being fairly tested.[2]

The crisis of Elizabeth's reign was at hand. As early
as September there were reports of an intended rising
which Sussex dismissed as lewd rumours. The queen,
not altogether unsuspicious of Sussex himself, ordered
him to tell Northumberland to go to court without delay,
and on November 10 she wrote to Northumberland and to
Westmorland requiring them on their allegiance to repair
to her at Windsor. These summonses drove the earls,
who feared that their traitorous dealings with Spain and
their intended revolt in September had been discovered,
to rise in the hope of thus escaping the block. The Queen
saw her danger and acted with promptitude, ordering
Hunsdon to go north, and encouraging Sir Henry Percy
to remain loyal.[3]

[1] C.H.M. i, 1260, 1263; For. ix, 116; C.S.P. ii, 1010, 1032; R.P.C.S. i, 653,
660–1. [2] C.H.M. i, 1329; For. ix, 461, 471–3, 477–80, 485, 489, 499;
R.P.C.S. ii, 37, 41–5; Bannatyne, 2; C.S.P. ii, 1181, 1195, 1197; Herries,
118; Spotswood, ii, 118–19. [3] Dom. Add. ii, 81, 85, 87–9; Span. Col.
ii, 96, 147, 158, 195–7, 199–201; C.H.M. i, 840*, 1400, 1405– 6 (1). *This
should be dated 1569.

V. THE RISINGS OF 1569 AND 1570

THE rising of 1569 which, though not strictly a Border revolt, is inseparable from Border history, was caused mainly by the religious innovations, and by the jealousy of the earls for the new men about the Queen. By November 20 it looked really dangerous, though much depended on whether help came from the Continent, from Scotland, or from the loose Borderers. A week later, however, Moray made a proclamation forbidding Scots to ride in England or have any dealings with Elizabeth's rebels, a prelude to more practical help. The real difficulty was that the Wardens of England were reluctant to send their troops against the rebels, because they feared not only Scots raids but also the possible rising of the earls' tenants in such places as Cockermouth in their rear. Sussex thought these fears vain, and by December 4 was pretty confident of success, and sure that the earls when beaten would flee into Scotland. Forster had taken Alnwick Castle without a blow, and fortified Warkworth Castle and Newcastle against the earls, but it was not till the middle of the month that affairs came to a head. The earls then marched from Durham towards Newcastle, and were met by Forster and Sir H. Percy at Chester Dean, midway between Durham and Newcastle, where there was a skirmish. Next day the rebels fled, and the army finally broke up at Hexham, the earls going to Naworth, whence at midnight on December 20 they fled with their principal confederates and a hundred horse towards Harlaw Woods in Liddesdale, guided by Black Ormiston and other outlaws. Moray, who was on the Border, at once started after them. 'The vermin be fledd into a forrayn covert', wrote Cecil on Christmas Day.[1]

The curious thing about the rising is that the English

---

[1] Dom. Add. ii, 111, 117–18, 125, 137–9, 160; R.P.C.S. ii, 66–7; C.S.P. iii, 32–3, 54, 57; For. ix, 523, 547, 553; Stow, 1123–5; Herries, 108; Bannatyne, 21; Holinshed, S., 510–11; Holinshed, E., 1839–41; Sadler, ii, 343.

Borders kept quiet all the while, so that Sussex paid off the extra footmen directly after the earls fled, to the disgust of Moray, who thought that the rising had branches yet unknown. Liddesdale did not prove a very comfortable refuge for the earls, for the very morning after their arrival they were driven to flee again by the principal men who had given pledges to the Regent. Elizabeth sent to him to treat for their capture and delivery, but they changed their names and apparel to make detection more difficult. Moray promised to do his best, and his practices were rewarded on December 24 by the delivery of Northumberland at the hands of the Hector Armstrong of Harlaw, whose name became a synonym for Border traitor. An attempted rescue by Scots, aided by men of Bewcastle, failed, and the earl was shut up in Lochleven Castle, where he remained till Morton sold him to Elizabeth in 1572. Moray was not strong enough to deliver him, as the capture was very unpopular on his Borders, and there was much other domestic trouble in Scotland, as the gaps in the Privy Council Register show.[1] But the great comfort to Elizabeth, and in a lesser degree to Moray, was the collapse of the rising. Its premature outbreak, the inefficiency of its leaders, their failure to seize Mary, the energy of Sussex and the Wardens, the loyalty or at least the indifference of the local nobles and gentry, the loyalty of the commons, and the co-operation of Moray all contributed to this. The Border Wardens up to this time had always emphasized the influence of the old baronial families. No prince but a Percy was said to be known in Northumberland;[2] but when the matter came to the proof in 1569, and in 1570 with the Dacres, the value of an old name was shown to have diminished. It is true that the House of Percy was divided against itself, but it is not unlikely that the earls, when they intrigued with alien enemies, went further than their tenants were willing to follow. The English Catholics were said to hate the very name of foreigner, and to wish the old religion to be

---

[1] Dom. Add. ii, 160–2, 165, 167; For. ix, 554–7, 559–60, 565–6; C.S.P. iii, 59–61, 64–5, 86; Herries, 119; H.J.S. 44–5; R.P.C.S. ii, 73.   [2] For. ix, 568.

restored in a way which would not hand them over to any other nation.[1]

1570. The next year was mainly occupied with the legacies of its predecessor. There were on the whole some seven hundred executions, the actual numbers being uncertain as the work of supervising them was divided. Perhaps less than half of those executed were Borderers, as the executions in Durham county alone numbered three hundred and fourteen. Each execution was held as near as possible to the home of the particular rebel, and most of the deaths were those of the meaner sort and by martial law. The vengeance was bloody, but not particularly so for those days. Attainders numbered fifty-eight, the queen taking the lands, even those in the Bishopric, but she had spent over £200,000 in suppressing the rebellion, though it lasted not above two months. It has been suggested that the executions led to decay, but this is hardly likely, as one of the causes of decay was over-population. The confiscations, however, increased the number of non-resident landholders.[2]

Before the tale of deaths was complete the Regent Moray, with whom Elizabeth was negotiating for the delivery of her rebels, was murdered on January 23. He left a reputation at which it is difficult to find a contemporary qualified to cast the first stone, and his death was a serious thing for England, as, in Hunsdon's opinion, he was the only stay and cause of the quietness of the Borders.[3] The very night of the murder Buccleugh and Fernyhurst, after burning the house of the betrayer of the Earl of Northumberland, made an incursion in England with intent to cause war, and the Earl of Westmorland in their company watched the burning of corn and hay at Mindrum.[4] On January 31 the same folk with Johnstone rode as far as Morpeth.[5]

---

[1] Span. Cal. ii, 157.   [2] Sharp, 144, 187–8; Dom. Add. ii, 174–85, 188; C.H.M. i, 250; Camden, 167; Stat. Realm, iv, pt. i, 549; Bradley, *Romance of Northumberland*, 30.   [3] Spotswood, ii, 120; For. ix, 597, 600, 635–6; C.S.P. iii, 77.   [4] Calderwood, ii, 513, 528; Spotswood, ii, 122–3; For. ix, 640, 657–8; Herries, 121–2; Pitscottie, ii, 221; Bannatyne, 4.   [5] For. ix, 661.

They failed to involve the two countries in war, but succeeded in encouraging Leonard Dacre, grandson of the late Warden, who claimed to be heir in tail male to his nephew George, who had been accidentally killed in May 1569, to try his luck. He had been in the counsels of the rebel earls, and Elizabeth had decided early in January that he would be safer in custody. The situation was complicated. Scroope doubted whether West March troops would fight against him, and Leonard was cunning enough to excuse himself from coming to Scroope to give Border advice, alleging that his leg was damaged. Moreover, he had ordnance, much victual, and many men at

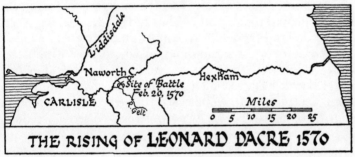

THE RISING OF LEONARD DACRE 1570

Naworth, and the Earl of Westmorland might well give up his nightly raids in England in order to help him with two thousand horse in conjunction with the men of Liddesdale and Teviotdale. There were various rumours, and the return of the rebels seemed to the men of the time not likely to be unwelcome, so Elizabeth, while raising troops and using clemency as a temporary measure, being fearful lest Dacre should escape into Scotland, ordered Hunsdon to proceed against Naworth.[1] Meanwhile, Dacre was raising men under colour of protecting his poor tenants against Scots raids.[2] On the night of February 18–19 Hunsdon was at Hexham ready to strike and all was uncertain, for if he were beaten the whole Border was likely to break. During the next night, while 'the beacons

[1] Dom. Add. ii, 193, 202, 211, 216, 218–20, 223, 226–8; For. ix, 686; Lodge, i, 495–7; H.J.S. 48; Calderwood, ii, 553; Sadler, ii, 409–10.   [2] Dom. Add. ii, 235, 237; For. ix, 691–2.

burned all night, and every hill was full of horse and foot crying and shouting as though they were mad', he made a forced march and was before Naworth at daylight on February 20, but, lacking ordnance, declined Dacre's offer to fight, and decided to pass by and join Scroope at Carlisle. Dacre followed him for four miles and, says Hunsdon, 'in a heath where we were to pass a river (the Gelt) his foot gave the proudest charge upon my shot that I ever saw; whereupon, having left Sir John Forster with five hundred horse for my back, I charged with the rest of my horse upon his foot and slew between three and four hundred'. A hundred prisoners were taken, and Dacre, narrowly escaping capture, was the first to flee, and never looked behind him till he was in Liddesdale, whence, later, he escaped to Flanders, to die in August 1573. The rebels numbered over three thousand, of whom over a thousand were horsemen, but few, if any, gentry. Hunsdon had only fifteen hundred men 'of all sorts', five hundred of them footmen. His victory was largely due to his rapid night march, as Dacre, who apparently used no scouts, did not expect him till February 22, by which time his forces were expected to number four or five thousand more out of Scotland alone. The lack of resistance to Sussex later on makes this very doubtful. The three hundred men from Berwick garrison did good service and the gentry of Northumberland under Forster behaved valiantly. It seems probable that some of Dacre's men who had been raised in the Queen's name joined him under a misapprehension, and therefore made little resistance and were ready to curse him after the fight. The Queen, urged by Hunsdon, spared all the meaner sort.[1]

[1] Dom. Add. ii, 237–8, 240–2, 244; For. ix, 699, 773; C.S.P. iii, 134; Arch. Bodl. F.C. 11, fol. 136–7; Holinshed, E., 1841; Stow, 1125–6. The last two err in dating the battle February 22.

VI. THE ENGLISH RAIDS OF 1570[1]

DURING Hunsdon's brief campaign the Scots had raided both East and Middle Marches, and taken over seven score prisoners. The West was also much unsettled. When, therefore, in thanking her officers, Elizabeth said she intended to take due revenge on the Scots for aiding her rebels, and proceeded to raise troops in the south, Hunsdon was overjoyed.[2] Having raised some thousand horse and three thousand foot, with the quality of which he was not satisfied, Sussex on April 10 issued the Queen's proclamation that she was sending the force merely to take her rebels and that it would treat all Scots 'lovingly and peaceably as her own', except the notorious outlaws who had invaded her realm and supported her rebels. He wrote a letter to Morton and his party to the same effect.[3] The Scots Lords made no sign of joining Sussex, but Mary's friends prepared resistance in the West, though in other parts they 'threshed their corn, fled with their cattle, and unthatched their houses'. Sussex having made plans for entry in three separate places, refused the rebel Lords' plea for a truce, stayed their messenger to Elizabeth, and started for Teviotdale on April 17.[4]

In writing an account of these invasions it is best to finish Sussex's first set of operations before describing what Scroope did in the West. If the account seems disproportionately long, it is well to remember that the subject is unique in Elizabethan Border history. On Monday April 17, then, at 6 p.m. Sussex and Hunsdon left Berwick, and entering Scotland at Wark at 3 or 4 a.m. on Tuesday, marched along Teviotdale 'burning on both hands at least two mile' and leaving neither castle nor

---

[1] See Maps X, XI, XII.   [2] Dom. i, 366, no. 12; Dom. Add. ii, 244, 246–7; For. ix, 699, 710, 737, 746.   [3] Dom. Add. ii, 268, 271; Sharp. 233–4; For. ix, 798, 800, 814; C.S.P. iii, 167–8; Calderwood, ii, 555–7; Arch. Bodl. F.C. 11, fol. 138–9; Bannatyne, 33–7; H.J.S. 55.   [4] For. ix, 799, 801, 814; C.S.P. iii, 169, 177–82; Calderwood, ii, 558.

tower nor town unburnt till they came to Jedburgh, where
they met Forster, who had entered Scotland at the head
of Coquet and burnt along Oxnam Water on each side of
the stream. Here the night was spent. Many of the towns
burnt were Buccleugh's, yet there were only three or four
small skirmishes, and some resistance at one of the towers,

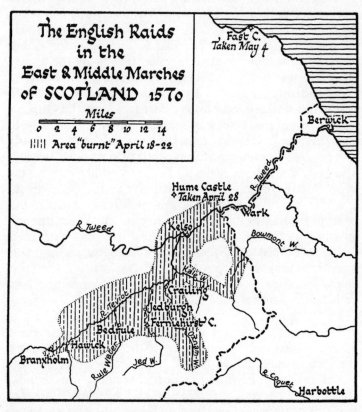

for Hume and Dacre, though in the field, durst not come
nigh Sussex. Next day, April 19, Sussex divided his forces
into two, one on each side of the Teviot, and marched to
Hawick, burning three or four miles on either side. They
failed to blow up Fernieherst Castle, but left it 'so torn up
with laborars (workmen) as it were a goodly flat'. On
arriving at Hawick, where they meant to spend the night,

they found 'the houses of the town unthetched, the thetch
set afire in the streets, and the people wholly fled', except
the keeper of Drumlanrig's castle, 'who had received the
goods of the whole town'. After quenching the fire with
some difficulty, the army spent the night there, and the
soldiers were forced to eat such victuals as they had with

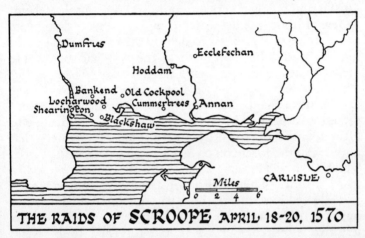

THE RAIDS OF SCROOPE APRIL 18-20, 1570

them. Next day, April 20, having finished firing the
place, except Drumlanrig's house and the goods therein,
the foot remained at Hawick, but, while Forster went with
his horsemen 'to burn the towns and villages adjoining',
Sussex and Hunsdon went to Buccleugh's principal house
at 'Branksam', where their powder finished the work
which the owner's fire had begun. Having burnt the
castles and houses of Buccleugh's friends and kinsmen in
those parts, Sussex and Hunsdon returned along the
Teviot to Jedburgh and burnt all the country farther off
from the river which they could not come to the day before.
Here they were joined by Forster and spent the night. On
Friday, April 21, the army was again divided. Sussex took
the direct road to Kelso, burning as he went, and Hunsdon
with the Berwick bands and other footmen, and a few
horse, 'went along Bowbent and Kele', leaving 'never a
house nor tower unburnt', unless its owner 'came in' and
offered pledges. Forster on Hunsdon's right hand did the

like. The three met near Kelso, where Sussex spent the night, but Hunsdon with his footmen went to Wark. Cesford came to ask them to spare East Teviotdale, but refused to give hostages, whereupon Sussex 'burnt all those places that belonged to any of the offenders', sparing those of Cesford and divers gentlemen, who had promised satisfaction for their servants and had done nothing themselves. Hume came the same night to Sussex to make peace, but, on his refusal to deliver the rebels, Sussex told him he would be dealt with as the rest had been. He meant to attack Hume Castle the next day, April 22, but owing to some negligence the horses that should have drawn his ordnance had returned to Berwick, so he went there too at once. On April 26 he left again and came to Hume Castle on April 27 and planted his artillery that night. All the forenoon of April 28 he battered the castle, which then yielded unconditionally after a vain appeal to Lord Hume. The garrison of about two hundred men was allowed to depart without bag or baggage. The place ought to have been able to hold out for a month. Sussex left two hundred men there and returned to Berwick, having fired divers towns and villages within three or four miles of the castle during the siege. Lord Hume's other Border stronghold, Fast Castle, yielded on May 4, before any artillery was planted against it. Between three and five hundred villages had been burnt, and terror caused the rest of the country to come in.[1]

Meanwhile Scroope had entered Scotland on the night of Tuesday, April 18, and encamped at Ecclefechan for Wednesday night. On April 20 he sent Simon Musgrave out to burn and spoil the country and meet him at Cummertrees, but Simon, when he had burnt the towns of Blackshaw, Sherington, 'the Bankend three miles of Dumfries', Lougher, Lougherwood, and Ecclefechan, met Lord Maxwell and Johnstone with their forces and the men of Dumfries at Old Cockpole. They had six hundred

---

[1] C.S.P. iii, 209, 270; For. ix, 841, 844; Sharp, 233–40, 508; Stow, 1126–7; Lodge, i, 507–10; Spotswood, ii, 128–9; Herries, 124; Bannatyne, 38; Melvill, M., 225–9; H.J.S. 55; Pitscottie, ii, 228–9; Holinshed, E., 1842–5.

foot and four hundred horse, but, after three hours' fighting, help came from Scroope at Cummertrees, and Simon
put the enemy to flight and chased them as far as Dumfries,
taking a hundred prisoners. Musgrave then joined
Scroope and they returned to Carlisle. This is Scroope's
account. The Scots version is different, and says that
Scroope did little beyond destroying castles at Dumfries,
Hoddam, and Annan, the people having gone away with

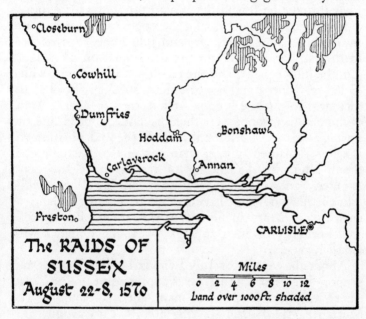

The RAIDS OF SUSSEX
August 22-8, 1570

Miles
0 2 4 6 8 10 12
Land over 1000 ft. shaded

their goods to the hills. It also asserts that Scroope had to
retreat, 'fearing distress in his army', and 'with loss of
many of his army who were cut off by parties'. Some of
the Scots, however, chiefly Armstrongs, came in to
Scroope.[1] The most astonishing fact, however, is that
'during all these invasions' the Scots dared not enter England, and no house was burnt nor cow stolen.[2]

These raids, of course, indirectly helped the King's

[1] C.S.P. iii, 188, 209; For. ix, 848, 853; Spotswood, ii, 129; Holinshed, E.,
1843; Stow, 1127; Trans. Dumfries and Galloway, N.H. & A.S. xxiii,
217–45.   [2] Dom. Add. ii, 296.

party in Scotland, though Elizabeth, while wishing to
keep it loyal to her, showed no inclination to declare herself definitely in its favour for fear of complications with
France.[1] When the raids were over, however, and the
Marian Lords began to gather forces at Linlithgow early
in May, Sussex ordered Scroope and Forster to feint or
actually to enter Scotland in the West and in Teviotdale.
In this way by keeping Herries, Buccleugh, and suchlike
men at home he repaid the Scots Protestants for Moray's
aid six months before, and Scroope went further and
ravaged the lands of Herries and Johnstone. Sussex went
further still and sent Drury into Scotland on May 11 to
join the king's party, and the result of this journey, which
ended on June 3 and is not strictly speaking Border history, was to put the king's party in the ascendant. Some
of the English troops were then disbanded, but Hume and
Fast Castles were retained, and till the end of June the
Borders remained quieter than any one could remember
them. But the disbanding of troops made the Scots
'stouter', and Herries grew busy on the West, while
Elizabeth's allowing Livingstone to enter Scotland as
envoy from Mary to her party encouraged Buccleugh's
and Fernyherst's men to raid Wark in company with
English rebels.[2]

About the middle of July Lennox became Regent and
proposed another English invasion, this time on the West,
where Leonard Dacre was maintained by some of the
Marian party. Elizabeth consented, and by August 18,
after delays caused by heavy rain, Sussex arrived in Carlisle. Further delays owing to rain and floods gave the
Scots time to collect their goods and flee, before Sussex,
who had ordered Hunsdon and Forster to feign to enter
their opposite Wardenries, entered Scotland with four
thousand men on August 22. He burnt Annan and
demolished the castle, and those of Dumfries, Hoddam,
Cowhill, Carlaverock, Closburne, 'Tynnell', Bonshaw, and
divers other places, so that not a stone house guardable in

[1] C.S.P. iii, 226.   [2] C.S.P. iii, 222, 233, 270, 274, 284, 330, 341, 345;
For. ix, 905, 907, 921-2, 973, 993, 1054, 1061-2, 1072, 1078.

any way was left to any ill neighbour within twenty miles of Carlisle. Drumlanrig's party was spared, and Sussex was back in Carlisle with great spoil by August 28. Maxwell and Herries, 'Mitchell Wyleis lauchful successoure', were the chief sufferers, but, though Sussex tried to spare the poor and the king's party, Morton's tenants of Preston under the Fell were spoiled. As a result Herries offered to be at Elizabeth's devotion, and Fernieherst, Buccleugh, and their faction offered to submit to the king.[1] The Scots Borders had been made too hot for Elizabeth's rebels, some of whom, including Westmorland, took ship from Aberdeen towards the end of August. The sequel to the two English rebellions was over, and the Borders in their wasted state were quiet enough for Sussex to leave for the south, which he did in November after disbanding most of the extra troops, and carrying on negotiations for an abstinence between the two Scots parties which was made difficult by the unreliability of their Border allies.[2]

[1] For. ix, 1087, 1121, 1192, 1196, 1205, 1212, 1222, 1240; C.S.P. iii, 372, 380, 424, 432, 436, 537, 540; Bannatyne, 51; H.J.S. 60; Holinshed, E., 1853; Calderwood, iii, 11.   For. ix, 1231, 1305, 1311, 1392; C.S.P. iii, 486–8; Dom. Add. ii, 321.

VII. THE SCOTS CIVIL WAR AND MORTON'S BORDER POLICY, 1571-5

FOR the next two and a half years Scotland was engaged in a civil war of which no man could foresee the issue. For the first part of 1571 the English Borders were quiet owing to Sussex's raids and the storms, which lasted well into February and seriously damaged Berwick bridge, and because the Scots Borderers were occupied with their own feuds and civil war, while Mary, who hoped for restoration and did not wish to anger Elizabeth, kept her friends quiet. The English garrisons, however, at Hume and Fast Castles were alert.[1] Some fighting took place in and around Jedburgh, but most of the civil war was fought outside the Borders, though not outside the sphere of influence of the English Wardens, who managed to keep such folk as Herries, Maxwell, and Lochinvar at home for a time, though in May they were able to take forces to Edinburgh. Drury went there twice to try to make peace, but failed, and there were again skirmishes on the Borders, chiefly between Fernyhurst and the men of Jedburgh.[2] In September many Borderers were in the fighting round Stirling in which Lennox was slain, and Buccleugh and Ormiston of the queen's party captured. Fernieherst, who had some broken Englishmen with him, escaped. Towards the end of the year Elizabeth seemed more inclined to side with the Regent, and in November Hunsdon was sent north, partly because raids were becoming more frequent, but mainly to negotiate for the delivery of Northumberland, a proposal to which Mar would by no means agree. Andrew Melvill also came to Berwick on behalf of the Marian party, but the negotiations did not affect the

---

[1] Dom. Add. ii, 336; For. ix, 1500, 1504-5, 1514, 1541, 1543, 1570; C.S.P. iii, 610, 616, 632-4, 638.   [2] Calderwood, iii, 155; H.J.S. 98; Diurnal, 241; Spotswood, ii, 170; For. ix, 1561-3, 1567, 1570, 1579, 1581, 1604, 1694, 1706-7, 1710, 1744, 1776, 1784, 1795, 1804, 1827, 1841, 1846, 1917; C.S.P. iii, 767, 865.

English Borders which were peaceful, though Hunsdon thought they would hardly remain so unless Mary was more hardly used and her escape made impossible.[1]

1572. The next year much resembled its predecessor in Border history. Hunsdon was mainly occupied in negotiations with the Scots parties, and there were but few raids. The first real thing of note was Hunsdon's success towards the end of May in buying Northumberland from Morton for £2,000. He was kept at Berwick for a time, and the absence of any attempts at rescue says much for the strength of the place. Finally he was sent to York, where he was executed at 3 p.m. on August 22.[2] His delivery doubtless helped to secure the surrender of Hume and Fast Castles to the Regent, though this was delayed till October 1573.[3] For the last five months of the year there was an abstinence between the Scots parties, from which, however, 'the haill thevis and brokin men' of the Borders were excluded, and the Regent meant to send men of war to Jedburgh and visit the Borders himself. Lack of money postponed the raid, and before he could raise it he died.[4] The effects of the news on the Borders were expected to be serious, and the English raised forces to keep the King's 'unfriends' at home, and, apparently to enter Scotland if necessary. However, nothing important happened on the Borders, and on November 21, Morton, who had been declared Regent, was formally elected.[5] On

1573. January 1 the abstinence was broken by the queen's party in Edinburgh, and Elizabeth's determination to aid the Regent, most likely formed soon after St. Bartholomew's day, became clear, and doubtless caused many men, including Buccleugh and Johnstone, to come in, and the Teviotdale folk to give pledges to Morton.[6] Finally, in April, Drury was sent into Scotland

[1] C.S.P. iii, 904, 912, 921, 935, iv, 24, 34, 50, 57; For. ix, 1970, 1984, 1989, 1992, 2012, 2015, 2061, 2114, 2132–4, 2192.   [2] For. x, 32, 56, 111, 218–19, 340, 384; C.S.P. iv, 199; Spotswood, ii, 177; Diurnal, 298; H.J.S. 107; Dom. Add. ii, 417, 419, 424.   [3] For. x, 393, 1211; C.S.P. iv, 737.   [4] For. x, 505; C.S.P. iv, 399, 426, 459, 470; R.P.C.S. ii, 158 ff.   [5] For. x, 626, 630, 639, 641, xxxvii.   [6] For. x, 744, 761; C.S.P. iv, 536; R.P.C.S. ii, 179.

with fifteen hundred troops with siege trains, and on May 28 Edinburgh Castle, in which was Lord Hume, surrendered. By June 13 the ordnance was back in Berwick. During the expedition the Borders were quiet, except Fernyherst's men, who 'comytted great Riotts and murders upon them of Jedworth', and the proud thieves of the West.[1]

The civil war being over, Morton at once turned his attention to the Borders and ordered a levy at Peebles on July 20. As former 'rodes' had been partial failures owing to the 'recet' of thieves with their cattle and goods by their 'previe freindis' in the incountry, steps were taken to prevent this, and the concurrence of the English Wardens requested. This they were ordered to give, and, after a postponement, the Regent came to the Borders in August, and, after having trouble with Fernyhurst and the West March rebels, he met with success about which contemporary estimates differ. Illegal bonds were quashed, sureties were taken, and the Wardens of both nations met in the Regent's presence and agreed to set all unlawful prisoners free. There seem to have been no executions, but the author of the *History of James the Sext* harps on the amount of money taken by the Regent at 'Justice Ayris'. The author of the *Diurnal* says that, though the Regent took four thousand men to Jedburgh, the thieves after he left the country on August 30, convened and harried it 'followand ay on the oist', but the Regent was pretty well satisfied with his work, though he did not regard it as complete, and so was Valentine Browne, who was in charge of Berwick.[2] The Borders remained quiet, and at the end of October Elizabeth thought fit to surrender Hume and Fast Castles, after removing the guns to England.[3] In November Morton again visited the Borders, held courts, and succeeded in capturing Black Ormiston and other outlaws. He appointed new Wardens for the

---

[1] C.S.P. iv, 596, 666, 694; For. x, 969, 987, 1009, 1038; C.H.M. ii, 127; Murdin, 246.   [2] For. x, 1024, 1055–6, 1117, 1131, 1136, 1145, 1161; R.P.C.S. ii, 242–4, 252, 266, 273–5, 368, 548; C.S.P. iv, 702, 712, 723; A.P.C. viii, 128; Spotswood, ii, 194–5; H.J.S. 149; Diurnal, 336–7; Pitscottie, ii, 308–9.   [3] For. x, 1211; C.S.P. iv, 737.

Marches, ordered 'Trews' to be held, and showed such a strong hand that Fernyhurst, to whom a quiet Border was a dull and unprofitable place, desired to go to France. Elizabeth for her part retained the guns she had had removed.[1]

1574. The next year was uneventful. The Borders were on the whole very quiet except for raids in September, and the Regent showed himself not only disposed to keep them so, though he made no journey thither, but also to do justice to England. The amity was well preserved in spite of delay in returning the Scots guns; and, though English pirates were troublesome, and Fernyhurst was maintained by Forster, and other rebels by the English West Marches, Morton made no reprisals for fear of spoiling his chance of getting an English pension. Elizabeth made some attempts to reform old domestic Border abuses, and felt so secure that she sent a hundred

1575. of Berwick garrison to Ireland.[2] These attempts were being continued and the Regent was quite satisfied with the justice he got from England, except that Forster persisted in his recet of the king's rebels, when in July an 'accident' took place which nearly shattered the amity.

[1] For. x, 1144, 1223–4, 1232; C.S.P. iv, 731–2, 744; R.P.C.S. ii, 300; A.P.C. viii, 158; Dom. Add. ii, 454. [2] For. x, 1297, 1313, 1335, 1411, 1421, 1445–7, 1455–6, 1470–2, 1483, 1515–19, 1564–6, 1602; C.S.P. iv, 750, 756, 778–9, v, p. 8, nos. 34, 37–8, 54–5, 64; A.P.C. viii, 205, 272, 275; R.P.C.S. ii, 367, 371–3, 421; Dom. Add. ii, 462–6.

VIII. THE RAID OF REDESWYRE

THE Redeswyre, some two and a third miles north-west of Carter Fell, is the watershed between the River Rede and the Carter Burn, which runs into Jed Water. Here, on July 7, a day of 'Trews' was held between Sir John Forster, Warden of the Middle March, and Sir John Carmichael the younger, who had been nominated Warden of the Scots Middle March by the Regent, but was regarded by Forster merely as Keeper of Liddesdale. Carmichael had failed to agree with Sir George Heron, Forster's deputy, at their last meeting, and therefore Forster decided to meet one whom he considered his inferior in office. The first at all trustworthy account of the happenings of that day was issued by Huntyngdon, Gargrave, Henry Gate, Rauffe Rokebie, and R. Bowes, who examined Forster on August 4 as a preliminary to their proposed meeting with the Scots Regent. In substance it is as follows. The meeting was for justice only, and almost all on both sides were unarmed and went abroad in each other's company. After friendly salutation a fit place was chosen on English ground, and justice was quietly done, only one bill being passed over. After courteously drinking to each other the officers began justice again, an English absentee being condemned by Forster for default. Carmichael demanded delivery for the same, and Forster offered to make it at the next meeting, whereupon Carmichael said, 'No more can I make further delivery to you, and it appears you cloak justice and are not willing that it should proceed'. He is said to have added, though he afterwards denied it, saying that the words were spoken before over their cups and that Forster took no offence, that so long as Forster's and the keeper's 'nolt' went quietly on the Borders there was nothing but maintenance of fugitives, rebels, and traitors. Forster denied this and said he was willing to do justice,

and Carmichael replied that he was as able to answer for
his office as Forster, and was of as good a lineage. Forster
retorted that he was Warden and Carmichael but a keeper,
whereupon certain lewd Scots murmured and said, 'Fye,
Fye, comparison, comparison', and then cried, 'A Jedworth, a Jedworth', and began the affray. The Scots
averred on the contrary, according to Forster, that certain
Tynedale men standing by him cried, 'A Tindale, a Tindale', and running together shot arrows amongst the
whole company and thus began the affray. Forster continued that though the beginners of the slaughter could
not be found, yet it seemed that many evil disposed persons with deadly feuds in their hearts seized the chance
and began the broil without the knowledge of Carmichael
or himself, and that they mutually agreed to pacify the
people. Forster said he quieted those about him, but
Carmichael failed, and came among his men with drum
and three 'pensils' against Forster and his company, who
were few in number, and put them back and followed the
chase into England. Some of the Scots took a prey of
cattle, Sir George Heron and five other Englishmen were
slain, and Lord Francis Russell and sundry others hurt,
while Forster, Collingwood, and some more, including
Russell, were taken into Scotland. The Scots had five
slain and divers hurt. All this time Carmichael, according
to Scots testimony, was trying to hold back his men, and
no Englishman charged him with doing any hurt with his
own hand. The craftsmen of Jedburgh were said to carry
drums and 'pensils' to meetings to call and keep their
people together, and for no other purpose. The commissioners' report concluded that the fray was due not to the
words of Forster or Carmichael but to the great number
of feuds among the people, and the number of evil disposed men gathered on both sides.

After the fray peace hung, as it were, by a twine or
thread, but was maintained, in Forster's opinion, because
Sir William Ker of Cesford, whom Forster calls Warden,
was content to bind up assurance with Forster while he
was in Scotland, though two of his men had been slain in

the raid. The Regent, on the other hand, said it was due to his taking Forster and his company to Dalkeith for their safety. Both of them probably contributed to the desirable end, as did also John Selby, Angus, who was in Jedburgh, and Huntyngdon. Elizabeth, though she used strong words, knew as well as the Regent that only outlaws and Marian Papists had anything to gain from war. Thus peace was kept, and an English commission gathered from Forster and his gentry, after their return, the account given above. It did not quite satisfy Huntyngdon, who thought Forster was trying to hide matters, thus confirming Killegrew's view that Forster was not so clean in the matter as he could wish. The commission met the Regent at Foulden in the third week in August and negotiations were so long that it was not until after Hunsdon's arrival that an agreement was reached on September 13, the Regent consenting that the cases should be settled by March Law, and that four of his own surname of Douglas, and four of Carmichael's should be entered to remain at Berwick during Elizabeth's pleasure. The eight pledges were delivered the next night, and on September 20 Carmichael, the Regent's cousin, was entered too, but was sent home again before the end of October 'with Honour and certain presents'. Thus was Elizabeth appeased.

There remains the question of responsibility for the fray, and unfortunately there is no extant account from Carmichael's hand. Scots partisans and English ones blamed each other, and moderate men like Huntyngdon blamed both sides. But Camden and Davison seem to have been right in laying the blame at Forster's door. His whole Border policy was selfish, and he appears to have been in league with the Regent's enemies. Carmichael, on the other hand, was no Borderer, and held no Border lands, and, when he did justice and daunted Border thieves, Forster may well have feared lest some of his own underhand dealings should come to light. Thus he may have arranged the fray, or at least done nothing to stop it, with the intent of getting Carmichael removed.

The case is not proven, of course, but it is thoroughly consistent with the careers of the two men.[1]

[1] For. xi, 214–16, 218, 220, 222–5, 234, 238–45, 256–7, 274–6, 279, 281, 283, 290, 292–3, 297, 309, 311, 328, 332–5, 350–2, 360, 394, 404; S.P. Borders, xix, 90, 146, 178–95; C.S.P. iv, 169–72, 174–5, 177, 179–80, 182–4, 186–7, 192, 195–7, 206, and p. 193; R.P.C.S. ii, 420, 459; Murdin, 166, 283, 286; Diurnal, 348–9; H.J.S. 153–4; Spotswood, ii, 198; Camden, 210–12; C.H.M. ii, 299–300, 316, 320; A.P.C. ix, 34; Pitscottie, ii, 321.

IX. MORTON'S RENEWED ATTEMPTS AT SETTLEMENT AND HIS FALL

DURING his remaining years of power Morton showed great energy in dealing with the Borders. Immediately after the agreement at Foulden he proclaimed a Border journey, and, after one or two postponements, during which he raised a tax and arranged for the concurrence of the English Wardens, he arrived at Dumfries on November 16. Here he did his work thoroughly, punishing the recettors of thieves' goods 'indifferentlie as the saidis thevis', causing 'execution of justice to be made apoun certain of the offenders, and mony greit offences bipast to be redressit', taking pledges, and giving instructions for their safe custody and convoy under the penalty of £2,000. This occupied about a month.[1] Of course some of the pledges escaped later and rode in England, but Scroope and Elizabeth were satisfied with what he had done and with his intentions as to the Middle Marches.[2]

1576. Though all the Redeswyre goods had not been delivered, the Regent's journey had produced a lull which enabled the English government to consider domestic matters, chiefly about Berwick, and to inquire into Morton's complaints against Forster, whom he vainly wished to be 'depryvit of his charge'.[3] This failure, however, did not prevent the Regent going to Jedburgh in November and doing nearly three weeks' work for justice and the amity, among other things ordering a list of the many thieves still at large to be compiled and sent to the Wardens of both realms who were to pursue and punish them. His good example was followed on the West, where Scroope and Maxwell met and made delivery for forty-two bills, an unprecedented day's work for their Marches.

[1] R.P.C.S. ii, 460, 462–3, 465, 467–9, 476–8; C.S.P. v, 208–9, 212; A.P.C. ix, 50.   [2] R.P.C.S. ii, 514, 525; A.P.C. x, 68.   [3] For. xi, 648, 655, 765, 781–2, 785–6, 843–4, 876; C.S.P. v, 228, 232, 238; A.P.C. ix, 71, 77, 85, 165; R.P.C.S. ii, 498.

The Redeswyre goods, however, do not seem to have been returned.[1]

1577. Another quiet year followed in Border history. In the earlier part of it the English government was again busied with inquiries into the necessary repairs at Berwick, Carlisle, Newcastle, and elsewhere.[2] On May 25 Maxwell resigned and was succeeded by Angus, who showed 'singular care . . . towards the furderance of justice' and of the amity. The Regent intended to visit the Borders in October owing to the partial failure of his system of pledges, but was prevented not by annoyance with English piracy or with Forster but by the internal state of his own country where 'soundry of the nobles' were 'infected with French traynes and gredy of innovation', and where there was a possibility of a fresh attempt being made in favour of Mary.[3] None the less,
1578. good quietness such as no man remembered seems to have continued on the Borders until Morton's fall in March, and it is noteworthy that one of his last official acts was the proclamation of a journey against the disordered Border peoples, though as no place is mentioned, he may have meant to use the levies for other purposes. James, who now took over the nominal rule of his kingdom, told Elizabeth that his first care, next God, would be the maintenance of the amity and good Border rule.[4]

The fall of Morton marks the renewal of the Guise attempt to restore Mary, and the amity was again in jeopardy. Morton, indeed, soon regained ascendancy, but his time was too much occupied for him to attend to the Borders, and so the Scots Borderers not only revived their old feuds but also made raids in Tynedale and Redesdale. The 'broken estate' of Scotland 'falling daily into dangerous condition by the great discords renewing still among the nobility, and presently threatening seditious effects',

[1] R.P.C.S. ii, 554, 567-9, 572; C.S.P. v, 241; Dom. Add. ii, 505.   [2] A.P.C. ix, 287-8, 336, 355-6, 364; Dom. Add. ii, 512-13, 530; For. xi, 1406, 1443, 1489; C.B.P. i, 15-16.   [3] R.P.C.S. ii, 613, 619-20, 626-40; A.P.C. x, 103-4; C.B.P. i, 18; C.S.P. v, 259, 269-70.   [4] R.P.C.S. ii, 674-5, 677; A.P.C. x, 143; C.S.P. v, 318.

was an excellent opportunity for Scots Border reivers, and
they used it, and were imitated throughout the realm.[1] In
August Hunsdon was sent down to his charge to confer
with Scroope and Forster for putting the Borders in readiness not only for defence but also to assist James with a
thousand horse and a thousand harquebusiers from York
and the Bishopric, if Bowes thought necessary. But
threats to burn the houses of Cesford and Sir James Hume
and their followers, if they would not refer their causes to
Elizabeth, proved sufficient to bring about a seeming
accord in Scotland.[2] It was during this lull that William,
Lord Ruthven, went to the Borders as Lieutenant, a
special tax being voted for maintaining a force
1579.   there. The accounts of his doings are scanty, but
when he returned in the third week in January
bringing with him Lord Maxwell, the Warden of the
West Marches, who had been troublesome, the Scots
Council voted that he had 'dewelie worthelie and suffi-
cientlie done and performit his dewitie'. There is no
record of English forces entering Scotland to aid him,
though the Wardens had been ordered to be ready if he
required them. The result was a lengthy inquiry into the
state of the West Marches, which ended in the superses-
sion of Maxwell by Herries.[3]

For a short time there was quiet, and Elizabeth thanked
Herries for his pains; but Morton's temporary overthrow
of the Hamiltons, some of whom fled to England after
Maxwell and Herries had openly consorted with them (a
course which led to Herries's dismissal in August), strained
the amity, as the fugitives were 'recetted' in England,
and the Scots retaliated by seizing Englishmen and their
goods in Kelso market. Smaller questions had hindered
justice and encouraged evil-doers on the East, but Elizabeth felt confident enough to send northern troops, including three hundred from Berwick garrison, to Ireland,

[1] C.H.M. ii, 533, 539; R.P.C.S. iii, 2, 9.   [2] A.P.C. x, 304, 306–7; For.
xiii, 171; C.R.B. vii; C.S.P. v, 375; C.H.M. ii, 589.   [3] A.P.C. xi, 5–6;
R.P.C.S. iii, 38, 41, 46, 62–8, 73, 75–86, 92, 133–4, 170; Spotswood, ii,
259–63.

their stay and final sending being governed not by Border affairs but by the course of events in Ireland.[1] A commission was suggested, and Errington went into Scotland to try to settle Border matters and to intercede for the Hamiltons, but no arrangements were made except for 'trews', and the arrival of young Esmé Stuart, Count D'Aubigny, the nephew of the Regent Lennox, who was sent by the Guises to plot against Morton and the 'Religion', boded ill for the amity.[2]

1580. The year 1580, the main interest of which in Scotland was the struggle between Morton and Lennox, as D'Aubigny soon became, opened on the Borders amid 'great justice with promise of greater progress'. But the English government showed wisdom in inquiring into the decay of horsemen on the Borders, for the state of the opposite realm was soon in 'doubtfull condition'. Elizabeth, however, persevered with her demand for a commission and was generally conciliatory, though musters were taken as a precaution. James did appoint commissioners, but postponed a meeting as Lennox's influence grew.[3] For a time the Borders remained quiet in spite of this, but in August nightly Scots raids began, and Elizabeth, who guessed that the Border influence of Lennox was the cause, sent Bowes to Scotland to demand his exclusion from the Council. He was recalled without getting it, and on December 31 the fall of Morton brought Lennox nearer to his goal.[4]

[1] C.S.P. v, 406, 409; C.H.M. ii, 732, 735; Camden, 235; A.P.C. xi, 224, 226, 228, 253–6, 264–5; R.P.C.S. iii, 207.   [2] Camden, 235; C.S.P. v, 444–7; C.H.M. ii, 784.   [3] C.R.B. xii, xiii, xxvi; C.S.P. v, 453, 456, 459, 463, 470, 483, 486, 491; R.P.C.S. iii, 262–3, 265; C.B.P. i, 42–3, 47–50, 54, 56; C.H.M. ii, 823; A.P.C. xi, pp. xv, 422–3, 425–6, 447, 453.   [4] C.S.P. v, 523, 573, 576, 581, 583–4, 592, 612; C.R.B. li, lvi, lxiv–v.

X. YEARS OF UNCERTAINTY, 1581–4

ELIZABETH made various attempts to save Morton, partly by sending an embassy and partly by raising a force to be sent into Scotland under Hunsdon. 1581. At the end of March Hunsdon was actually given leave to enter Scotland, but the order was revoked on April 10. Meanwhile the Scots had paid considerable attention to their own Marches, outwardly for the furtherance of justice, but really to strengthen Lennox's position. For instance, Cesford, Warden of the Middle Marches, replaced Carmichael as keeper of Liddesdale, and soon afterwards Johnstone was denounced rebel and Maxwell became Warden of the West Marches. The Scots Council, moreover, ordered a general levy for Border service, with the obvious intention of resisting any English invasion, and proclamation against intercourse with England was made. Perhaps Elizabeth found the job too big for her, and at any rate she gave the Scots that impression, and Morton was executed on June 1.[1] Angus and his friends fled to Carlisle, where they were entertained with courtesy, and the Borders remained quiet, there being only one notable Scots raid; but, if Scots authorities can be trusted, Angus made extensive raids on the West, and even took Langholm Castle and led the captain away prisoner into England, besides burning divers villages and taking away much booty. Apparently these raids were made with Johnstone's help.[2]

1582. Lennox no doubt had meant to do much, but within fifteen months of Morton's execution the Raid of Ruthven, August 23, 1582, deprived him of power. Among the charges made against him were the permission of great outrages on the Borders and of great raids on

---

[1] C.S.P. v, 649, 651–2, 785, vi, p. 4, no. 4; Camden, 261–2; R.P.C.S. iii, 344–8, 355–6, 374, 376; H.J.S. 183; C.R.B. lxxx.   [2] Camden, 263; C.S.P. vi, 30–3, 35, 40, 51; A.P.C. xiii, 200, 263–4; A.P.S. iii, 191 ff.; H.J.S. 184; R.P.C.S. iii, 448–9.

England, and neglecting to take advice for quieting the Marches. His Border friends, such as Maxwell, now Earl of Morton, Herries and Hume, who afterwards both changed sides, and Ferniherst, persisted in making raids and practising to raise war between the two realms,[1] while Elizabeth comforted the Lords around the King with promises of the aid they requested, and was rewarded with some attempt to quiet the Borders, the King calling on the Wardens and barons to meet him at Edinburgh in November. Few of them came, Morton being the most notable absentee, with the result that he was put to the horn and replaced by Johnstone. The King seems to have had some intention of visiting the Borders in person with a levy, but after postponing it till December 26, he stayed at home.[2]

1583. Lennox having left Scotland before the end of the year, the new Scots government seemed to favour the amity and was met by Bowes on behalf of Elizabeth with offers of justice to English pirates, a poor counter to the 'golden tools' which French emissaries were using as part of a huge Guise plot against England.[3] Johnstone, who had replaced Morton as Warden, was trying to arrange to do justice with Scroope. Cesford, on the other hand, was delaying things as much as he could, and these two cases are typical of the uncertainty of Scots relations. James was outwardly friendly to England and ordered his Wardens to do justice as Scroope and Forster wished, but it was not clear how far he might be influenced by 'Manningville', the agent of the Guise's scheme for invading England in the summer.[4] Such was the situation when on June 27 occurred the counter-revolution which took James out of the hands of the Ruthven Raiders, but it still remained uncertain whether James would accept a French pension or make a league with England and hope for an English one. Bowes was not optimistic, and the English Council again inquired into decay on the Borders.

[1] R.P.C.S. iii, 506-8; C.S.P. vi, 144-5, 154-6; C.R.B. xc.   [2] C.R.B. xcvii, civ, cxix, cxxii; R.P.C.S. iii, 527-8, 531.   [3] C.B.P. i, 141, 145, 147-9, 151-2; C.S.P. vi, 279, 288; C.R.B. clii, clv, clvii, clxiv-vi, clxx-i, clxxiii. [4] C.B.P. i, 153; C.S.P. vi, 369, 393; C.R.B. clxxvi, clxxviii, clxxxiii, clxxxviii.

There do not seem to have been any Border outrages, except one on the English Middle Marches in August, but Bowes could get no satisfaction from James, so Walsyngham was sent to Scotland to deal with a very fickle situation.[1] After audiences with James, he left Scotland, convinced that it was the Scots government, and not the Borderers, except the loose men, who were unfriendly to England. The government had even sounded several Scots barons and towns on the question of war. Besides having five days at Durham, during which he conferred with the Lord President, Scroope and Forster, Walsyngham learnt much of the state of the Borders on his northward journey from the complaints of Englishmen who met him by the way, some of them showing the bloody shirts of their friends slain by the Scots. On his way south he was met with pitiful complaints of the raids made during his sojourn in Scotland, and asked the Council to move the Queen lest the Borders be weakened.[2] Raids continued, especially on the West and Middle Marches, where the raiders 'sett nother by prince nor Warden'. Johnstone seemed willing to do justice if he could, but Cesford was still dilatory, so that, as the Queen refused to allow horse to be levied in Yorkshire, it was only by reprisals that Scroope's men forced the Scots to rob in their own realm rather than in England. The men of Tynedale, encouraged by the 'shooting' of meetings, burned and killed in Scotland also.[3]

1584. The 'tickle' and unsettled state of the Borders continued for the first few months of the next year. Liddesdale, in spite of English revenges, raided within three miles of Hexham, and there was 'doinge on both sydes' of the Middle Marches. The Scots Council made some kind of effort to improve at least the internal state of its own Marches and even ordered speedy redress for Liddesdale outrages on England.[4] But this was not enough to prevent

---

[1] C.R.B. ccxix, ccxxvi, ccxxix, ccxli; Dom. Add. iii, 90, 92; C.S.P. vi, 588, 590, 616, 623-4. [2] C.S.P. vi, 626, 628, 630, 643, 653; Dom. ii, 120; C.R.B. cclxiv-v. [3] C.S.P. vi, 657, 678, 680; C.B.P. i, 174, 176-7, 180-3, 185-7, 190. [4] C.B.P. i, 198-9, 201-3; C.S.P. vii, 36, 204; R.P.C.S. iii, 628, 634, 638.

Elizabeth's approving and indirectly supporting the attempt of Mar and Angus to gain control of the king. James tried to raise Border troops for use against them and to seize Fast Castle, but, though Scroope and Forster were ready to keep unfriendly Borderers at home, Davison was not sent in time with money, and the plot failed, and on April 27 Mar, Angus, Glamis, and some forty others came to Wark, where Selby, the deputy Warden, received them till Elizabeth's pleasure was known. They were not the only important fugitives 'recetted' that year, for James Melvill fled to Berwick and preached, being much struck with the 'fectfull professioun of trew Christianitie', which he found there. He afterwards left for Newcastle to preach to the exiled Lords.[1] Morton and Herries made proclamation for pursuit of the rebels whom Elizabeth refused to deliver, and raids began with renewed vigour, both sides growing loose. Orders were given for the levy of ten thousand foot and four hundred horse in Yorkshire against Scotland, and a tax was levied for Border defence, while the Scots forbade intercourse with England. Neither side, however, wished for war, and Davison, who was sent into Scotland, was able to arrange for a commission to settle the more important Border disputes. There were plenty of these, Scroope alleging that he had had no redress for five years, and Arran that the English daily heaped insupportable wrongs on the Scots. In July Hunsdon went north, and, after conferring with the gentry about fortifying the Borders, had a conference with Arran at Foulden on August 13, but, to the delight of Mary's friends, nothing was accomplished, and there was not even a cessation of raids during the meeting.[2] Hunsdon then busied himself with nine other commissioners in viewing decays within twenty miles of the Northumberland frontier and taking musters. He had sundry meetings

[1] C.B.P. i, 206, 212-13, 216, 218; C.S.P. vii, 55, 73, 75, 79-80; Camden, 292-3; Autobiog. 168, 172, 181, 196.   [2] C.B.P. i, 220, 222, 224-5, 228-9, 231, 234, 238, 250; C.S.P. vii, 127, 134, 138, 156, 159, 172, 179, 184, 212, 223-4, 236, 239, 248-50, 257, 259, 271; Dom. Add. iii, 119, 125; H.M.C. x, iv, 302-3; C.H.M. iii, 97; Melville, M., 329; Calderwood, iv, 171; H.J.S. 205-6.

for East Teviotdale redress, and things seemed somewhat better, though Forster could get no justice from his opposite as there was 'muche adoe betwene Pharnihyrst and Cesforde for the Wardenrye', whereby thieves were encouraged. In October Patrick, Master of Gray, was sent to Elizabeth to deal about Border incursions, the Scots queen, and the banished Lords, whose presence in Newcastle was a continual source of worry to Hunsdon. He obtained an official answer favourable to the amity and a private assurance that, when the time was ripe for upsetting Arran, the banished Lords would be allowed to return home.[1] While his embassy was in progress there were many Scots raids and English reprisals, the latter with government sanction. James, who was in great dislike with all his Wardens, Hume, Cesford, and Johnstone, acknowledged that Cesford by his 'oversight' had encouraged Liddesdale raids, and therefore made Fernyhurst Warden in his stead with extra troops and the large allowance, for a Scot, of £1,000 Scots. The new Warden's difficulties were great and he made no improvement, his March being raided by his own countrymen from the West, but his opposites Scroope and Forster, by taking assurance with some surnames of Liddesdale, Ewesdale, and Teviotdale, seem to have kept their own Marches quiet. They were again ordered by the English Council to proclaim peace, arrange 'trews', and collect a list of unredressed bills for a future commission.[2] It may be well to note that the Bond of Association was signed by the gentry of Cumberland and Westmorland, and by towns like Carlisle and Kendal.[3]

[1] Dom. Add. iii, 127–8; C.B.P. i, 253–5, 258–9, 267; C.S.P. vii, 344, 396, 418–19, 421; Brown, ii, 199.   [2] Dom. ii, 208; C.S.P. vii, 346; C.B.P. i, 264–6, 268, 270–2, 278, 280; C.H.M. iii, 116; R.P.C.S. iii, 699; Ham. P. ii, 468.   [3] Dom. Add. iii, 133.

XI. THE DEATH OF RUSSELL AND THE FALL OF ARRAN, 1585

THE next year was of great importance not only in Border but also in international history. England and Scotland were soon to be drawn together by the proclamation of the Holy League in France, and Arran was 1585. to fall. The year opened with some little show of Border justice, but this was much interrupted on the West by the sudden increase in fury of the Johnstone-Maxwell feud, and the Scots outlaws took advantage of it to do many small injuries to Scroope's charge. Three or four hundred in that part of Scotland were at disobedience, but Liddesdale was quiet owing to the captains and bands in waiting.[1] There was a smaller disturbance on Fernyhurst's March, where the gentry, especially those who supported the imprisoned Cesford, were disobedient.[2] A commission was really necessary, and, when Edward Wotton was sent to James to conclude a League in answer to the Holy League, and to intrigue for Arran's fall, the fixing of a date for such a commission was among his instructions. His work was much complicated by the continuance of the Johnstone-Maxwell feud, which made things very hard for Scroope. Johnstone was the Warden from whom he must get justice if he wanted it, and Maxwell, the rebel, was an enemy of Arran, and as such was to be joined by Angus and his friends when the time seemed ripe for Arran's overthrow. Things went well for England, however, and on July 31 an offensive and defensive League was agreed upon to be operative in case either of the realms was invaded, and Border questions since the King's accession were to be settled by a commission, and all others abolished within six months of the treaty.

[1] C.B.P. i, 281–3, 289, 291, 293, 299; Laing, i, 35, 37, 39, 44–9; R.P.C.S. iii, 721–2, 725; Ham. P. ii, 469–71.   [2] R.P.C.S. iii, 726.

Wotton had thus finished half his work, and the other half was made easier by the events of July 27.[1]

On the top of the Cheviots, near the watershed between the Coquet and Bowmont Water, is a hill called Windy Gyle, just two thousand feet above sea-level. The frontier ran through its summit, and a road, still traceable and named Clennell Street on the Ordnance Maps, led from England to Scotland past a place called Cocklaw. Here, where it crossed the old boundary, is a cairn, said to mark the spot where Russell fell. The only English statement of the facts of that day that is at all credible, for reasons which will soon be obvious, is a letter written by Forster to Walsyngham from his house nigh Alnwick on July 28.[2] He begins by stating that Russell came to the meeting 'for certain particuler causes of his own, against my will'. Russell had not attended a day of 'trews' for almost two years, and Forster does not seem to have expected him. The truce began, and then, continues the letter, 'yt chaunced a sodden accident and tumult to arriese amonge the rascalles of Scotlande and Englande, abowte a lyttle pyckery amonge themselves'. Meanwhile, Russell was apart with the Wardens who were calling bills, but soon went aside with his own men and was talking to a gentleman when he was 'sodenly shott with a gonne and slaine in the myddest of his owne men'. No one else was slain, the letter continues, and after 'this mischevious chaunce' Fernyhurst, the Scots Warden, with Forster and the gentry of both realms, 'stoode together and made a quietnes, and the opposite Warden as willinge as I in all the tumult', and then made a proclamation deferring redress for a day or two. Pledges were given on both sides, 'and so we parted quietly owte of the field'. Inquiry failed to reveal the shooter of that 'unhappie shotte'. Forster also wrote to Scroope that the shooting was 'accidentall',[3] and on July 31 he wrote to Wotton at Edinburgh

[1] C.S.P. vii, 587, 615, 619, 632, 636, 644, 653, viii, 31, 38, 40, 43; C.B.P. i, 303–5, 308, 311–15, 317, 320–1, 327; Moysie, 52; R.P.C.S. iii, 733–5, 741, 745–6, 759; Laing, i, 53; Ham. P. ii, 492–3.   [2] C.B.P. i, 330.
[3] S.P. Borders, xxiii, 226.

to inform him of the 'mischevous and unfortunate mis-
chaunce'.[1]

Now Wotton saw that, to use pastor Melvill's words,[2]
God had 'provydit in lyk manner a motive' for the removal
of Arran and the return of the exiled Lords; and the Scots
who were well affected to England thought that Elizabeth
would do well to take great offence at the murder, as if it
had been plotted by Arran and Fernyhurst, and have Arran
sent to England, though she must not go so far as to make
James despair of the amity.[3] It was then, probably without any reference to London, that Forster, doubtless
acting on Wotton's suggestion, drew up his later and lying
accounts of Russell's death,[4] in which he states that it was
'a prepensed matter, devised before'. It could not have
been. There is no evidence that the Scots expected Russell
at the meeting, and, on the other hand, there is evidence
that Forster hardly expected him.[5] Elizabeth adopted the
views of her ambassador and Warden, though Walsyngham acknowledged privately that there was no evidence
that the affair was not accidental. Arran was warded for
a few days at Wotton's request, and later Fernyhurst, who
steadfastly denied Arran's complicity, was committed to
ward at Aberdeen. Soon after, Arran set about gathering
forces, but Elizabeth, greatly to Wotton's discomfort,
would not loose the banished Lords. Finally, in October,
a commission of both sides met on the frontier to decide
the case.[6] While it was sitting, as there seemed little
chance of the delivery of Fernieherst, even if he were
declared guilty, Elizabeth recalled Wotton, who left of his
own accord before he got her letter, and let slip the
banished Lords, with the result that they met at Kelso and
arranged to take the whole of the Border forces with them,
Forster agreeing to prevent any raids from England.
Bothwell, Hume, young Cesford, Drumlanrig, Maxwell,
and indeed 'the haill Bordouris, East and Wast', 'resorted

---

[1] S.P. Borders, xxiii, 219.   [2] Autobiog. 222.   [3] C.S.P. viii, 46.
[4] C.B.P. i, 331, 337.   [5] C.B.P. i, 330.   [6] C.S.P. viii, 57, 60, 133,
187; Ham. P. ii, 495, 528, 536; Melvill, M., 344; Camden, 313–14; H.J.S.
207; Moysie, 53; R.P.C.S. iv, 4; C.B.P. i, 357–9, 361–9; Bell, 134–141.

unto them without delay'. They took Jedburgh, and
marched to Stirling, which they entered on November 1
or 2. Arran escaped, but, though James tried to raise
troops against them and issued proclamations, he failed,
and by November 4 the revolution was complete and the
returned Lords in favour.[1]

For the rest of the year there is little evidence about
Border matters. The Johnstone-Maxwell feud continued,
though Johnstone himself was a prisoner closely warded
by Maxwell, who ruled the March. The revolution of
November 4 led to the passing over of all the enormities
with which Maxwell was charged, and to his becoming
Warden *de jure* as well as *de facto*. At the end of the year
he disgusted many of those who had helped him to power
by assembling a number of priests at Dumfries and going
in procession by night with two or three hundred persons
to Lyncluden Church where Mass was said. Afterwards
Mass was celebrated in his house at Dumfries and the
town preacher silenced. He had in all nine Masses on
Christmas Day, it was said, and nine on New Year's Day,
and continued them openly. The ministers informed the
king, with the result that Maxwell was warded first of all
in Edinburgh Castle, and then less closely in the city.[2]
Owing to the revolution Cesford became Provost of Jedburgh and Warden, and entered into divers commodities
that Ferniherst had. He did nothing to redress disorders,
and Forster did not think he could, as the thieves would
not obey him.[3]

[1] C.S.P. viii, 165, 167, 170, 172, 174, 176, 182, 194-5; C.B.P. i, 370, 373-9,
381, 383; R.P.C.S. iv, 28-30; Calderwood, iv, 378-9, 381, 383; Stow, 1187;
Autobiog. 222-3; Spotswood, ii, 330-1.   [2] C.B.P. i, 333-4, 338, 341-2,
349, 392, 404-9; C.S.P. viii, 202, 224; A.P.S. iii, 387-95; Spotswood, ii,
325-6, 337; H.J.S. 209-10, 216; R.P.C.S. iv, 54 (note).   [3] C.B.P. i, 395,
399.

XII. THE MAKING AND TESTING OF THE LEAGUE, 1586–8

THE League, to which a Convention at St. Andrews had given its consent on the previous July 31, had not yet been finally concluded, and Arran, who had no cause to be Elizabeth's friend, was reported to be intriguing with the new French ambassador. Randolph was therefore sent into Scotland to show James the danger of the French and of Maxwell, and to urge the completion of the League, and redress in the Russell case. He was promised honourable amends for the murder, and in return promised the king a pension of £4,000 a year.[1] The West March of Scotland was still troubled by the same feud, but the English were not damaged thereby, and therefore were none the less eager for the League which the French ambassador was trying to prevent. The opportune death of Fernieherst at Aberdeen, before April 5, removed another possible cause of disagreement, and Forster was satisfied with Cesford's efforts, and expected redress from Bothwell, the new keeper of Liddesdale. Thus for a time the Borders, except the Scots West March, were quiet.[2] Proclamation was then made in Scotland for the collection of complaints for the meeting of commissioners in June, and the English Wardens received similar instructions, the commissioners' duty being to deal with unredressed Border causes as well as to conclude the League.[3] The Scots delayed the meeting, and in the interval much spoil was done, especially in the East, where some of the queen's poor tenants were reduced to begging their meat in Berwick. Liddesdale made two big raids, and Forster considered the situation 'verie ticklie'.[4]

[1] C.B.P. i, 409–10, 415; C.S.P. viii, 258–9, 297, 299, 302.   [2] C.S.P. viii, 308, 326–7, 329, 337, 362, 386; C.P.B. i, 418–19, 421; R.P.C.S. iv, 55–6, 81–2.   [3] R.P.C.S. iv, 68; A.P.C. xiv, 135–6; C.B.P. i, 431; C.S.P. viii, 444–5, 460.   [4] C.S.P. viii, 459–60, 462–3, 470, 497, 512, 557, 653, 681; C.B.P. i, 439.

At last the commissioners met at Berwick Tolbooth on June 27, and the Scots, besides finding fault with the League, wished redress to begin from 1567 instead of 1573, thinking that the injuries done by the English in 1570 would countervail what the Scots had done since. However, the League was concluded on July 5, the question of Border redress being postponed till the commissioners had consulted their princes, the Scots having no commission for redress.[1] They had much to answer for, the bills against them for the last thirteen years, with double and 'saufe', amounting to £58,000, besides maims and slaughters, and Maxwell's refusal of the Western Wardenry was likely to cause a big increase when the dark nights came.[2] The rest of the year, however, seems to have been fairly quiet. Maxwell acknowledged himself Warden before the end of August, and agreed to do justice with Scroope, who kept on his guard as Maxwell was suspected of foreknowledge of the Babington plot and was known to have consorted with Jesuits. The English Wardens tried to stop men connected with the plot from escaping into Scotland, but neither the accusation of Mary nor her condemnation had much effect on the Borders at first, probably because no Scot thought the sentence would be carried out. The sole recorded effect is the repeated postponement of a day of 'trews' by Cesford. Angus, lately made Lieutenant of the Borders, held courts in Jedburgh and hanged sixteen persons, taking pledges for the rest, but Huntyngdon seems to have neglected his orders to inquire into charges against Forster.[3]

1587. The next year was to see the League pretty thoroughly tested. Maxwell was reported to be having frequent intelligences with Jesuits in England, and the Scots were making 'greate bragges of warr' which Forster did not think would be executed, even if Mary's head were stricken off. Little had been done on the Scots West

---

[1] C.S.P. viii, 493, 522, 524, 562, 564, 567, 603–4; Rymer, xv, 805; Camden, 322 ff.; Bell, 119–23; Calderwood, iv, 587; Moysie, 57; Spotswood, ii, 346–8.
[2] C.S.P. viii, 647, 705; C.B.P. i, 441, 443.   [3] C.S.P. viii, 754, ix, 207; C.B.P. i, 442–4, 446–7, 449–55, 457–8, 461, 463–5, 470, 472–3; R.P.C.S. iv, 111, 114, 124, 132, 146–8; Calderwood, iv, 605; Dom. ii, 361.

March by Hamilton, who, though he hanged twelve thieves and warded sixty others, held no meeting with Scroope and punished none of Maxwell's friends before his sudden departure. Doubtless owing to this Scroope was given fifty horse 'for the present necessitie'. Then on Wednesday, February 8, Mary was executed, and as soon as news reached the Borders the passages were shut and spies could not operate.[1] It is not unlikely that James was inwardly joyful at the news which he was slow to credit, but though Cesford assured Forster that the King 'had nane uther meaning . . . bot observing the peax', Scots threats were plentiful, and James refused to receive Robert Carey whom Elizabeth sent north to explain matters. The English government and its Wardens took certain precautions, but Scots opinion was so much divided that, though a proclamation was issued against intercommuning with Englishmen, the only tangible act of hostility seems to have been the hanging of 'one pece of a roape and a libell' at the chamber door of Carey's messenger in Edinburgh.[2]

The 'stormye and contageouse wedder' may have helped towards the maintenance of Border peace, but anyhow Forster and Cesford met twice and did great justice, after which Forster, seeing that his March had never been more quiet than since Mary's death, visited Huntyngdon at Newcastle, where he was cleared of all the charges against him, but advised to retire on account of age. Huntyngdon thought that two hundred extra troops were necessary for Border defence, but Forster said the Scots could do nothing yet.[3] James busied himself at the beginning of April with the reduction of his own West Marches, and, though he failed to catch Maxwell, got good rule for the most part. He seems to have taken more pledges than his own castles could hold and therefore sent them to various lairds to keep. After this journey Maxwell came in and

[1] C.B.P. i, 474–5, 478–81, 483–4, 494; R.P.C.S. iv, 146–8; C.H.M. iii, 491.
[2] Moysie, 60; C.S.P. ix, 280, 286, 293, 313; Calderwood, iv, 611; Thorpe, 542; C.B.P. i, 485–7, 490–1, 495, 497; C.M. 6–7; C.H.M. iii, 489, xiii, 334.
[3] C.B.P. i, 490–501; Dom. Add. iii, 205; C.H.M. iii, 506; C.S.P. ix, 321.

promised to depart over sea, which he did, after giving very little more trouble, and found a temporary refuge in Spain.[1]

Then came three troubled months, May, June, and July, during which there were thirty-seven raids, mostly on the English Middle March, whence over seven hundred oxen, four score horses, four hundred sheep, and thirty prisoners, besides goods were taken. These raids may have been due to the grievous dearth of corn, which was so great that it cost twelve pence a day to victual a man; there is no evidence that James promoted them, but he may well have winked at them, hoping that they would cause Elizabeth to grant his demands for a northern duchy and the English succession, but for the present they were answered by English reprisals.[2] In August Hunsdon was sent to James, and, though he parted from him 'in doubtful terms', his embassy and the sentence against Davison made James show some disapproval of raids on England, and Angus's coming to the Borders made them quiet.[3] Thus Hunsdon had an opportunity of inquiring into the charges against Forster, who was ordered to surrender all books, &c., and sequestrated from his March, which Hunsdon took over. The inquiry was interrupted by fresh threats of war from Scotland, and precautions were taken against them, but at the end of September it was resumed, and Forster gave acceptable answers to most of the charges which Hunsdon thought had proceeded from 'meare mallys' on the part of Sir Cuthbert Collingwood. Some of the charges were 'fryvelous', and Forster's delinquencies were but 'tryffells in respect of deserving either deprivacion or the prince's displeasure'. The spoils were due rather to the poverty and unfurnished state of the country, to disagreement among the gentry, and to refusal to follow fray.[4] Having finished with Forster, who was not reinstated at once, Hunsdon again turned his attention

[1] C.B.P. i, 503, 505, 507, 512, 540; H.M.C. Rep. iii, 422; R.P.C.S. iv, 158–9.
[2] C.B.P. i, 514; C.H.M. iii, 555, 572.   [3] Spotswood, ii, 377–8; R.P.C.S. iv, 209; Thorpe, 546; C.B.P. i, 536.   [4] C.B.P. i, 453–5, 493, 534, 539–41, 543, 546–7, 550, 552, 554, 556; A.P.C. xv, 221, 223–4; C.H.M. iii, 584; N.D. xl.

to James, whom he thought deceptive and to be trying to gain time till he could get money from France or Spain. It seemed that, under cover of suppressing their own Border thieves, the Scots might be planning a big invasion of England with Continental aid, and James was actually considering a Spanish offer of the wages of thirty thousand men for three years, as a loan, if he would invade England. Hunsdon was only given three hundred more men out of the thousand he required to daunt the Scots, but, as things got no better and there was a big raid under Buccleugh, Cesford, Johnstone, &c., with two thousand men as far as Eslington, Elizabeth decided at the end of November to send Huntyngdon as Lieutenant-General to raise ten thousand troops for defence against Scotland if required. Hunsdon refused to serve under him, saying he 'never saw any servys', and adding, 'for seurly I will ley yn pryson rather'. The threat was enough for James, who in December discountenanced raids and sent to Hunsdon to say that he had 'byn gretly sollycyted bothe by France and Spayne with many grete offers . . . yet hathe he never yeldyd', and to hint that Elizabeth might make 'sum honorable offer' to him. Thus the year closed in quiet; the League still held, and its strongest bolt was Philip II's assertion of a claim to the throne of England.[1]

1588. The earlier part of 1588 was important for two matters. On January 25 John Carmichael, Alexander Hume of Huttonhall, and George Young, Scots commissioners, met Sir John Forster, Sir John Selby, and Richard Lowther at Foulden to settle Border causes. Hunsdon, who was present when the meeting was continued in Berwick, found the Scots far more ready than he expected, and by February 24 they had finished, having filed many large bills, and arranged for the arrest of the defendants and for giving pledges, but without having made any appreciable addition to the Laws and Customs of the Borders. Forster with his 'longe experiens and perfettnes

[1] C.B.P. i, 555, 557–61, 565, 569–72, 574–5, 577–8; A.P.C. xv, 254–5, 267 273–4; C.S.P. ix, 396; R.P.C.S. iv, 221–2, 234; H.M.C. x, pt. iv, 303; C.H.M. iii, 606; Calderwood, iv, 641.

in Border cawses' proved invaluable, and Hunsdon advised his restoration as Warden.[1]

The second matter, that of the Scots West March, had a closer connexion with the Armada. William, fifth Lord Herries, had been made Warden in the previous June, but had proved negligent and shown leanings towards popery. He was denounced rebel, and levies were raised against him, but he submitted, and on March 5 gave bonds for good behaviour. About ten days later, Lord Maxwell was reported to have returned to Scotland and not to have gone to the King. He did not, however, rebel at once, and in the interval James prorogued his West March journey and went to Jedburgh with large forces to deal with the delivery for filed English bills and with escaped pledges. He entered sundry Teviotdale gentry in England, took measures against the 'recet' of Maxwell, and returned to Edinburgh by way of Halidon, Langton, and Berwick, where he was greeted with a salute of guns, conferred with the captains, and paid for drinks for the men.[2] About the middle of May Maxwell rebelled, seized the castles of Langholm, Lochmaben, Carlaverock, &c., and proved too strong for Herries, who went to Edinburgh for aid. By May 28 James was at Dumfries in his own interests and those of England, for it was thought at the time that the Armada might go to the West of Scotland and land a force to join Maxwell and enter England by the Borders. Maxwell escaped into Galloway with an hour to spare, and all the castles but one surrendered. Lochmaben Castle held out till June 8, 9, or 10, when it surrendered, either after two or three shots, or a long bombardment by English artillery borrowed from Carlisle by arrangement with Sir Robert Carey, who was then on an embassy to the King. Six of the garrison were hanged, though James is said to have promised them their lives. Maxwell was soon caught and taken to Edinburgh, and seventeen of those who had been in the ship with him were hanged. After burning

[1] C.B.P. i, 582–9, 593–4, 596, 602; Bell, 102–8; C.S.P. ix, 433.   [2] R.P.C.S. iv, 188, 244, 247–8, 257–8, 271–2, 274–5, 278, 367–8; Calderwood, iv, 676–8; Moysie, 65–6; Spotswood, ii, 381; C.B.P. i, 599.

Langholm, &c., and holding courts and taking various cautions at Dumfries, the King returned to Edinburgh on June 27, leaving the country in charge of Angus, who died at the end of July. The journey had been most successful, especially in the capture of Maxwell, which made the creation of a diversion on the West Marches unlikely, even if the Armada succeeded in landing troops.[1]

The English officers in the north had started their preparations against the Armada at the beginning of the year. Their naval forces were small, but Newcastle supplied three ships and one pinnace, which were eventually ordered to join the Lord Admiral. Huntyngdon, who viewed armour and weapons, found that he would have some six thousand men, and perceived in every place a cheerful disposition to serve the Queen and to furnish themselves as well as they could. Later, when Hunsdon had gone up to court to command the troops about the Queen's person, it was noticed that the Borderers, though they would have been willing to serve against Scotland, were loath to enter on what might mean service of all kinds. Huntyngdon, however, trained his men as well as he could, being hindered as to the 'shott' by lack of powder and match. He kept the six thousand at York ready to march at an hour's warning, but had only four hundred horse, which he thought too few, especially as Tynemouth seemed defenceless.[2] During July Border history is almost a blank, but, when the Armada went north after Gravelines, Huntyngdon was ordered to convey 'some good quantytye' of victuals, powder, and shot from Newcastle and Berwick to Holy Isle in readiness for the Lord Admiral. There was no powder at all at Newcastle, and only a few brass pieces fit for service, so that Huntyngdon, who did not know how well the navy had done its work, and felt sure that the Spaniards knew the weakness of the north and had friends there, as they had, was far from

---

[1] R.P.C.S. iv, 285–92; H.J.S. 236; Moysie, 87; C.B.P. i, 607, 609, 613; Calderwood, iv, 678–9; Spotswood, ii, 383–4; Thorpe, 550; C.H.M. iii, 687; Camden, 406–7; C.M. 7–8; Melvill, M., 360.   [2] Dom. Add. iii, 239, 250; A.P.C. xv, 390–1, xvi, 41, 100, 129–30, 212–13; C.B.P. i, 604–6, 608, 611; Camden, 405.

confident.[1] In Scotland, at the same time, orders were
given to be ready to receive and resist any attempted
Spanish landing, and beacons were prepared on Windy
Edge, at Hume Castle, &c.[2] It was not till the end of
August that the fate of the Armada was understood, and
in the interval there was considerable alarm. On August 9
twenty great ships of unknown nationality were seen off
Eyemouth, and two days later it was reported at Newcastle that sixty 'sayle' of Spaniards had been newly seen
off the west coast.[3] During the whole of the week there
were rumours of Spanish landings in the Moray Firth, or
Firth of Forth, a trying state of affairs for Huntyngdon,
who found so many of his men 'in effect all naked' for want
of furniture, as it was only on August 13 and 14 that the
Council ordered munitions to be sent north. On the
nineteenth Forster heard that the Spanish fleet lay 'hove-
inge near the haven of Aberdeen', and that James had
ordered his subjects to be ready for it. On August 20
Bowes heard that it had landed in the Shetlands, and on
the same day Elizabeth seems to have been getting ready
six thousand men to send to Scotland if necessary.[4]

But the danger was over for the year, and during the
crisis the Borders had been quiet, save for some few
Teviotdale thieves who broke into the keeperless castle
of Harbottle and 'carried awaie much goods without
either showt or crie'.[5] James had supported Elizabeth
well—knowing, as he said, that Philip meant to favour him
as Polyphemus promised to favour Ulysses—and was
given £3,000, some of which he promised to spend 'for
the suppressynge of the troubles of the Borders', which
began 'to aryse in every march' in September. He made
John Carmichael Warden of the West March. The
promised disorders do not seem to have come to a head,
and the lengthening nights passed quietly except in Bewcastle, if lack of evidence means quiet, as it should. The
commission, the King's two journeys, and, most of all, the

[1] A.P.C. xvi, 211–13; C.B.P. i, 619; Span. Cal. iv, 170, 427.   [2] R.P.C.S.
iv, 306–8, 314–16.   [3] C.B.P. i, 620.   [4] C.B.P. i, 621–3, 625, 627–9;
A.P.C. xvi, 231, 233–4, 236.   [5] C.B.P. i, 627.

knowledge that owing to the good amity offenders could and would be punished, must have combined to keep the Borders quieter than they had ever been. The League had stood its hardest test well.[1]

[1] C.B.P. i, 628, 633, 638; A.P.C. xvi, 338–9, 360; R.P.C.S. iv, 322–3; Camden, 419.

XIII. THE END OF THE POPISH DANGER, 1589–94

LITTLE of importance occurred on the Borders during 1589. There was domestic disorder as usual on the Scots West Marches,[1] and threats against England on the part of Francis Stuart, Earl of Bothwell, who, as

1589. a nephew of Mary Stuart's Bothwell, and son of a natural son of James V, had no love for England. He had, however, to abandon his plans against the East and Middle Marches, as Lord Hume and the chief gentry of Teviotdale refused to take part in them. He therefore left the Borders for a time.[2] Jesuits and seminary priests were equally unsuccessful in their attempts to cause disorder,[3] and Francis Dacre, who went to Scotland to found an alliance with some of Elizabeth's 'unfriends' there, failed too.[4] On October 22 James sailed for Denmark to fetch his bride, and left the Scots Wardenries in the hands of John, Lord Hamilton, with the advice, at his option, of the Earl of Glencoe, Lords Boyd, Maxwell, Herries, and Hume, Cesford, and other chief barons 'luiffaris of justice and good order'. Hamilton was to live at Jedburgh, or Dumfries, and have £10,000 Scots, one-tenth of the marriage tax, towards his expenses.[5] Maxwell, who had been released under caution, was ordered to see that none of the West Marches troubled England in the absence of Carmichael with the king; Bothwell gave a bond to keep good rule, and, as a result, the Borders were never more peaceable.[6]

1590. In the beginning of 1590 the English government paid some attention to the augmentation of arms and munitions in the north, but its measures were taken against Spain rather than against Scots raiders. The latter

1 R.P.C.S. iv, 346, 396–7. 2 C.B.P. i, 642; A.P.C. xvii, 149–50. 3 A.P.C. xvii, 264–5; C.B.P. i, 646–7. 4 C.B.P. i, 652; Dom. Add. iii, 266, 285–6, 289; Bell, 193–5. 5 R.P.C.S. iv, 423–7, 430, 432–3. 6 R.P.C.S. iv, 412, 432, 437; C.B.P. i, 651, 653; C.H.M. iii, 949.

were not altogether inactive, there being two big bills
against them, which, however, were filed and sworn when
Cesford met Forster on March 12. Good agreement also
existed between the West March deputies. None the less,
Bowes was afraid that the raids were part of a 'practyse to
wrake the Borders', and suspected Herries and Maxwell
of being ready to take men to Ireland to stir up a rebellion
against the Queen. Hume and Bothwell were also thought
to be practising something.[1] On May 1 James arrived at
Leith with his bride, after six months' absence, during
which the Borders had been more than ordinarily quiet,
and about the middle of June his council tried to put the
law of 1587[2] into force by appointing a special committee
to meet weekly in Edinburgh to hear and determine all
Border causes and send a monthly report to the King. All
other commissions of justiciary were meanwhile suspended, and the committee dealt with pledges, cautions,
the inhabitants of the debatable lands and other matters.[3]
In September Scroope was able to settle all the complaints
against Carmichael's Wardenry for the last two years,
greater justice than had been done for a long time, but the
East March bills against Liddesdale and the unredressed
bills filed by the Berwick commissioners made no
1591.   progress[4] until early in the next year the efforts
of Bowes induced the Scots council to attend to
them. In spite of difficulties owing to feuds among the
Kers and outrages by the Johnstones, it succeeded in en-
forcing delivery for all filed Liddesdale bills except one.[5]
Carmichael had done many good offices for England, and
it is probable that at least the latter of two outrages suffered
by the English West March about this time was insti-
gated by Bothwell, who escaped from Edinburgh, where
he had been imprisoned for witchcraft, to the Borders in
June. The King followed him, took possession of all
his houses, and put Buccleugh, whose ill deeds against

[1] A.P.C. xviii, 364; C.B.P. i, 657-64, 666, 668, 671; R.P.C.S. xiv, 371-2.
[2] cap. 59.   [3] R.P.C.S. iv, 478-80, 529-30, 544, 790-4, 807 ff.   [4] C.B.P.
i, 685; Thorpe, 853.   [5] C.B.P. i, 700-3; R.P.C.S. iv, 580, 585-6, 592, 623,
803-6; A.P.C. xxi, 30-1.

England were still unredressed, in his place as Keeper of Liddesdale. Bothwell himself escaped, only to return again in August and be pursued by the King once more. This time he fled to Caithness as some of his followers obeyed the King's proclamation, and for the rest of the year the Borders seem to have been quiet, the wildest spirits being with Bothwell in his daring but unsuccessful attempt to seize the King and Queen at Holyrood on December 27.[1]

1592. For some two months Bothwell's whereabouts was unknown, though it is not unlikely that James's secret night raid on his Middle Marches, which failed, was intended to capture him. Scotland was very much troubled at the time, so much so that Bothwell and other outlaws, who were said to be attending race meetings on the English West Marches, found it safer to dwell at home, as the English Wardens were jealous against 'recet'.[2] The Liddesdale men, as was usual when their own country was troubled, were raiding England, so that the death of the experienced Lord Scroope on June 13 was particularly unfortunate, though James gave public orders for the peace to be kept. Scroope had ruled the most difficult of the English Marches well, being particularly successful in keeping a firm hand on the various factions which were to give his son so much trouble. Richard Lowther was given a commission as Vice-Warden.[3] Bothwell thought it a favourable opportunity, and appeared in the Scots West March, took Lochmaben Castle, and sought to strengthen himself there. Soon he was ready with the chief surnames to ride against the King. He had the aid of at least thirty English thieves, but his forces may have been kept small by the fact that many of the Borderers were a-summering. Anyhow his attempt at Falkland on June 28 failed, and he fled back to the West Marches, whither James prepared to pursue him. Maxwell's efforts

[1] Dom. Add. iii, 322; C.B.P. i, 709, 711–12, 714, 718, 723, 740–1; Calderwood, v, 133; R.P.C.S. iv, 643–4, 648–9, 662, 666–8, 705–6 (note); Moysie, 87; Melvill, M., 397; Camden, 400–1.   [2] C.H.M. iv, 175, 183, 188, 208–10; C.B.P. i, 742; A.P.C. xxii, 300–1.   [3] C.B.P. i, 745–7; Dom. Add. iii, 332–5, 341; R.P.C.S. iv, 758; Camden, 468.

in winning Johnstone and other important gentry over to
the King's side were rewarded with his re-creation as Earl
of Morton and Warden of the West Marches, which Carmichael willingly resigned. James's presence on the Borders led to no fighting, as Bothwell retired to the Hermitage, a stronghold at any time and doubly strong in that
stormy September, hoping to get his peace by Elizabeth's
means.[1] At last, in October, James went to Jedburgh with
two or three thousand men to chastise Bothwell's party.
He had with him Morton and Hume, but, as Bothwell
was perhaps in England, and James was not resolute
against any one else, very little was done beyond the taking
of bonds from some of Bothwell's alleged recettors, the
casting down of a few houses, and the appointing of
Lennox as Keeper of Liddesdale.[2] For the rest of the year
there is little evidence except Lowther's letters about the
West Marches, where there was great riding, spoiling, and
taking of prisoners. Morton, who had trouble with his
own barons, showed no desire to do justice.[3] The amity
was outwardly maintained, but the English government
sent a commission to Huntyngdon and others for the
defence of the Borders, and a good store of munitions to
Berwick early in the year. Perhaps it had its suspicions
that James was privy to a Papist plot to invade England
through Scotland, as indeed he was.[4]

1593. As long as Morton and Bothwell maintained
their Border influence there was a chance for Popery on
the Borders. Morton's Wardenry was disturbed inter-
nally, and in the beginning of the year his broken men used
the chance, offered by the non-residence of English officers
and Lowther's incapacity as Warden, to make people
within twenty miles of Carlisle so fearful that they kept
their cattle in their houses by night.[5] Though Morton

[1] C.B.P. i, 749–63, 765–6, 769–70, 773, 777; R.P.C.S. iv, 762–3, 765–9, v,
11–13; H.J.S. 250; Pitcairn, i, 275, 280; Moysie, 96–8; C.H.M. iv, 230,
232–3.   [2] C.B.P. i, 779–80, 783–6; Spotswood, ii, 424; R.P.C.S. v, 14;
Moysie, 97–8; Calderwood, v, 176–7.   [3] C.B.P. i, 787–8, 790–4, 801.
[4] MSS. Bodl. Add. C, 175; Gough Adds. Gen. Top. 8⁰, 120; C.B.P. i, 744;
C.H.M. iv, 214; Span. Cal. iv, 617.   [5] R.P.C.S. iv, 767; v, 39–40;
C.B.P. i, 799, 802, 809; A.P.C. xxiv, 53–4; Dom. Add. iii, 346–8.

showed more disposition to put down disorder, and the West Borders became temporarily more settled in and after March, the new English Warden, Thomas, Lord Scroope, was from the first suspicious of his opposite, who was fortifying Carlaverock Castle and showing kindness to Johnstone. But, even if Morton was still practising with Spain, he was able to do nothing, and before the end of the year he was killed in what is usually called the last of the great Scots Border fights.[1] This took place on December 6 at Dryfe Sands, near Lockerbie.

In the previous July Johnstone had made a great depredation on the lands of Lord Sanquhar and the laird of Drumlanrig in Nithsdale, and slain eighteen of his pursuers. As Morton was then friendly with Johnstone, the aggrieved parties thought he would be remiss in granting redress, and therefore, knowing that he loved to be followed, offered him their services against Johnstone, against whose surname the Maxwells had a long-standing feud. They were able to procure a commission from James, as Johnstone had favoured Bothwell, and a band was made, but, being negligently kept, fell into the hands of a Johnstone of Cummertrees, who took it to the laird. Morton, finding denial useless, said he must obey the King's orders. Both therefore raised forces, and Johnstone was able to get help from Teviotdale and the English Grames. Morton, however, succeeded in raising two thousand men and was lying in Annandale beside Lockerbie, with the intention of besieging Johnstone's house of Lochwood and rooting out the surname, when Johnstone with forty horse came in sight of the Maxwell host, and was pursued by eighty of Morton's 'skurrouris'. These he cleverly led into an ambush of some three or four hundred men 'lyand darnit in a wood', and they were soon in full flight towards their main body, which being ignorant of the enemy's numbers, and seeing its own men in flight, fled altogether. Morton fled unarmed, and, being a tall man and heavy, was soon caught. Johnstone is said to have given the first stroke, and the Warden fell from

[1] C.B.P. i, 802, 804, 845.

his horse and was cruelly slain with sundry of his special
kin and friends. Others were drowned, and in all two
thousand were put to flight by four hundred. The King
took his Warden's death ill, and ordered Herries and
Drumlanrig, who had escaped from the battle, to abide at
Dumfries and repress stirs till he could go there in person
next February. He could not go at once owing to his
business with Bothwell and the Popish lords.[1]

Bothwell had spent the early part of the year in Eden-
hall and elsewhere in Scroope's March, where he had
'greate receipte and good favour', attending horse races,
and even sending to Scroope to desire a conference.
Scroope gave him no open countenance, and even proclaimed against him, but let him know certain secret
things contained in a letter from Burghley. He was also
reported to have visited Kelso and Newcastle. Then
suddenly on July 24 he was reconciled to the King at
Holyrood in a way scarcely compatible with the royal
dignity, James being in his nightgown. It is not surprising, therefore, that, though acquitted of witchcraft by his
peers, he soon lost favour, and once more wandered about
making the English Border officers particularly anxious.
Nothing else of note happened this year except a journey
by the King to Jedburgh, where he did little; but the Borders were quiet enough for Scroope to get leave to go up
to court after All Hallowmas, leaving his Wardenry in the
hands of Sir Robert Carey, his deputy.[2]

1594. Early in 1594 Bothwell sent a petition to Elizabeth asking that her ambassador might intercede for him,
and for leave to take refuge in England if necessary.
Apparently he got no satisfactory answer, and therefore
intrigued with Ochiltree and Johnstone, the latter of
whom James won over by pardoning him for the slaughter
of Morton at Dryfe Sands. The King then ordered Hume,
Cesford, and Buccleugh to pursue Bothwell, and they

[1] C.B.P. i, 918; Moysie, 109; H.J.S. 296–300; Calderwood, v, 290; Spotswood, ii, 445–7; Birrel, 31; R.P.C.S. v, 112–13.   [2] C.B.P. i, 802, 831,
845, 853, 862, 865–6, 868, 872–4, 878–83, 885, 892, 905, 908, 910, 917;
R.P.C.S. v, 78–9, 97–8, 101; Dom. Add. iii, 352, 355–6; Camden, 471–2;
Spotswood, ii, 438; Moysie, 105.

raised about a thousand men and went to Kelso. Bothwell apparently slipped away into England, and, when they had gone, entered Scotland with four hundred [1] well armed horse, and rode to Dalkeith, where he attacked the King's forces. He was beaten, and when pursued took refuge in England. He found no favour in England and retired to the Hermitage, whence he tried to stir up raids, and, failing, made an attempt early in July to seize the King at Linlithgow, but a poor woman betrayed the plan. He returned to Liddesdale, and there was 'as yt were in manner of a truce' between the King and him till after the baptism of Prince Henry, and reconciliation seemed not impossible. [2] There were all sorts of 'scarebogles' about Spanish armies coming to his aid, and he was in communication with the Papist earls, but did not join them till driven to desperation by Elizabeth's doing nothing for him. A new proclamation was made against him, three or four of his recettors were hanged, and James went north in pursuit. Bothwell soon returned to the Borders, and was 'little herd of as a man able to doe nothinge', after which he disappeared from Border history and died in penury in Naples many years later. With him (Morton being dead) disappeared the last chance of Spain and the Pope using the Borderers as a powerful aid in overthrowing England. But the might of his name was such that rumours of his coming caused Border unrest as late as April 1600. [3]

Nothing else of much account happened this year. There were renewed charges against Forster, and both Robert Carey and Rafe Gray tried unsuccessfully to get his job. Border justice as a whole was again wanting, chiefly because there were either no definite Scots officers, or they were not obeyed, but there were no big raids,

[1] This is Moysie's estimate : Forster and J. Carey say about sixty, but he may well have raised the rest in Scotland.   [2] Camden, 480–1; Moysie, 113–15; R.P.C.S. v, 137–8, 139 (note); H.J.S. 302; C.B.P. i, 933–4, 939–41, 950, 956, 962, 964; Spotswood, ii, 450–1; C.H.M. iv, 509, 541, 553; H.M.C. x, pt. iv, 306; Dom. Add. iii, 366–8.   [3] C.B.P. i, 971, 973, 980, 987, ii, 1162, 1168; R.P.C.S. v, 173–5, and note; Birrel, 33; C.H.M. v, 17–18; Dom. v, 413, 418.

partly because Forster took assurance with the opposite gentry, till the long nights began, when the Scots rode almost every night in Hunsdon's Wardenry, Cesford looking on occasionally and enjoying the slaughter.[1]

[1] C.B.P. i, 931, 935, 939, 958–61, 967, 987; Dom. Add. iii, 365–6, 370; Thorpe, 654.

XIV. THE DISMISSAL OF FORSTER AND THE CASE OF WILL OF KYNMONTH

THE departure of Bothwell did not bring peace to the Borders though there was little international trouble at first. Herries was definitely given the Scots West Marches, and, in spite of little being done when 1595. Scroope met him, the Borders remained quiet except for outrages by Buccleugh and those under his protection, which were done daily in June, about which time Cesford became active again in the East Marches. No justice was done, and the Scots became so bold, especially in Forster's charge, that they took 'markett folkes horses and goodes in the daye tyme'.[1] The Privy Council, on receiving complaints from the Bishop of Durham and others, told Forster plainly that he would be deposed unless he could repress disorders. Scroope received milder treatment, his defence being helped by R. Carey, who wrote, 'we are macht with a people without laues, and we are bound to keepe laues, only force must bridell them'. As things got no better, Burghley wrote to Eure on September 1 to supersede Forster, a thing he was loath to do. According to Robert Carey there had been no redress on those Marches for six or seven years, all but three or four of the chief men paid 'black maelle', and the poor who could not were daily spoiled. He laid the fault at the door of Forster, who, being ninety-four years of age, entrusted everything to a drunken bastard son as his deputy. It is not surprising then that Eure asked for 'a large and severe commission' and a force of horsemen.[2] Forster answered the charges in a way which was clever and not very incriminating, but he did not satisfy Huntyngdon, who wrote, 'Sir John did winde like an eel', and that he had 'betraied' or 'abused' the Queen, but the gentry got nothing but good advice, which did not make

[1] C.B.P. ii, 11, 13, 42, 62, 67, 71–2, 76–7, 80, 82, 86, 89; N.D. xlv–vi.
[2] C.B.P. ii, 97, 103, 110–11, 114–15, 119, 129, 131.

up for the serious lack of horses which the musters showed, for the lack of able preachers, for March justice being 'clean out of joint', for the strength of the enemy, for the weakness and destruction of the country, the scarcity, the intrigues, for the very unsafe place of abode, or for Forster's attempts to make the task as hard as possible, all of which problems faced the new Warden.[1]

These were the circumstances in which the last of Elizabeth's Wardens who was not an 'inland' man left office. They did not tempt her to repeat the experiment. Eure went to his Wardenry at the end of the year, and set to work with a will. He was in the prime of life, and with the advice of experienced Borderers set a general watch on the fords and passages of the whole March, wrote to Buccleugh and his opposite Warden hoping for justice and good neighbourhood and, getting favourable replies, mustered his Wardenry, hunted out felons and March traitors, and generally did his best.[2] Little else of note happened on the Borders this year. There was trouble in Berwick between civilians and soldiers, and frequent complaints about the victualling of the town. Later in the year this latter was temporarily remedied, and considerable repairs to the walls, gates, and bridge were taken in hand.[3] On the West nothing but fair words were obtainable from Herries, and nothing but a warrant for a hundred Berwick soldiers from the English government. The King apparently intended to take some order between the Maxwells and the Johnstones in October, but did not, and the Maxwell faction with three or four hundred men went from Dumfries to Lockerbie hoping to avenge Dryfe Sands, but were disappointed, for Johnstone gathered his men and met them, slaying some fourteen or twenty and taking many prisoners.[4] The year closed with rumours of a Spanish invasion, against which James, now definitely anti-Spanish, issued proclamations. They worried John

---

[1] C.H.M. v, 430–1, 458–60, 477, 493–4; C.B.P. ii, 138–40, 145, 147, 168–71, 173, 184; Dom. iv, 168.   [2] C.B.P. ii, 174, 179–80, 187; C.H.M. v, 551–2.
[3] C.B.P. ii, 1–3, 5–9, 12, 19, 24–7, 31, 86, 96, 105, 107, 137; A.P.C. xxv, 5–6, 39–40.   [4] C.B.P. ii, 124, 128, 132, 157; Calderwood, v, 385; Moysie, 124–5; Spotswood, ii, 465.

Carey and Scroope considerably, and the latter was also
troubled by Scots raids, the Berwick soldiers not having
            reached Carlisle.[1] These rumours continued into
1596.   1596, and led Cesford to arm and his men to
            raid England twice within a mile of Alnwick.[2]
During the first three months of the year most of the
extant Border documents concern Eure's attempts to
govern his Marches. He succeeded in getting Forster
sent to Durham, but that did not reduce the difficulties,
as every gentleman of worth in the shire was near of kin
or allied to the ex-Warden. Eure's conferences with them
must have been mere formalities, as they wished to show
that the March could not be governed without the aid of
the Forster party. The Queen showed her acceptance of
Eure's service, but it is hard to see what he had accomplished.[3]

James was taking order for the holding of justice courts
in his Marches,[4] and the rest of the Borders were apparently quiet, when in March a notable thief, William Armstrong of Kinmont, was captured by the English in
circumstances which were much in dispute. The Musgraves, who took him, asserted that a certain Blacklock
was taken away out of the office of Bewcastle by certain
men not answerable to any laws, and that when they (the
Musgraves) pursued them to the house of Peter of the
Harlaw, where 'Kynmonth' was staying, Will, though
told to go his way, persisted in trying to raise the country
by shouting 'A Harlaw, A Harlaw'. The Musgraves were
thus forced to pursue him for their own safety, and, after
resistance, took him and gave him to Salkeld, Scroope's
deputy, who shut him up in Carlisle Castle. Moysie, on
the other hand, says he was taken at a 'trew' to Buccleugh's
dishonour 'as he comptit'. Will was not actually taken at a
'trew', but later in the same day, but the English were
technically in the wrong, as the use was that those present

<hr>

[1] C.B.P. ii, 161, 175, 178, 181, 185, 190; R.P.C.S. v, 235, 242, 266, 274;
Camden, 495.   [2] C.B.P. ii, 202–3, 205.   [3] Dom. iv, 160; C.B.P. ii,
196–7, 199, 202, 206, 209, 211, 213–14, 217–19, 226–7, 232–4, 236, 239,
244–5; C.H.M. vi, 60, 92.   [4] C.H.M. vi, 8–9.

at a 'trew' had assurance till the next sunrise. Kinmont
in 1582 had been strong enough to resist his own Warden,
Johnstone, and ten years later was said to have a hundred
of his surname, all able men, dwelling about him. He
and his sons and complices had done many grievous murders and spoils in England, including the great raid on
Tynedale at Michaelmas 1584, when the damage amounted
to £2,000, and the great foray at Haydon Bridge three
years later. He dwelt outside Buccleugh's office, and was
not taken within it, according to Scroope, yet it was
Buccleugh who tried to obtain his freedom, first of all by
peaceable means, and, when Scroope 'behaved himself so
straitly in this matter that he would do no kind of reason',
approached Bowes, the English ambassador, and James
in vain. Therefore at dead of night on April 13 he made
a 'proude attempt' on Carlisle Castle. Scroope says the
Scots had five hundred horse, 'armed and appointed with
gavlockes and crowes of iron, handpeckes, axes and skail-
inge lathers'. The Scots own estimates vary from three
score to ten score, and Spotswood, who gives the latter
estimate, adds that Buccleugh might have made prey of
all the goods in the castle and taken the Warden prisoner,
but forbade plunder. According to Scroope the Scots
came to the postern gate, undermined it speedily, quietly
made themselves possessors of the 'base courte', broke
into Kynmonth's chamber, and carried him away, leaving
two of the watch for dead, and hurting one of Kynmonth's
keepers. Buccleugh was the fifth man to enter the Castle,
and, before the inner watch was roused or resistance could
be made, the Scots were outside the postern again. Birrel
says that Kynmonth was lying in irons, which is unlikely
as he was on parole. He also says the deed was done with
shouting, crying, and sound of trumpet, which is more
unlikely still, though Moysie also mentions a trumpet.
As a feat it may have been worthy of Wallace, as Birrel
thought it was, but its success seems to have been founded
on the bribery of the watch by Scroope's enemies, the
Carletons and Grames, though Scroope at first thought
they were asleep, or sheltering from the stormy night.

The Queen on hearing of it stormed not a little, but refused Scroope leave to take revenge.[1] The well-known ballad was possibly written by Sir W. Scott.[2]

James proposed to refer the matter to commissioners, but Elizabeth would not let it be treated as an ordinary Border matter; she clearly believed that some of the Grames might be guilty, and had some of them sent up to London, but would not let Scroope come up to confront them, whereupon he offered his resignation, and soon afterwards repeated the offer. He made, apparently with the Queen's leave, an unsuccessful attempt to take some of Kynmonth's rescuers, but only burnt empty houses and took four unimportant Armstrongs. Other reprisals failed also, and for a time the matter rested. The Grames were finally made to sign eleven articles and sent back to the Borders, arriving on September 24, but not submitting in a way which satisfied Scroope.[3]

The Borders were in a very 'tickle' state all this time, perhaps worse than for many years. Eure found his task quite beyond him: the juries refused to convict nine-tenths of his prisoners: the people made private bands with Scots, and the Scots raided those who did not. 'Trews' there were in name, but not in effect. The Scots also rode day and night unceasingly in the East Marches, and the only remedy seemed to be 'to doe one evill turne for another'.[4] Things were not improved by the death, on July 22, of Hunsdon the nominal Warden of the East Marches.[5] He was, wrote Camden, 'a man of great Spirit, but cholerick and passionate'. But, though he owed much to his kinship with the Queen, he had shown considerable force and ability in his work on the Borders, and fully merited his honours and moderate estate. Much of the trouble caused

[1] C.B.P. i, 156, 169, 174, 237, 556, 595, 744, ii, 250–3, 257, 264, 346, 699; Moysie, 126–7; H.J.S. 366–71; Spotswood, iii, 1–5; Birrel, 37, 41, 44; C.H.M. vi, 84–5.   [2] F. Elliot, *Further Essays on Border Ballads*, 107–151.
[3] C.B.P. ii, 282, 285, 296, 310–11, 317–20, 325, 330, 332, 336, 340–1, 344, 346, 360, 378, 380; R.P.C.S. v, 298–9, 302, 304, 307; A.P.C. xxv, 35–6, 105–8, 155–7, 161, 167–8; Dom. iv, 253.   [4] C.B.P. ii, 292, 294–5, 298, 303, 305, 312, 322, 331; N.D. xlvi; C.H.M. vi, 247, 261.   [5] A.P.C. xxv, 4.

by the Scots, and many of Forster's misdeeds, might have been prevented if Hunsdon had been a constant resident at Berwick.[1] The government now made the mistake of trying to save money by keeping the office vacant, and letting the two Careys do the duties as deputy warden and deputy governor. They thus lacked authority, and this, added to Eure's difficulties, and to the weakening of Scroope's position by the lenient treatment of the Grames, some of whom did not submit till the following January, meant that there was not on the Borders an officer of sufficient reputation to deal successfully with Cesford or Buccleugh. Lastly the case of Kynmonth had bred an utter lack of confidence between opposite officers, and the Scots Wardens took assurance with each other to take revenge on various English officers, while the English Wardens made reprisals with the leave of the Privy Council.[2]

[1] Camden, 528.   [2] C.B.P. ii, 329, 333, 362, 365–9, 371, 373–5, 397, 479; Dom. iv, 291; C.M. 51.

XV. THE COMMISSION OF 1597

IT had been plain, then, for some time that the ordinary methods of Border justice had failed completely, and a commission had been suggested, and both sides had busily collected rolls of spoils and answers to the allegations of their opposites in preparation for one.[1] On October 2 Elizabeth gave a commission to the Bishop of Durham, Sir W. Bowes, Francis Slyngesby, and Clement Colmer to meet the Scots, but they could not at once, and in the interval the Queen let R. Carey use his discretion in upholding her honour. None the less, in spite of there being extra horse in pay on the Marches, disorders went on, and Cesford even boasted that he would take Berwick in revenge for the hanging of some Scots thieves. Though the English commissioners were ready, James delayed the meeting, alleging his objection to Book v, Canto ix of the *Faerie Queen* as one of his excuses, but at last on November 27 a meeting was arranged for January 12 at 'Fowldon Kirk'. It was none too soon, for, as Eure wrote in December, 'the Border groweth wylde and disorderlie since the delay of the commissione, our bills increaseth, justice decreaseth, corne fayleth, peoples hartes are gone, my discomforth in my charge followeth—these are the news of the Borders'. It was no exaggeration for the Middle Marches, but Scroope found his own office quiet enough for him to spend a few days in his house at Bolton.[2]

1597. On January 14 the English commissioners met the Scots, the Bishop of Dunkeld, Sir George Home of Wedderburn, Andrew Ker of Fawdonside, and George Young, who, 'with much adoe', agreed to come to Berwick and treat there. Violent disagreement came at once about

1596, Oct.

[1] C.B.P. ii, 354–6, 379, 381, 383–5, 398–9, 410; A.P.C. xxvi, 182–3, 202–3.
[2] C.B.P. ii, 400, 402, 406, 435–6, 440, 447, 451, 453, 456; C.H.M. vi, 475; R.P.C.S. v, 323–4 and note.

Sir R. Ker's invasion of the previous September 19, which seemed likely to end the proceedings, but wiser counsels prevailed, and 'in amycable sort' the commissioners fixed dates for the trial of East and Middle March bills.[1] The work before them was immense. There had been scores of horrible murders, twenty of which were alleged against Buccleugh, and about sixteen against Cesford, and the value of Scots spoils since 1587 was said to be £100,000, of which nearly three-quarters had been done by Liddesdale and Teviotdale under Buccleugh and Cesford. The time also was hardly propitious. Not only were there fights between Scroope's servants and men on Eure's March, but the thieves did not desist from making daily attempts on both sides in every Wardenry.[2] However, after much wrangling the commissioners decided to pass over questions of form and proceed to substance rather than separate with nothing done, and divided themselves into two courts for the trial of bills. There were at once two difficulties, that of vowers, which the English could hardly get, and that of the number of murders and hugeness of the spoils, which made it likely that the accused would become outlaws when the time of delivery drew near, and exceedingly trouble both realms.[3] However, by shelving the bill for Cesford's invasion, and for Scroope's, they managed to file most of the East and Middle March bills by February 19, appointing the Wardens, or deputies, to sit every weekday till they had finished the rest, which was no small task, as only two hundred and twenty-seven East March bills out of some five hundred English ones for that March alone had been settled.

The commissioners prorogued their sittings till March 10, when they were to meet at 'Greatney Kirk', and the Scots Council was satisfied.[4] The feelings of the English Council were expressed by a warrant to Eure to retain his eighty extra horse for another three or four months, and they were justified, as the meeting between Eure and

[1] C.B.P. ii, 475–8, 481; R.P.C.S. v, 360–1. [2] C.B.P. ii, 482–3, 485, 492; N.D. xli. [3] C.B.P. ii, 490–1, 493–4. [4] C.B.P. ii, 514–15, 519–20; R.P.C.S. v, 365–6.

Cesford which the commissioners had fixed for March 1 was abortive, and Scots raids continued even after the meeting of the commissioners at 'Gretney Kirk' on April 12, and their adjournment to Carlisle.[1] Meanwhile, the commissioners met daily, made an agreement about pledges, indented a large number of bills, and fixed dates for 'trews', at which the rest of West March complaints, amounting to £12,000 against Scotland and £13,000 against England, should be settled.[2] Finally they concluded a treaty of thirty-six clauses,[3] which they signed on May 5, proclaiming that they would see that their princes carried it out. Confidence, however, was sadly lacking on the English side. The Scots were a people 'at whose handes wee cannot obtayne what we would desier, but must take what we can gett'. Slaughters had had to be left to the princes, and Johnstone alone of the Scots Wardens had given the commissioners any help. However, the filing of some two thousand bills, even if delivery was likely to be 'slow enoughe', and the arrangements for the exchange of pledges were something. The English despondency may have been partly due to overwork, for the Bishop and his fellows had also inquired into domestic Border affairs, the case of the Carletons, the Selby-Gray affair, and the religious state of the country, inquiries which had produced several charges against Eure, which he answered to his own satisfaction, but not to Burghley's. Copies of the treaty were sent to the Wardens, of whom Scroope already regarded it as a failure, and asked for extra soldiers to guard his Marches.[4]

None the less, in spite of provocations and raids by both sides,[5] Lord Eure, Sir R. Carey, and Sir W. Bowes met Lord Hume, Sir G. Home of Wedderburn, Buccleugh, and Cesford at the West ford near Norham at 9 a.m. on June 25, to exchange pledges. Twelve hours were spent there, but the meeting was abortive, as most of the Scots

[1] C.H.M. vii, 76, 79–80, 90–1; C.B.P. ii, 543, 561, 569, 577, 588, 590, 592–3, 595–6.   [2] C.B.P. ii, 594, 599–603, 606–11, 614, 617–18; N.D. xlii. [3] Bell, 124–32.   [4] C.B.P. ii, 573, 605, 610, 613, 631, 633–4, 636, 638, 640–2, 645, 652, 660, 680–1, 760; A.P.C. xxvii, 35–7, 293–5; C.H.M. vii, 230. [5] C.H.M. vii, 238–42, 250–1; C.B.P. ii, 650, 654.

and four of the English pledges were absent.[1] Raids and counter-raids followed, and the Scots Council prohibited them, while the more practical English government wrote to Essex in Ireland to send back all the principal Borderers in his army, by whose absence the frontiers were weakened.[2] The English, however, still held to the pledge scheme, and the Marches became somewhat quieter, partly owing to the plague, which necessarily postponed any present attempt to exchange pledges. The interval was used for a further inquiry into the charges against Eure, none of which seems to have been substantiated, with the result that he was left in office till he resigned early in the next year. He had taken office in an utterly decayed March, and his predecessor's party made his position untenable.[3]

On September 29 a second meeting for the delivery of pledges failed, owing to the absence of some of the Scots, and delivery was postponed till October 8, when Sir W. Bowes, with some three hundred men, met the Scots with five times that number, and five hours were wasted in waiting till 3 p. m. for the coming of Buccleugh. After much conference, as night was coming on, Buccleugh delivered himself and was given to the gentleman porter to take to Berwick. Bowes went on delivering the English pledges, one of them a corpse, till it grew too dark to read, and sundry of the 'Tyviotdales' crept up to where the commissioners were, and one of them 'dischardging a pistoll . . . bended downe his bodye towards the earth and cried with a pityefull voice that he was slayne'. A tumult arose, during which Hume did his best to protect Bowes, and a few of his men were slain by Englishmen, who mistook them for 'Tyviotdales'. The uproar was apparently a trick of Cesford's to prevent delivery of his pledges, and was so far successful, but the English pledges already delivered appear to have escaped in the tumult. Bowes,

[1] C.H.M. vii, 262–3, 268–9, 271, 274–6; C.B.P. ii, 662, 667–9, 671, 673.
[2] C.B.P. ii, 675–6, 683, 685, 692, 694, 697, 699–702, 705; R.P.C.S. v, 404–5; Dom. iv, 479.   [3] C.B.P. ii, 736–9, 741, 743, 753–8, 762–4, 792, 794, 796, 804, 813, 820, 836, 838, 841, 854, 860–2, 881, 894; C.H.M. viii, 73–4; A.P.C. xxviii, 443, 458, 489; Arch. Bodl. F.C. 11, fol. 370.

after supping with Hume, rode to Berwick along the right
bank of the Tweed, and arrived at 11 p.m., an hour after
Buccleugh.[1] Burghley could see no remedy for this
'desastur by Norham ford', but by 'Sesford rendiryng of
himself to the Quene to answer for all his pledges, and that
must be doon by the Kings commandment'. The 'desastur' was followed by Scots raids. In November, however,
the King made a journey to the West, hanged fourteen or
fifteen 'lymmeris and notorious theifes', took pledges of
the surnames, and left Lord Ochiltree as Lieutenant and
Warden at Dumfries, where he remained five or six
months holding courts, pacifying the country, and slaying
three score or more notable thieves, thus keeping the
country in great quietness.[2] The East, on the other hand,
remained disturbed; for instance, John Carey, while writing
a letter, was 'caled dowen iii severall tymes to see the freshe
bledinge, bluddey woundes and hortes' given by the Scots
during the night. Hume said he was willing to arrange
about delivery, but seemed 'too much affected' to Cesford.
The Middle March was in a yet worse state, the chief
spoilers of it being Englishmen who joined with Scots.
Eure was in London answering charges. At last, in
December, the Council decided to send Sir R. Carey back
as Warden of the East March, and the question of pledges
was again taken up, and Sir W. Bowes went to Berwick to
deal with it.[3]

1598. After some vain negotiations he went to Edinburgh, where, largely by promising to re-enter Buccleugh,
he indented with the king for a delivery at Foulden on
February 13. The English pledges were delivered on that
day, and the next day, after long waiting and a parley,
Hume delivered Cesford to John Carey on Halidon Hill
'as the freinde of all the world he loved best, with great
entreatie of letting passe former unkyndnesses, and to
receyve him to his favourable custodie'. Cesford himself

[1] C.B.P. ii, 761, 765–7, 772–3, 783–6, 788–90, 1550; N.D. xliii–v; Spotswood,
iii, 67; Birrel, 44.   [2] C.B.P. ii, 791, 803, 806, 815–19, 822, 832–3, 839–40,
844, 846–52, 857–8, 863–4, 868; Moysie, 135–6; R.P.C.S. v, 421–7, 432–3.
[3] C.B.P. ii, 815, 826–7, 830–1, 837, 854, 872, 875, 877, 879–80; A.P.C. xxviii,
174.

showed an earnest desire to remove Elizabeth's hard conceit of his behaviour, and grounded his apology on the 'unskillful inconstancie of his opposites'. He appeared to Bowes as the most dangerous of all the Borderers, and there seemed no alternative to winning him over, as to make him harmless would be very difficult. On March 21 Buccleugh was set free in exchange for his young son, and went to collect his pledges, some of which he delivered before the end of March. Cesford was liberated some time, apparently, between May 11 and June 3, on which day he delivered his pledges, and with that this chapter about the commission may close.[1]

[1] C.B.P. ii, 882, 884, 900–11, 924, 929, 941, 1022; C.H.M. viii, 23–4; Dom. v, 30; Thorpe, 750.

XVI. THE LAST FIVE YEARS, 1598–1603

IN March there was a redistribution of Border offices. Lord Wyllughby d'Eresby replaced Sir R. Carey, and became, in addition, Governor of Berwick, and Carey, against his will, succeeded Eure. Sir W. Bowes had suggested a more radical change by means of the amalgamation of the two Marches, and letting each of two 'choyce' gentlemen rule half Northumberland as deputy, and get half of the fee of the Warden of the Middle Marches, but the plan was not tried, and would hardly have succeeded. The only really valuable note it contained was that the Governor and Council of Berwick should 'be tied to better residence' there.[1] Wyllughby, directly after his arrival at his charge, began to gain knowledge of it and send criticisms south. It seems to have been very quiet, while Carey's March was much disturbed, and Carey found his house at Woodrington an inconvenient residence.[2]

He had not time to settle down before, on August 3, an international Border fray took place in his Wardenry, and the accounts of it vary so much that the truth has been lost. The Scots, according to their own accounts, were sixty in number and unarmed and were merely hunting in England, not knowing any objection, when they were assaulted in warlike manner by four hundred Englishmen, pursued four miles into Scotland, and lost several hurt and slain, besides fifty nags and 'the gentlemens carriadge'. Carey said they numbered two hundred, four score of them armed with 'calyvers' and horsemen's pieces, that they brought a hundred men to cut wood and carried it away as usual, and that only two of their meanest men were slain. The Scots must have known that unlicensed hunting was illegal, as some of them had asked Wyllughby's leave, but James complained to the Queen, and

[1] C.B.P. ii, 913, 920, 922, 933.
[2] C.B.P. ii, 936, 941, 944–5, 949–50, 962, 968, 970; C.H.M. viii, 261.

Carey's two deputies, Fenwick and Woddrington, were warded with the Bishop of Durham, and not released till the next May, in spite of the Warden's and the Bishop's intercession for them.[1] It says much for the new officers and for the effects of the treaty that there was no open revenge from Scotland. Redress for the bills filed by the late commission was, however, another matter. 'Trews' on both the Middle and East Marches were spoilt by the groundless claims of the Scots that the English should come into Scotland. Nevertheless, the Borders remained quiet, except in Carey's March, where the Scots made at least twenty great raids in a month, while Fenwick and Woddryngton were confined in Durham. Carey said he could not suppress the Scots without their aid. The west was kept quiet, partly by the plague, which in Scroope's absence touched the deputy's personal servants, and partly by Angus's efforts as Scots lieutenant.[2]

1599. Calderwood states that in the next year there were 'diverse incursiouns' upon the Borders,[3] but they only lasted for a short while. The first part of the year was peaceful, in spite of the efforts of the Scots pledges to escape, and of Scroope's doubts of Angus's power and will to do justice. On the East, likewise, there was no trouble, except from the Dunkirk pirates, who had lately come to the coast with twenty-four great ships, chased all the poor fishermen ashore, stripping naked all those they took, and interfered with the Berwick corn trade and Newcastle coal trade.[4] Otherwise Border peace was undisturbed till May 23, when, in a fray at Bewcastle, Mr. Rydley and two of his friends were murdered, and twenty-six men and thirty-two horses taken. The outlaws also became busy in the Middle Marches in Carey's absence, and two were slain and three captured within a

[1] C.B.P. ii, 974, 978, 986–9, 992, 1006, 1020, 1025, 1035–8, 1041–3, 1049, 1054–5, 1066; Birrel, 47; C.H.M. viii, 287, 314–16; A.P.C. xxix, 68, 269–70; Mar and Kellie, 48–9.   [2] C.B.P. ii, 961, 963, 969, 980, 983, 985, 991, 993–4, 997–9, 1001–3, 1010, 1020, 1026, 1030; Dom. Add. iii, 390; R.P.C.S. v, 503, 511; C.H.M. viii, 485.   [3] v, 771.   [4] C.B.P. ii, 1040, 1046–50, 1056, 1058–61; R.P.C.S. v, 537, 543; C.H.M. ix, 16–17, 104–7, 137–8; Dom. v, 193.

mile of Newcastle. The Armstrongs of Liddesdale, who now held Buccleugh in contempt for his dealings with England, wasted the West March bordering on them, and entered the Middle March, while the Teviotdale thieves seemed to have received 'lowse reynes' from Cesford. It is not unlikely, however, that Cesford, like Buccleugh, was held in contempt for his dealings with England. Anyhow there were internal troubles in his charge and in that of his western colleague.[1]

The way in which James's increasing hopes of the English succession were teaching him wisdom is shown by the case of a certain Ashfield, an Englishman, who had 'cunningly abused' Wyllughby by taking horses through the Borders, and been well entertained by James. When the ambassador told Wyllughby, he sent his cousin Guevara into Scotland with five or six horse, and, by making Ashfield drunk, they managed to get him into a coach and bring him to Berwick. James wrote to demand 'spedie reparacioun' and put an embargo on Wyllughby's ship and its crew in Leith, and restraint upon the English ambassador. Wyllughby retaliated, and sent Ashfield up to London under guard, and James merely put Sir W. Bowes in Edinburgh Castle. In earlier days he would have encouraged Border raids, had he failed, as he did, to get Ashfield back.[2]

For the rest of the year most of the Wardenries were quiet, and Cesford gave Wyllughby some extraordinary justice, and 'himself voluntarily put out th'offenders unknown and unsuspected to the partie greived'. He also gave some good justice to Sir R. Carey, and most people thought the sudden change was due to his desire to get some ease for his pledges. On the East there was either no stealing or riding, or instant redress if there was any, and by November there was not an unsatisfied bill between Sir R. Carey and Buccleugh. Most of this peace was due to those in authority, the Scots Council proclaiming against raids into England, and making death the penalty for

[1] C.B.P. ii, 1065–8; R.P.C.S. vi, 2, 4. [2] Spotswood, ii, 79–80; C.B.P. ii, 1072–6, 1079–80, 1085.

theft or 'recet', but it is interesting to note that the discretion shown by a simple fellow in not resisting, when taken unlawful prisoner at a 'trews' between Wyllughby and Sir Alexander Hume, prevented a fray. When sent home he said that 'his life was not worthe so muche as the hassard of that daies worke betwene the nations'. Hume delivered the culprit, and the amity continued. A duel between Cesford and Sir Henry Woddryngton was prevented by the latter finding discretion the better part of valour.[1]

The one unquiet part of the Borders was the Scots West March, where the inhabitants rode and spoiled one another, but there was only one raid on England at first, and that was possibly arranged by Lowther, the friend of the Carletons. The Scots Council tried to pacify the March by making Herries and Drumlanrig responsible for the wrongs done by their men. Later there were raids by the Grames on Scotland, and by Angus's broken men on Gilsland, for which no redress was done. Angus seems to have worked hard, and was promised 'one hundreth hieland men . . . to be interteyned upoun the expenssis of the said outlawis rentis and leving', though there is no evidence that he got them. In October there were raids by the Grames on the Johnstones with Angus's privity, and divers spoils of worthy persons by the Scots, but the public appointment of Sir John Carmichael as Warden, three months after his being chosen privately, seemed to promise future peace and justice, though Scroope thought it would hinder justice because Carmichael would naturally take no burden for bygones.[2]

1600. The next year was another quiet year for all the Borders except the West, and even that was quiet at the beginning.[3] James made a Border journey towards the end of February, partly to hunt, partly, it seems, to do justice. But there is no record of his doings, beyond the

---

[1] C.B.P. ii, 1085, 1087, 1090–4, 1100, 1102–5, 1108, 1112, 1116–17, 1121–2, 1126–7, 1131; R.P.C.S. vi, 13; A.P.S. iv, 181–2.   [2] C.B.P. ii, 1072, 1082, 1084, 1095, 1107, 1113, 1118–20, 1133, 1139, 1143; R.P.C.S. vi, 17, 27, 31–2, 44–6, 56–9, 63, 65–6, 68, 834–6, 851; xiv, 384–5.   [3] C.B.P. ii, 1141–2, 1145–6, 1151–2; C.H.M. x, 64; R.P.C.S. vi, 834.

fact that he was much annoyed because Guevara, attending on the Borders as deputy to see good rule kept and to prevent creeping in, dared to come into his royal sight. James, who had not forgotten Ashfield, could not see a joke against himself.[1] In May the English Wardens were all in London, and on Sunday afternoon, May 25, considered the case of the pledges and other Border causes, but, as the next four pages of the Acts of the Privy Council are blank, there is no record of their decisions. In their absence the West Marches were 'full of trouble', but the other two were quiet, in spite of rumours of Bothwell's return.[2] It is interesting to note that the Scots who had been 'damnified in the huntinge action' had met Fenwick and Woodryngton and agreed to be good friends, a proceeding for which James, who still demanded justice, warded such of them as he could catch.[3] The Dunkirkers were again troublesome in June,[4] and, to add to the troubles of the West, Carmichael who, like Lowther, was worried by 'th'insolent base disobedient' folk, 'wes slaine be the Armstrangis and Carliles, he doing and executing his office of Wardenrie'.

He was riding from Annan to Langholm to hold a Warden Court, and fell into an ambush of sixteen Scots and two Englishmen, and was shot 'with a gonne'. James at once made Herries Warden, and promised to come to the West shortly. The murderers and their dependants made raids on England to the annoyance of Lowther, who found resistance hard, as the gentlemen 'of the factyon' would not obey him. Over a year afterwards, on November 14, 1601, Thomas Armstrong was convicted of the murder, and, after his right hand had been struck off, was hanged, and his goods escheated to the King. On February 13, 1606, another Armstrong was hanged for the same murder.[5]

Both Privy Councils paid considerable attention to the

[1] C.B.P. ii, 1148; C.H.M. ix, 46–8, 60.   [2] C.B.P. ii, 1158, 1162, 1167–8, 1170–82; R.P.C.S. vi, 105; Dom. v, 413, 418; A.P.C. xxx, 349.   [3] C.B.P. ii, 1173, 1195.   [4] C.B.P. ii, 1181, 1190.   [5] Birrel, 49; R.P.C.S. vi, 117–18; C.B.P. ii, 1183–4, 1186, 1188–9; Pitcairn, ii, 364–5, 504–5.

affairs of the West, and, when Scroope returned in July, he found his March out of order; for instance, the six-year-old son of the sheriff of Westmorland was carried away into Scotland in the daytime from a house within three miles of Carlisle.[1] The Middle Marches of England had never been so quiet as they were till the end of July, when Carmichael's murderers began their raids, but these did not last long, and for the rest of the year the whole Border, including the West, seems to have been quiet, nor did the escape of some pledges from York disturb it.[2] There was, however, a big domestic storm at Berwick, and loud complaints were made against Wyllughby's alleged attempts to exceed his rightful powers. His health was very poor at the time, and may have affected his actions, but his boast, 'it is enuff for me that my heart beares me record that I am honest to England', seems to have been borne out by his deeds, and the Queen, by committing the Master of Berwick Ordnance to the Fleet, showed that she would allow no contemptuous demeanour towards him.[3] The improved relations between Elizabeth and James are shown by the fact that the receipt of the two young brothers of Gowrie, who came to Berwick on August 11, and apparently stayed in England, was not made an excuse for disorder or delay of justice on the Borders.[4]

1601. Wyllughby's last few months of life were exceedingly troubled. Apart from his differences with his council at Berwick, he was involved in a dispute with Sir R. Carey, because some East March captains exceeded their orders and tried to take a certain Ogilvie out of Carey's Wardenry without acquainting Carey. The Privy Council tried to smoothe the matter over, but these upsets must have had a bad effect on Wyllughby, who was already sick and weak in body. An added trouble was the continued presence of the Dunkirkers off the coast, preying upon Berwick victualling ships; and, while Wyllughby

[1] R.P.C.S. vi, 121, 128, 136–8; A.P.C. xxx, 473–6; C.B.P. ii, 1196–8, 1200, 1203, 1206.   [2] C.B.P. ii, 1195, 1205, 1211, 1247–9, 1260–1, 1263–6, 1285, 1301; R.P.C.S. vi, 155.   [3] C.B.P. ii, 1252–3, 1255–7, 1267–8, 1272–3, 1275–8, 1283, 1289–90, 1293–4, 1298–1300, 1303–4, 1307–9; C.H.M. x, 380.
[4] C.B.P. ii, 1217, 1221, 1230, 1235, 1243.

was engaged against them in a ship manned at his own cost, there were sundry affrays in Berwick where his firm hand was missed. Worry and overwork had so undermined his constitution that a great cold, which he caught while his ship was lying at the haven mouth awaiting a wind, brought on a 'feaver' which was fatal to his body, which was so weak for want of sleep and food. He died suddenly and unexpectedly on June 25, without having settled the Dunkirkers.[1]

The year on the whole was quiet on the Borders,[2] but in March, soon after Scroope left his Wardenry, the Scots with English outlaws started making daily and nightly raids, though they did not do so much damage as the Carleton faction, which, it was hoped, the execution of two Carletons at York would deter for the future. There were also many outrages in the East during the short interval between Wyllughby's death and the appointment of Sir John Carey as his successor as Warden. Lord Roxburgh, lately known as Cesford, was found by both the Careys to be very ready and forward for justice, and justice was obtained from the officers of Liddesdale, and bonds from the chief riders of the Scots West March.[3] In some cases justice was unobtainable, and James authorized Lowther, in Scroope's absence, and Sir R. Carey to pursue with fire and sword such thieves as their opposites would not answer for. Woodryngton, Carey's deputy, took advantage of this to burn some houses and drive the owners to lie in 'bogges and woodes', while Carey himself lay in the English highlands as near to them as he could to prevent further troubles. The strength of the amity, not only between the princes but also between the Wardens, was such that this retaliation did not hinder ordinary justice.[4]

1602. The year 1602 was not unlike its predecessor. International justice was on the whole well carried out,

[1] C.B.P. ii, 1313–19, 1327, 1339, 1343–5, 1355, 1364, 1367–8, 1388–9; C.H.M. xi, 14–15.   [2] C.B.P. ii, 1320, 1344, 1395; C.H.M. xi, 85. [3] C.B.P. ii, 1341–2, 1400, 1402–6, 1408–9, 1418; A.P.C. xxxi, 472–3, xxxii, 54–5; C.H.M. xi, 275, 295; Watson, 130–1; H.M.C. xv, pt. vii, 51.   [4] C.B.P. ii, 1348, 1353–4, 1369–70, 1372–3, 1378.

quiet was maintained, and there was little stealing till the end of the year, when Liddesdale grew active.[1] The great need, according to Sir J. Carey, was domestic justice, which was in peril owing to the lack of competent J.P.s.[2] The Scots West March was the only part of the Borders which was seriously unsettled, and James made two journeys thither. In February he came and took bands from Herries and others not to assist Maxwell, and proclaimed against Papistical practices.[3] At the end of September he came again, and was for some time in an evil temper against Scroope. He held justice courts at Dumfries, and numerous cases involving spoil, oppression, destruction of corn, manslaughter, &c., were tried. At Peebles there was only one case for trial, and at Jedburgh nothing very important, so by November 4 the King was back in Edinburgh, having taken a general band, against thieves, with the Border lairds. According to Birrel he also visited Duns 'qr he gart hang maney theives'. Maxwell was kept a prisoner in Edinburgh Castle.[4] Scroope had been free from raids all this time, but, being unable to get justice from Johnstone, had invaded Scotland openly and plainly by his officers, and spoiled and killed Scots for three months, a proceeding which in earlier years would have led to retaliation, and of which the English Privy Council hardly approved.[5]

1603. There is really no more Border history. Maxwell escaped from Edinburgh Castle and went to Dumfries in March, where he put Johnstone in great fear.[6] But Scroope's Wardenry was quiet enough for him to get leave to go to court.[7] Sir R. Carey was there already, and his brother at Berwick had very little to report. Thus, when Elizabeth died on the last day of the old year, 1602–3, the Borders seem to have been quiet. Sir R. Carey took the

---

[1] C.B.P. ii, 1439, 1446, 1450, 1453–4, 1456, 1467, 1476, 1479–82, 1489, 1512; C.H.M. xii, 115; R.P.C.S. vi, 395.   [2] C.B.P. ii, 1470.   [3] R.P.C.S. vi, 347, 351–2, 355–8; C.B.P. ii, 1447–8.   [4] C.H.M. xii, 384–5, 415, 458–9, 504–5; Birrel, 57; C.B.P. ii, 1491–2, 1495, 1498–1500, 1502, 1504, 1507–8; R.P.C.S. vi, 467–8, 475, 825–31, xiv, 398–9.   [5] C.B.P. ii, 1522, 1525; C.H.M. xii, 504–5, 529–31.   [6] R.P.C.S. vi, 311; C.H.M. xii, 662. [7] C.B.P. ii, 1536; C.H.M. xii, 612–13.

news to Holyrood, arriving there on Saturday evening, March 26, two days in advance of the authorized messengers. Proclamations against Scots riding in England on pain of treason were made, and steps were taken in England for safeguarding the country. These seem to have been effective.[1] The Borders as Borders had ceased to be. On April 7 the charge of the Marches of England and Scotland, which had now become 'the verie hart of the countrey', was committed to the Council of Scotland resident in Edinburgh, and on May 7 James arrived in London, with Lords Roxburgh and Hume, of Border fame, in his company.[2]

It is undeniable that in these last four or five years the Borders had improved. The prime causes were the evident failure of Spain and her satellites, and James's growing conviction that, if he kept in the good books of England, nothing could prevent his succession to the throne. The firebrands of the Borders, Cesford and Buccleugh, had both been warded in England for a short space, thus tasting the power of Elizabeth, and they seem to have felt with James that, if they also helped to preserve the amity, they would on his succession share in richer and more peaceable spoils which were to be won in London. Thus the disorder which took place was caused by the broken men, who had nothing to hope for from the Union of the Crowns, and this was kept within smaller bounds than before by the energy of resident English Wardens like Wyllughby and the two Careys, aided by the co-operation of Scots authorities. Without that the laws of 1597 would have been useless. Ridpath states that after the Union of the Crowns the Borders enjoyed 'a quiet and order which they had never before experienced',[3] but that is another question, and the writer hopes, given time and facilities, to investigate it.

[1] R.P.C.S. vi, 548, 554 (note), 883; C.M. 79–80; H.M.C. x, pt. iv, 308; Bell, 231–2.   [2] R.P.C.S. vi, 560–1.   [3] Ridpath, 484.

APPENDIX

A LIST OF WARDENS, 1558–1603

THE EAST MARCHES OF ENGLAND

1558 THOMAS, 7TH EARL OF NORTHUMBERLAND (1528–72)

He was Warden under Mary and was kept in office by Elizabeth, his patent being granted on January 18, anno 1.[1]

On November 8, 1559, he went to London, leaving Sadler to act in his absence, as his deputy. Sadler received no patent.[2]

1559 WILLIAM, 13TH BARON GREY DE WILTON (?–1562)

His patent was granted on December 22, 1559.[3]

Sadler had charge of the East and Middle Marches during Grey's absence in Scotland. Grey was only resident for a short time and then made efforts to resign. He died early in the morning of December 15, 1562, in the south.[4]

During the vacancy Sir John Selby acted as Warden, and Sir Thomas Dacre as Governor of Berwick.[5]

1563 FRANCIS, 2ND EARL OF BEDFORD (1527–85)

He was appointed about November 20, 1563, and his patent was granted on February 24, 1564. He was recalled on October 9, 1567, and left Berwick on October 27, 1567.[6]

Sir William Drury, the Marshal, took charge of Berwick and the East Marches during the vacancy.[7]

1568 HENRY, 1ST BARON HUNSDON (1524?–96)

His patents as Captain of Berwick and Warden were granted on August 25 and 26, 1568.[8] He was absent from his charge for many years towards the end of his life, and died in the south on July 23, 1596.[9]

During the vacancy Sir R. Carey had charge of the East March and his brother, John, of Berwick.[10]

[1] C. Pat. Rolls P.R.O. Eliz. 1–16, fol. 11; Rymer, xv, 472, 475.   [2] For. ii, 161, 187, 213, 274; Sadler, ii, 65.   [3] C. Pat. Rolls, *ut supra*, fol. 35; Grey, 53–8.   [4] For. ii, 483, iii, 405, 653, 734, iv, 950, 1010, 1035, 1057; C.S.P. i, 616; C.H.M. i, 627.   [5] For. vi, 914, 1012, 1416, 1422.   [6] C. Pat. Rolls *ut supra*, fol. 130; C.B.P. i, 537; For. vi, 1422, vii, 1753, 1790–1.   [7] For. vii, 1790–1.   [8] C. Pat. Rolls, *ut supra*, fol. 223, 239.   [9] C.B.P. i, 537; For. vii, 2453–4; C.S.P. ii, 778.   [10] C.M. 51; C.H.M. vi, 342.

1597 SIR ROBERT CAREY (1560?–1639)

He was Hunsdon's seventh and youngest son, and on November 26, 1597, was given a patent as Warden with fees as from the previous midsummer.[1]

In the following March he was displaced in favour of Wyllughby.[2]

1598 PEREGRINE BERTIE, 11TH BARON WYLLUGHBY D'ERESBY (1555–1601)

His patent as Governor of Berwick granted on March 13, 1598, to be in force from March 25, is in the Border Papers.[3] I have failed to find his patent as Warden. He died suddenly on June 25, 1601.[4]

William Selby was made 'interim' Governor of Berwick, and Sir John Carey was sent down to Berwick, where he arrived on July 4, 1601.[5]

1601 SIR JOHN CAREY (1550?–1617)

He was Hunsdon's second son, and received his patent as Warden on July 11, 1601, and remained in office till the Queen's death.[6] The note of the grant of his patent in the Calendar of Patent Rolls [7] is undated. He and his brother were the only two Wardens of the East March who were not also Governors of Berwick.

THE MIDDLE MARCHES OF ENGLAND

1558 THOMAS, 7TH EARL OF NORTHUMBERLAND
Vide East March.

1559 WILLIAM, 13TH BARON GREY DE WILTON
Vide East March.

1560 SIR JOHN FORSTER (1501?–1602)

He was made Warden, on the advice of Grey and Norfolk, on October 19, his patent being granted on November 4.[8] He survived one inquiry into the many complaints made against his rule in the autumn of 1586,[9] but was sequestrated from office on September 2, 1587, till he had answered the charges made against him. Hunsdon took his place.[10]

---

[1] C. Pat. Rolls, Eliz. anno 40, fol. 5; Dom. iv, 359; C.M. 53.   [2] C.M. 54.
[3] P.R.O. vol. 37, fol. 35; C.B.P. ii, 920.   [4] C.B.P. ii, 1389.   [5] C.B.P. ii, 1390, 1398; A.P.C. xxxii, 12.   [6] C.B.P. ii, 1402–3.   [7] P.R.O. Eliz. anno 43, fol. 16.   [8] C. Pat. Rolls, Eliz. 1–16, fol. 44; For. iii, 665; C.B.P. ii, 122.   [9] C.B.P. i, 422–5, 501.   [10] C.B.P. i, 537; A.P.C. xv, 221.

1587 HENRY, 1ST BARON HUNSDON
       Vide East March. His patent was granted on August 31,
       1587.[1]

1588 SIR JOHN FORSTER
       Forster was restored about August 20, 1588.[2] He was
       finally dismissed about September 6, 1595, but ordered to
       continue in office till his successor came to the March.[3] For
       the dates of his birth and death see C.B.P. ii, 129, 1438.

1595 RALPH, 3RD BARON EURE (1558–1617)
       He accepted office on September 6, 1595, and was granted
       a commission on October 9. He resigned sometime after
       January 22, 1598.[4]

1598 SIR ROBERT CAREY (1560?–1639)
       He entered office in March 1598, and his patent was
       granted on March 25, anno 41.[5] He was still in office when
       the Queen died.

THE WEST MARCHES OF ENGLAND

1558 WILLIAM, 3RD BARON DACRE OF GILLESLAND (?–1563)
       He was Warden in Mary's time, and Elizabeth granted
       him a patent on January 11, 1559, as Warden, and one as
       Captain of Carlisle two days later.[6] The last note of him as
       Warden is in a letter from Mary Stuart to Elizabeth, dated
       January 5, 1563.[7]

1563 HENRY, 9TH BARON SCROOPE OF BOLTON (1534–92)
       His two patents as Warden and Captain were granted on
       April 6, 1563.[8] He died in office on June 13, 1592.[9]
       Till the next appointment Richard Lowther held office as
       Vice-Warden, but had no patent.[10]

1593 THOMAS, 10TH BARON SCROOPE OF BOLTON (1560?–1609)
       His patents were granted on March 23, 1593,[11] and he
       was still in office when the Queen died.

---

[1] C. Pat. Rolls, Eliz. anno 29, fol. 4.   [2] C.B.P. i, 627.   [3] C.B.P. ii,
111, 119, 154.   [4] C. Pat. Rolls, Eliz. anno 37, fol. 19; C.B.P. ii, 119,
133, 894.   [5] C. Pat. Rolls, Eliz. anno 41, fol. 12.   [6] A.P.C. 1556–8,
373; C. Pat. Rolls, Eliz. 1–16, fol. 8, 10.   [7] C.S.P. i, p. 676.   [8] C. Pat.
Rolls, Eliz. 1–16, fol. 102, 103; Bell, 196.   [9] Dom. Add. iii, 341.
[10] Dom. Add. iii, 332; A.P.C. xxiv, 19.   [11] C. Pat. Rolls, Eliz. anno 35,
fol. 24, 35.

THE WARDENS OF
THE EAST MARCHES OF SCOTLAND

1557 ALEXANDER, 5TH BARON HOME (d. 1575)
He was given a commission as Warden of the East and Middle Marches by the Regent Mary on October 21, 1557,[1] yet 'the lard of Cesfurde' was paid £100 for his fee as Warden of the two Marches, 1558.[2] Home was Warden on May 21, 1559,[3] and Hunsdon mentioned him as Warden on February 1, 1570.[4] During the troubles in Scotland he sided with the Queen, and his office seems to have been vacant, though Randolph wrote to Sussex on September 25, 1570, that Lord Ruthven had been made Warden.[5]

1573 SIR JAMES HOME OF COLDENKNOWIS
He was appointed on November 6.[6] In 1578 he showed himself hostile to Morton, and, shortly before September 15, was dismissed.[7]

1578? GEORGE HOME OF WEDDERBURN
Sometime in 1579 he was ordered to be paid his fee for having been in office a whole year. He was still Warden on April 9, 1580, but before August 1581 he was warded and probably dismissed.[8]

1582? ALEXANDER, 6TH BARON HOME
He is first mentioned as Warden on July 26, 1582, and held office till early in 1599, when he resigned and left the realm.[9]

1599 SIR ALEXANDER HOME OF MANDERSTON
Appointed on April 26.[10]

1600 ALEXANDER, 6TH BARON HOME
On July 28 he is mentioned as Warden, the late Warden having become his deputy. He held the office till the Union of the Crowns, and on July 7, 1603, was made Lieutenant and Justiciar over the three Scots Marches.[11]

---

[1] H.M.C. 12th Rep. App. 8, 98–9.   [2] A.L.H.T.S. x, 393.   [3] For. i, 717.   [4] For. ix, 686.   [5] C.S.P. iii, 483.   [6] R.P.C.S. ii, 300.
[7] C.S.P. v, 383.   [8] H.M.C. Home of Wedderburn, 49, 50, 52.
[9] R.P.C.S. iii, 501, v, 552.   [10] R.P.C.S. v, 552.   [11] R.P.C.S. vi, 136, 883.

THE WARDENS OF THE
MIDDLE MARCHES OF SCOTLAND

1558 SIR WALTER KER OF CESFORD (1510?–1583?)

He is mentioned as Warden in April and October 1558 and in August 1559.[1] The last mention of him in office is in October 1569,[2] but there is no record of his leaving office. Apparently he was followed by his second son.

1573? WILLIAM KER OF CESFORD (1543–1600)

In November 1573 the Regent wrote to Elizabeth that he had made three new Wardens, but did not name them.[3] Spotswood says that Sir John Carmichael was the new Warden here, but there is no other record of it,[4] and if 'guardiano' is, as it appears to be, an obvious mistake for 'guardiani' in two grants of March 22, 1574, William Ker was then Warden.[5] The last mention of him as Warden is on February 21, 1584,[6] and soon afterwards he was warded, and succeeded by

1584 SIR THOMAS KER OF FERNIHERST (d. 1586)

He was appointed on November 13, 1584,[7] and soon after the death of Russell, on July 27, 1585, he was removed, and his predecessor was reinstated.[8]

1585 WILLIAM KER OF CESFORD (1543–1600)

He apparently remained in office till he died; but as early as 1590 his son Robert acted with him,[9] and is actually named as Warden in the Register of the Privy Council on October 3, 1594.[10]

1600 SIR ROBERT KER OF CESFORD (1570?–1650)

He was created Baron Roxburgh on December 23, 1600,[11] and was Warden till the Union, though, when he was intending to leave the realm, Sir Andro Ker of Grenheil was made Warden in his place on August 3, 1602.[12] There is no evidence that Sir Andrew acted as Warden.

---

[1] A.L.H.T.S. x, 347–8, 393; C.S.P. i, 532.   [2] R.P.C.S. ii, 73.   [3] C.S.P. iv, 732.   [4] Op. cit. ii, 194.   [5] Reg. Mag. Sig. 1546–80, nos. 2213–14. [6] R.P.C.S. ii, 634.   [7] R.P.C.S. iii, 699.   [8] C.B.P. i, 393; R.P.C.S. iv, 45.   [9] R.P.C.S. iv, 530.   [10] R.P.C.S. v, 178.   [11] R.P.C.S. vi, 187 (note).   [12] R.P.C.S. vi, 440–1.

THE WARDENS OF
THE WEST MARCHES OF SCOTLAND

1557 SIR JOHN MAXWELL OF TERREGLES (1512–83)
He was appointed on May 24, 1557,[1] and became 4th
Baron Herries in 1566. In 1568 he was in rebellion, and
Scroope asked Moray to appoint an officer opposite.[2] Moray
appointed, on June 21, 1568,[3]

1568 JAMES DOUGLAS OF DRUMLANRIG (1498–1578)
He was not in office long, and from October 1569 to
April 1573 there seems to have been no Warden whom
Scroope would acknowledge.[4] On April 24, 1570, Herries
openly proclaimed himself Warden in Mary's name,[5] and
three years later came to an agreement with Scroope.[6]

1573 JOHN, 8TH LORD MAXWELL (b. 1552?)
He was Herries's nephew and one of the three new Wardens.[7] He was in office as late as November 29, 1576,[8] but
on December 6, 1576, John, Lord Herries, is mentioned as
Warden for the time being,[9] and on May 25, 1577, Maxwell
is mentioned as having resigned.[10]

1577 ARCHIBALD, 8TH EARL OF ANGUS (1555–88)
On May 25 he was made Lieutenant-Governor of all the
Marches, as well as Warden of the West.[11] He resigned.

1578 JOHN, 8TH LORD MAXWELL
He had been in prison, but came out on Morton's fall, and
was reappointed Warden.[12] He was deposed and replaced by

1579 JOHN, 4TH BARON HERRIES
who became Warden on January 23.[13]

1579 JOHN JOHNSTONE OF DUNSKELLIE (d. 1586)
He was appointed on August 24, 1579, and denounced rebel
and deposed in April, 1581.[14]

1581 JOHN, 8TH LORD MAXWELL
He was reappointed on April 29, 1581, and deposed for
'slewthfulnes' on November 19, 1582.[15]

[1] Ex. Rolls. Scotl. xix, 414.   [2] For. viii, 2105.   [3] C.S.P. ii, 717;
R.P.C.S. ii, 631.   [4] For. ix, 485, 1727, 1818; C.S.P. iv, 174–80.   [5] For.
ix, 848.   [6] For. x, 866.   [7] Spotswood, ii, 194–5; C.S.P. iv, p. 625.
[8] C.S.P. v, 241.   [9] R.P.C.S. ii, 569.   [10] R.P.C.S. ii, 613.   [11] R.P.C.S.
ii, 613.   [12] R.P.C.S. ii, 677–8; C.S.P. v, 313.   [13] R.P.C.S. iii, 76.
[14] R.P.C.S. iii, 207, 374.   [15] R.P.C.S. iii, 531.

1582 JOHN JOHNSTONE OF DUNSKELLIE

Was reappointed on November 19, 1582,[1] and ceased to be Warden some time before August 21, 1585,[2] probably before September 16, 1583, when he was ordered to render Langholm Castle to the Earl of Morton.[3]

1585 JOHN, 8TH LORD MAXWELL, EARL OF MORTON

He proclaimed himself Warden on November 15, 1585.[4] Part of his period of office was spent in prison,[5] and he refused to act in August 1586.[6] In April 1587 there was no Warden.[7]

1587 WILLIAM, 5TH BARON HERRIES (1555?–1603?)

He was appointed on June 9, the clerk entering his name as 'Johnne Lord Hereis'. In February 1588 he was denounced rebel, but submitted and remained in office.[8]

1588 JOHN CARMICHAEL (1542?–1600)

He was appointed on September 13, and, during his absence with James VI in Denmark, Maxwell acted in his place. He resigned.[9]

1592 JOHN, 8TH LORD MAXWELL, EARL OF MORTON

He was reappointed on July 11, but was slain at Dryfe Sands on December 6, 1593.[10] For some time there was no definite Warden.[11]

1595 WILLIAM, 5TH BARON HERRIES

He wrote to Scroope in January that the King had made him Warden, but Scroope did not know whether to acknowledge him.[12] On May 27, 1596, Lord Sanquhar, Sir John Gordon of Lochinvar, and Alexander Stewart of Garlies were charged to be Wardens and justices conjointly within the West Marches.[13]

1596 SIR JAMES JOHNSTONE (b. 1567?)

He was appointed on July 28.[14] On August 21, 1597, Scroope wrote that the office was vacant.[15]

1597 ANDREW, 3RD LORD STEWART OF OCHILTREE

He was made Warden and Lieutenant on November 28.[16]

---

[1] R.P.C.S. iii, 531.   [2] C.B.P. i, 340.   [3] R.P.C.S. iii, 598.   [4] C.S.P. viii, 202; C.B.P. i, 392.   [5] R.P.C.S. iv, 54.   [6] C.S.P. viii, 705. [7] C.H.M. iii, 516.   [8] R.P.C.S. iv, 188, 247, 258.   [9] R.P.C.S. iv, 322; C.B.P. i, 653, 664.   [10] R.P.C.S. iv, 767; C.B.P. i, 918.   [11] C.B.P. i, 935, 947, 960, 967, 992; Thorpe, 657.   [12] C.B.P. ii, 11, 13.   [13] R.P.C.S. v, 292.   [14] R.P.C.S. v, 304.   [15] C.B.P. ii, 739.   [16] R.P.C.S. v, 424–5.

1598 WILLIAM, 10TH EARL OF ANGUS (1554–1611)
He was appointed on July 3.[1]

1599 SIR JOHN CARMICHAEL
Reappointed on September 18,[2] and murdered on June 16, 1600.[3] William, 5th Lord Herries, his successor, was apparently never proclaimed Warden.[4]

1600 SIR JAMES JOHNSTONE
The victor of Dryfe Sands was appointed on August 13, and was the last Warden.[5]

[1] R.P.C.S. v, 466. [2] R.P.C.S. vi, 33. [3] C.B.P. ii, 1183. [4] R.P.C.S. vi, 117–18; C.B.P. ii, 1196. [5] R.P.C.S. vi, 155.

GLOSSARY

ABSTINENCE. Armistice or truce.
AVOWER. One who bears witness to the guilt of one of his fellow-countrymen.

BACKBILLING. Malicious retaliatory billing.
BAND. Bond or assurance.
BARMEKYN. A walled enclosure, round a tower, used for the protection of cattle.
BAUGHLE, *vide* p. 105.
BEDSTOCK. Bedstead.
BIGGING. The act of building.
BILLING. Laying a bill of indictment.
BROKEN MEN. Outlaws, or men for whom no responsible person would answer.
BROKERS. Agents.

CLEARE. To declare guiltless.
CODDIS. Pillows.
CONTAGEOUS. Pestilential.

DOUBLE. Restitution which was twice the value of the damage proved.
DURANCE. A strong, hard-wearing cloth.

FEAD. Feud.
FEEDE. Feud.
FEOD. Feud.
FILE. To avow the truth of a bill of indictment.
FOSTYONE. Coarse cloth.
FOUL. Guilty.
FURNITURE. Military equipment.

GAVLOCKES. Probably iron crowbars.
GENT. Gentry or gentlemen.
GROGRAYNE. Coarse woven material.

HACKBUT. Primitive handgun.
HEADSMEN. Head men, or chiefs.
HORN, to put to the. To outlaw.

KYFE. Coif ; close-fitting cap.

LIMMER. Rascal or rogue.
LYMMERIS. Rascals or rogues.

MANURE. To cultivate or occupy (land).
MARCH DAYS, *vide* Trews.

OISTIS. Parties of armed men.

PASS UPON THE INQUEST. Serve on a jury.
PATLETTS. Neckerchiefs.
PENSILS. Small pennons or tapering flags.
PULLYN. Poultry.

RAILES. Garments ; possibly night-dresses.
RANK RIDERS. Marauders ; raiders.
RECETTING. Receipt of stolen goods, or harbouring a robber or other offender.
REIF. Plunder, or plundering.

SAVEGARD. Outer skirt worn by horse-women to preserve their frocks.
SAWFIE. Allowance for expenses, equal in value to the damage proved.
SHEYLD. The summer hut of a Border shepherd.
SHOOTING A DAY OF TRUCE. Not meeting the opposite officer on the agreed day.
SKURROURIS. Scouts.
SORNING. Forcibly billeting oneself upon a person or his lands.
SPEIRE. Inquire.
STAMMELL. Rough woollen cloth, red in colour.
STOUTH. Plunder or plundering.
STRAKYN. Coarse fabric made of flax.
SUMMERING. Pasturing cattle on the uplands in summer.
SURNAME. Family or clan.

THREAPLANDS. Debatable lands.
TICKLE. Uncertain ; difficult to handle.

TREWS. Meetings of opposite Wardens, or deputies, on the frontier for the administration of justice.

TRUCE, Days of, *vide* TREWS.

VALUE FOR VALUE. Redress not exceeding but just equaling the value of that given by the opposite Wardenry.

VILIPENDED. Held cheap or of small account.

VOWER, *vide* AVOWER.

WATCHES. Watchmen, or the watches which they kept.

INDEX